Morocco
OVERLAND

ROUTE GUIDE – FROM THE ATLAS TO THE SAHARA
4WD – MOTORCYCLE – VAN – MOUNTAIN BIKE

CHRIS SCOTT

with contributions from
JOSÉ BRITO & TIM CULLIS
and additional material by
ERIC DE NADAI, FRANCK SIMONNET
& RAF VERBEELEN

TRAILBLAZER PUBLICATIONS

Morocco Overland Routes

MA – Anti Atlas routes
ME – Eastern routes
MH – High Atlas routes
MO – Ocean routes
MS – Saharan routes
MW – Western routes
━━ – MS10 Desert Highway

Atlantic Ocean

Casablanc

El Jadida

See MH Routes Overview

Safi

Marra

Essaouira   Chichaoua

Ag

See MA Routes Overview map, p176-7   Aoulouz

Agadir

Taliouine

Igherm

Tafraoute

Tiznit   Tat

Ousemlal   Akka

Sidi Ifni

Timoulay

See MO Route Overview map, p230-1   See MW Routes Overview map, p208-9   Fask   Ait Herbil

Guelmim

Tiglite   Assa

Tan-Tan

Tarfaya   Msied

Route MO2 continues to   *WESTERN SAHARA*
Nouadhibou, Mauritania

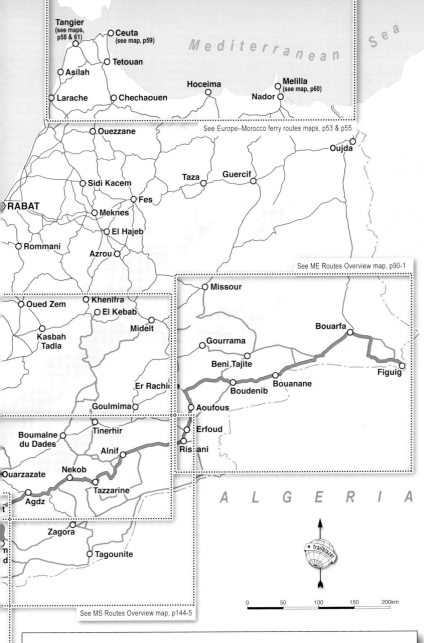

Tangier
(see maps, p58 & 61)
Ceuta (see map, p59)
Tetouan
Asilah
Larache
Chechaouen
Hoceima
Nador
Melilla (see map, p60)

Mediterranean Sea

See Europe–Morocco ferry routes maps, p53 & p55

Ouezzane
Oujda
Taza
Guercif
Sidi Kacem
Fes
RABAT
Meknes
El Hajeb
Rommani
Azrou

See ME Routes Overview map, p90-1

Missour
Oued Zem
Khenifra
El Kebab
Midelt
Bouarfa
Kasbah Tadla
Gourrama
Beni Tajite
Bouanane
Figuig
Er Rachidia
Boudenib
Goulmima
Aoufous
Boumalne du Dades
Tinerhir
Erfoud
Alnif
Rissani
Ouarzazate
Nekob
Tazzarine
Agdz
ALGERIA
Zagora
Tagounite

trailblazer

0   50   100   150   200km

See MS Routes Overview map, p144-5

Colour section (following pages)

● **C1 Top**: Entering the Tazegzaoute gorge on Route MA3. **Middle**: Road riding along the Desert Highway: MS10 (© Raf Verbeelen). **Bottom left**: Lunch at a High Atlas auberge, Aït Ayoub on MH13. **Bottom right**: Basic desert auberge near Foum Zguid, MS7.
● **C2 Top**: The Rekkam plateau (ME). **Middle**: Desert camp, Erg Chebbi (© Matthew Kelham). **Bottom**: Tree spotting on Route MS6 (© Raf Verbeelen).
● **C3** The crumbling citadel of Ighern Warfaln (MA6, MA13) viewed from over the valley on Route MA12.
● **C4** Gnarly stage between Agadir Melloul and Assaragh on Route MA13 (© Robin Webb).

C2

CHRIS SCOTT (below) first passed through Morocco in 1982 on an XT500 motorcycle while returning from his first aborted Sahara trip, an adventure he relates in his early memoir, *Desert Travels* (available on Kindle). Since that time he's undertaken several other trips in the Sahara, including *Desert Riders* in 2003 (on DVD) and the second known crossing of the Majabat al Koubra in 2006. For the full list of his other achievements go to www.sahara-overland.com and click his picture.

His other books for Trailblazer include the *Adventure Motorcycling Handbook* (now in its 6th edition), *Sahara Overland* and the *Overlanders' Handbook*.

C4

CONTENTS

Morocco Overland – Route guide: from the Atlas to the Sahara
First edition 2009, this second edition June 2013

Publisher
Trailblazer Publications
The Old Manse, Tower Rd, Hindhead, Surrey, GU26 6SU, UK
info@trailblazer-guides.com
www.trailblazer-guides.com

British Library Cataloguing in Publication Data
A catalogue record for this book is available from the British Library

ISBN 978-1-905864-53-9

Editor: Nicky Slade
Series Editor: Bryn Thomas
Proofreading: Anna Jacomb-Hood
Typesetting and layout: Chris Scott
Cartography: Nick Hill
Photographs: © Chris Scott 2013 (unless otherwise credited)
Index: Patrick D Hummingbird

Acknowledgements

As well as those included on the title page and credited elsewhere, thanks also to
Matthew Kelham for additional pictures and to BMW Motorrad UK, Vines of Guildford,
Metal Mule and Enduristan for equipment and loan of the BMW 650 GS SE.

A request

The author and the publisher have tried to ensure that the information in this book is as up to date
as possible. Nevertheless, things are certain to change; even before the ink is dry. If you notice any
changes or omissions that you think should be included in the next edition or have any other feed-
back, please email the author at the website below or via Trailblazer (address above).

Warning

**Mountain and desert travel is unpredictable and can be dangerous.
Every effort has been made by the author, contributors and the publisher to ensure that
the information contained herein is as accurate as possible. However, they are unable
to accept responsibility for any inconvenience, loss or injury sustained by anyone
as a result of the advice and information given in this guide.**

Additional online content: mapping, imagery and GPS downloads at:
www.morocco-overland.com

Photos – Front cover: KM125 on Route MA13
Title page: The dramatic climb out of the Smouguene gorge (Route MA2)

Printed on chlorine-free paper by D'Print (☎ +65-6581 3832), Singapore

INTRODUCTION

'...had to get away to see what we could find.' **Marrakech Express**

As a tourist destination Morocco is well established. Long before Crosby, Stills, Nash & Young sang their carefree Sixties hit, and half a century before Bergman turned away from Bogart on that foggy airstrip in *Casablanca*, European tourists had lifted the veil on the 'African Orient'. They crossed the Straits of Gibraltar, intrigued by the mysterious medieval allure of cities like Tangier, Fes and Marrakech, a traditional Islamic culture that had fiercely resisted colonisation, and the promise of the mountains and desert beyond.

Today our fascination with Morocco, so close and yet so different, shows no sign of abating. 'Sand, sea and souks' coach tours continue to ply the well-worn tourist tramlines, while cheap air fares have popularised weekend city breaks to upmarket Marrakech *riads* or villas.

Morocco Overland shows you another side of Morocco, where the adventurous driver, rider or cyclist can safely explore the snowbound passes of the High Atlas or the dusty *pistes* of the Sahara. In between visiting the well-known highlights, the sites, cities and beachside resorts, you can trace a network of easily navigable routes far from the hassle-prone, trinket-clad tourist hotspots.

In doing so you have a chance to experience the wilderness of southern Morocco at your own pace and on your own terms. Explore the jebels, palmeries and ruined kasbahs of canyon-bound Berber villages lost in time, and by doing so encounter a traditional and hospitable people, light years from the populated, Europeanised north.

Along the way you'll also learn the capabilities of your own machine and acquire many other new skills, all while lunching on a grassy meadow by a mountain stream or overnighting at the base of a dune with little more than the wind, sand and stars between you and Timbuktu.

1 PLANNING

When to go

Morocco is a **year-round destination** but, depending on the season, some regions will be more agreeable or accessible than others. The short version is this: in summer the desert south of the Atlas will be extremely hot, in winter tracks over the High Atlas may be snowed over, and at any time of year heavy rain can render mountain tracks impassable. Flooding or its consequent damage is the least predictable but most likely cause of inaccessible tracks and briefly closed main roads in southern Morocco.

Some guidebooks suggest the spring thaw sees a high risk of floods across the Atlas. It sounds plausible but anywhere in the world, mountain snow melts steadily and there's not that much of it in Morocco anyway. A sustained period of **heavy rain** will have a much greater impact and this can happen at any time of year, but most commonly in late summer into early autumn.

There's not much you can do about flooding, but unless you know better or are habituated to high temperatures, certainly on a bike you'd do well to **avoid Morocco in mid-summer**, or at least plan to stay in the mountains.

Climate patterns

Between them the influence of the Atlas mountains, the Sahara, the Atlantic and the Mediterranean all complicate the Moroccan climate. The snow-bound summit of Jebel Toubkal (North Africa's highest mountain) is just 200km from the dunes of Chegaga and many routes in this book can take you from 2500m (8000ft-plus) passes down to the baking desert in a couple of hours. On one trip in April I experienced scorching 40°C winds south of Foum Zguid and met some bikers a few days later who were riding through snow over the Rif Mountains at around the same time. In a car with air-con, heating and wipers, the weather is not such a big deal, but on a bike – with or without an engine – it certainly is.

North of the High Atlas the country experiences a predominantly Mediterranean climate of hot, dry summers and cool, wet winters. Snowfall is likely in the Middle Atlas with winter rainfall most prominent north of Casablanca and particularly in the Rif. Heading south from the Mediterranean ports, from November to March there's a one-in-three chance you'll get rain on any one day.

By the time you get to Marrakech it's less than one-in-five and over the Atlas in Ouarzazate the chances of getting wet are negligible. Ouarzazate is Morocco's **driest and hottest** big town and can experience temperature variations of 58°C (though not necessarily in the same year) and an annual average rainfall of less than half an inch (< 12mm). Places further from the sea and at lower elevation like Figuig or Zagora are drier and hotter still.

© Eric De Nadai

The **wettest and coldest** town is the alpine-style resort of Ifrane at 1665m/5463ft in the Middle Atlas, with average daily lows barely above freezing from December to March and with a lot of rain and snow from November to April. If you find yourself heat struck in mid-summer Morocco, head for the cool cedar forests of the Middle Atlas.

The desert wind

In the desert, winds are almost always present and when strong and from a certain direction can reduce visibility to a few kilometres and render all landscapes hazy. The season begins in February with hot **sand winds** blowing for days at a time. As the months progress and temperatures rise, summer skies are often muddied by the heat-borne haze.

The term '**sandstorm**' is often misused for conditions that are merely very windy with some dust and sand blowing about; a pretty permanent situation in the Sahara which occasionally escalates to the 'sand wind' described above. Just like a regular thunderstorm, a true sandstorm is a relatively short and intense event, lasting maybe a few hours. It will be associated with a wall of sand coming at you and briefly engulfing you in zero visibility. A sprinkle of rain often accompanies this dramatic event. Although, like thunderstorms, they're more common at the height or end of summer, in 30 years I've only experienced this twice in the Sahara. One time was in May 2008 near Merzouga when with little warning, a tsunami of sand hundreds of feet high rolled towards us and wrapped the rocking car in a sandy fog.

DAYLIGHT HOURS IN WINTER

When the clocks go back in the UK in late October, Moroccan time is the same but because it's more or less halfway to the equator from the UK, daylight hours vary less with the seasons. So it is that while the sun may set at 5.45pm in late October or February, it's also light enough to travel from 6am onwards. By getting into a 'farmer's' schedule of sleeping and rising early, you can still make use of up to 12 hours of daylight at these times of year. Moroccan hotel staff may not see it this way of course, and getting an early breakfast may require some persuasion.

In mid-winter the **shortest days** are still about 10 hours long, with sunrise around Christmas in Ouarzazate at 7.20am and sunset at 5.30pm. Depending on your **altitude**, when camping at this time of year, it can be the dawn temperatures that decide how early you manage to get up, but with the way the clocks are set in Morocco, it pays to get going soon after dawn and so make the most of the best part of the day.

In southern Morocco I find the most violent sand winds seem to come predominantly from the south or south-east in the transient seasons of spring and autumn, bringing with them the dust from the Western Sahara plateau. Such a day can often end in rain which quickly rinses the skies, bringing a following day of ragged clouds and clear air until the next front comes through.

The Atlantic influence

While the Atlantic coast of Morocco from Tan-Tan southwards sees the Sahara unroll to its very shore, temperature extremes are mitigated by the ocean. Places further north like Essaouira and particularly Agadir have the most agreeable climates in Morocco, with moderate rainfall and temperatures all helping make Agadir the country's main beach resort. Down in the Western Sahara, Laayoune recorded 44°C one day in June 2007, but generally the ocean suppresses such extremes and summer temperatures here don't usually exceed the mid-30s. Dakhla (a special case, situated at the end of a peninsula) never sees frost and gets temperatures above 30°C on no more than a couple of days a year. At this time, however, right along the Atlantic Route **strong winds** as well as cloud and fog are regular features.

AND WHEN NOT TO GO

Particularly on a motorbike or bicycle, avoid the **Moroccan Sahara** between June and September. At this time from Tangier southwards anywhere in Morocco below 1500m can have a 40°C day and south of the Atlas these sorts of temperatures occur daily for a month or two.

In winter expect to get **rained on** in the north as well as in the High- and Middle Atlas ranges where **snow** is also a distinct possibility above 2000m. However bad that might get, at this time at least you have the benefit of knowing that this book's routes south of the High Atlas (ie: most of them) will probably experience near **ideal conditions**: clear skies but with little chance of getting dangerously dehydrated while riding a bike.

In between these seasons – **October to November** and **February to March** – you have the greatest chance of exploring anywhere without getting comprehensively frozen, soaked or baked. Late autumn in particular can be a good time with light winds, warm temperatures and clear skies.

Good **weather websites** covering Morocco include 🖳 www.weather online.co.uk/Morocco.htm and 🖳 uk.weather.com/global (click 'North Africa') which features sunrise and sunset times (see box on previous page).

PLANNING YOUR TRIP

Where to go

Even if this is not your first trip to Morocco, chances are you'll want to see something of the north during your visit, at the very least one of the big cities like Fes or Marrakech, or more manageable large towns like Asilah or Chefchaouen, both an hour or two south of Tangier Med port.

The Standard Morocco Tour

For drivers and bikers, the standard Moroccan visit involves crossing the Straits of Gibraltar on a quick ferry to **Tangier Med** port, heading down towards the Middle Atlas or **Marrakech**, crossing the **Atlas**, often via the popular **Aït Benhaddou** piste then heading over to the **Todra Gorge**. From there it's common to cross over **Jebel Sarhro** to Nekob via Route MH4 and either continue south to **Zagora** to take Route MS6 east to Merzouga, or find some other way to end up at **Erg Chebbi**. A return might include a crossing of the Atlas such as MH2 or via Midelt with a stop in **Fes**. **Essaouira** on the coast north of Agadir might somehow be thrown in the mix too.

A tour like this is just manageable in a fortnight and hits all the buttons in Morocco. It could also be described as following the main tourism axis with the most chance of encountering high prices and hassle in the bigger towns and cities. In the busy seasons it can also feel a bit like a procession, reducing the impression that you're out exploring the wilds, though if it's your first time, knowing you're not alone can actually be comforting.

For Morocco, Erg Chebbi is a natural wonder for sure, but other than that, consider using this book to find a creative way to cover the same regions, or break off the axis altogether to do your own thing. There is more on the regions at the start of each of the six zones from p86.

... AND WHERE YOU MIGHT NOT WANT TO GO: THE RIF

Although no one will stop you going there, one region worth being aware of is the cannabis cultivation area in the Rif mountains, centred around the town of **Ketama** on the N2 junction, east of Chefchaouen.

Following a post-independence Berber rebellion in the 1950s (and a brief 'Republic' in the 1920s, crushed by France and Spain), the government turned its back on the Rif, stifling economic development in the area. As a result cannabis, once grown all over Morocco, has boomed here, making it the biggest source of hash in the world, with cannabis pollen recorded on the Spanish mainland and the ever-expanding cultivation threatening local forests.

Despite EU pressure, the state turns a blind eye to the illegal enterprise, but deprivation has led to poverty, crumbling roads and neglected and sometimes hostile towns. It may be a lucrative business but the peasants who do all the work are as poor as any in Morocco.

There are no armed drug gangs terrorising each other as elsewhere in the world, but those travellers who don't blunder in naively regularly report that their initial curiosity soon vanishes on being chased by youths in an aggressively-driven Mercedes trying to sell a block of hash or inviting them for a smoke – usually in exchange for their valuables.

What can I do in...

These suggestions assume you're UK-based. If you're in Portugal or Spain you can do a bit more; if you live on the outskirts of Alice Springs your options are much more limited. Even then, many recognise once they get back that they planned over-ambitiously and tried to do **too much in too short a time**.

For ideas of what can be done in a **two-day rental** see p75. For suggestions on combining many of these routes into two dozen **day trips** by returning to the same place in the evening – particularly aimed at motorbikers looking to enjoy a ride without carting full baggage – see p81-3.

A week or less

Quite a lot actually, but you'll need to fly in and rent a vehicle out of Agadir, Marrakech (see p73) to make the most of your time. All three cities are well placed to make the most of their adjacent regions, giving you up to five great days on the piste. Doing it this way will be hectic of course, but the costs may well be the same as trying to cram a fortnight in with your own vehicle. A

FIRST TIME IN MOROCCO

In the current climate of what some call Islamophobia, it's understandable to feel a little apprehensive about visiting Morocco if you've never been to a Muslim country or had a chance to meet Muslim people.

Particularly around Algeciras port in southern Spain or in Ceuta, the flavour of what lies ahead can start to get intimidating, which is one reason why the alternative Spanish ports of Tarifa, Málaga and Almería can be more relaxed departure points.

Once off the boat and with the immigration formalities completed, the biggest hurdle is behind you, but the **culture shock** still requires some acclimatisation. Until you get your bearings, or even when you do, the relatively crowded north may not be to everyone's taste. South of the Atlas it's altogether another world and is partly why a book like this was written.

If you're unsure about dealing with it all it's not a bad idea to head directly south and get a feel for the country and the people. Then dally through the north on your way back by which time you're a little more streetwise.

Islamic customs

It's worth recognising that not all Muslim countries follow the strict mores of places like Saudi Arabia or Iran. North African countries in particular interpret religious strictures much more leniently and even meld Islam with older, pre-Islamic practices.

This moderate form of Islam partly accounts for the success of tourism in places like Morocco, Tunisia and, until recently, Egypt.

When you start to meet genuine people (as opposed to the irritating touts who zone in on you) there are some customs worth adopting. They really add up to no more than politeness and local etiquette.

- When asking directions or initiating a conversation with a stranger, slow down, turn off a noisy engine, then start with a *bonjour* or *salaam aleikum* and shake hands, rather than yelling 'Ay-oop, which way to Ouarzazate!?'.
- In remote and traditional settings such enquiries have the most successful and accurate results with older men.
- If you speak in French there's more chance of being understood. In the remote villages women may not speak French.
- If invited into someone's living room or tent, be ready to take your shoes off.
- For anything more than a tea, for example a meal, a lift or some other form of help, offer payment or some sort of gift. It does not have to be extravagant.
- If eating communally from a bowl (as one does with cous-cous) do not use the left hand.
- If the talk turns to Islam, as it can do, it's better to profess some religious belief than being an atheist or agnostic.
- If in doubt, do as others do.

more relaxed alternative is having a normal week's holiday and renting for a couple of days to do some routes. It's a great way to dip your toe in the sand and see if you like the idea of overlanding in Morocco.

Two weeks
This is the practical limit for a visit in your own vehicle from the UK or northern Europe. Falling within a typical holiday allocation, it's what many people try, usually just once. You'll need to get cracking and have a good plan; from Dover to Algeciras is 2250km or nearly 1400 miles. To squeeze every last hour from what are technically 16 days away, if the ferries line up and by leaving work on a Friday night, you could be in Morocco by Monday lunchtime and in the desert a day or two later. This could give you, at the very best, nine days in the Atlas and the Sahara, or more reasonably a week on the piste with a rest day or two or a visit to a big city or a resort. Although this is an intense schedule, a week on the piste is actually a pretty satisfying immersion as long as the weather remains good and you have no vehicle problems.

Renting a decent 4WD like a Toyota 105 for two weeks gets pretty pricey unless you have a car full of people to share the cost, or if you choose to hire a well-used and inexpensive 4WD you must accept the risks entailed in driving in remote regions. The 650 motorbike rental out of Marrakech adds up to around €600 or so a week, still pretty good compared to riding down in midwinter, but sometimes frustrating when it comes to additional gear.

A month
With up to four weeks at your disposal you need not dash from work to the ferry port like a lunatic and so can enjoy a relaxing tour, ticking off your pick of the routes in this book as well as taking the chance to visit some other places in Morocco, Spain and France. Between Figuig and the Atlantic you could easily explore a dozen routes as well as a few of your own, highlighting the full potential of the region and without needing a holiday afterwards to get over it. Or of course you could make a dash to Mauritania.

More than a month
By choosing the right season and using your typical three-month Moroccan visa to the limit, you can slowly explore the Atlas ranges and the Saharan plains, park up in remote spots or villages that take your fancy, get to know some locals, go trekking with them or go mountain biking and generally immerse yourself in the Moroccan experience. Or head off to West Africa for the winter. All you need is the time, the money and the inclination.

Documents, money, costs and phones

For Morocco your paperwork adds up to no more than your **passport** and your **vehicle ownership document** as well as motor insurance and travel insurance documents. Your passport must be valid for at least six months after the date you expect to leave Morocco and, unlike some other North African countries, the presence of Israeli stamps is not a problem.

Your **vehicle registration** – in the UK called the V55 or 'logbook' – is your vehicle's 'passport' and even though back home you may only ever see it when buying and selling the machine, to enter Morocco it's **essential**. If for some reason the vehicle is not in your name you'll need a letter of explanation in French (and better still, Arabic) with official-looking stamps stating you have permission from the owner; in my experience it shouldn't be a problem.

In general the owner of the vehicle must be present at the Moroccan border and this particularly goes for other people's motorbikes in the back of a van. If vehicle owners are not present, even with the vehicle logbooks and written permission from the owners, you can expect delays at the port while you persuade them you're not an unlicensed tour operator or transporting stolen bikes to Mauritania.

Visas

Currently citizens of EU member states as well as Canadians, Americans and Australians don't need a visa and can stay in Morocco for up to **90 days**. This period can be renewed at police stations or by simply leaving the country and re-entering. Some east European nationals as well as South Africans will require a visa which must be applied for in advance and which lasts a month. In the UK they cost about £18. Apply at your nearest Moroccan embassy well before your planned departure.

Motor insurance

A few years ago in the UK it was easy to get a Green Card extension of your domestic motor insurance to cover Morocco, just as you can still do for Europe (although your basic insurance will cover you in the EU, even without a Green Card). Low-risk **UK campervan** drivers have less difficulty with Moroccan cover and the situation is better on the continent, but nowadays some UK motor insurance companies don't offer this service. However, buying insurance in Morocco is easy enough and costs the same.

Some entry ports like Tangier Med (see map on p61), but not Fnideq at Ceuta or Nador, have insurance booths selling *Assurance aux Frontières*. It's also said to be possible to buy it at Algeciras port. If not, you can buy it once out of the port in an adjacent town (from Fnideq it's Tetouan – look out for the blue '*Axa Assurance*'). If you get stopped by the police as you leave a port – which is not uncommon – explain you're heading for or even ask for the nearest '*bureau d'assurance*'. It may seem unorthodox to venture out on the streets without motor insurance but this, as you're about to find out, is Africa.

The cost of insurance is the same fixed rate wherever you buy it and the periods are fixed at one or three months with prices at the time of writing as follows:

	10 days	1 month	3 months
Cars and motorcycles	620 dirhams (dh)	950 dh	1950 dh
Camping cars	1260 dh (est)	2750 dh	5000 dh

For **exchange rates** see opposite. A document not unlike your D16 (see p58) will be printed out with your details alongside French and Arabic explanations. Keep it with your D16 to present if asked at a roadside checkpoint.

What's actually covered following an accident you'd hope never to find out; probably no more than the legal minimum protection to a Third Party, or more realistically something to show at a police checkpoint to avoid a fine.

Some worry that this does not cover **damage** to or **theft** from, or of, their vehicle and is one good reason to resist decking out your Defender like the Battlestar Galactica. Such insurance can be bought from expedition specialists in the UK but it can be extremely expensive (on the continent it's less so). When overnighting in big cities, if your hotel has no parking (often the case in the traditional small hotels in the city-centre medina or old quarter) you're best off paying for **secure parking** in attended lots or garages while taking the usual precautions you'd take anywhere else. The guidebooks reviewed on p24 give basic details of secure parking sites in cities like Fes or Marrakech.

In the UK at least, insurance cover for breakdowns, repairs or **vehicle recovery** is not available as it is, say, for Dutch members of the Royal Dutch Automobil Club and probably other continental nationals. This does mean you can be on your own if you strike vehicle trouble and is where the true and not so glamorous meaning of the word 'adventure' can become apparent. For ideas on what to do when things go wrong, see from p64.

Money and costs

Exchange rates for major currencies against the Moroccan dirhams seem to change little over the years and at printing time were as follows:

    £1   13 dirhams (dh)
    €1   11 dh
    US$1 8.6 dh

Officially it's not possible to buy Moroccan dirhams outside the country but there'll be exchange bureaux or banks at Algeciras, on some ferries and at the ports. They're all legitimate, offer the same rate and provide you with a receipt, but as anywhere it pays not to let your guard down when the notes are being dished out and to count them back in front of the seller. There's no black market for currency in Morocco, though that won't stop shady individuals at the ports or in bigger cities trying to suggest otherwise.

Once on the road it's easy to withdraw further funds with credit or debit cards from banks or **ATMs** outside banks in many Moroccan towns. It's not unusual to find that, despite guarantees in advance, on arrival one of your UK bank cards isn't recognised by a Moroccan ATM so if you have several cards, **bring them all** to be on the safe side and try them out sooner rather than later. Some of these ATMs even recognise and accept major foreign currency bank notes (as opposed to plastic cards) and will return a receipt plus dirhams in notes and a tinkle of coins. In the deep south ATMs will only be found in the biggest towns like Erfoud and Rissani, Zagora, Tata and Guelmim.

Away from ATMs, **foreign credit or debit cards** are barely used for purchases in the south of Morocco, certainly not in local stores, fuel stations or at less than high-end hotels. Travellers' cheques leave you dependent on finding a bank that's open, so good, old-fashioned **cash** in the form of **euros** or of course dirhams is the best currency in Morocco. If you run out of dirhams, in places it may be possible to pay in euros.

Some costs

As a tourist, and certainly in touristy places down south such as Boumalne du Dades, Erfoud and Zagora, you can expect to be overcharged a little for ordinary purchases where prices aren't clearly marked. Overall though it's not something worth getting worked up about as the **cost of living** is less than half that of the UK.

Remember too that, as anywhere in the world, costs will be higher and the range of products smaller in remote places. Very occasionally, in places not normally visited by tourists, you may be charged a local rate for something like a meal which can come as quite a shock. Then again, at other times a kind local may offer a service or assistance for nothing or humbly request 'whatever you think it's worth'. Even in tourist souks, getting blatantly ripped off is rare and depends partly on your attitude, gullibility, patience and sometimes, your proficiency in French.

Motoring

Straits ferry; 4WD & 2 passengers	from €200 return
Motorcycle and rider	from €100 return
Diesel	8.5 dh/litre
Unleaded petrol	11 dh
5L motor oil	from 90 dh
Car tyre repair	from 30 dh
DIY car wash	from 30 dh
Replace broken leaf spring	around 500 dh
Motorcycle rental per week	from 3500dh for a 250 to 10,000dh for a GS1200
4WD rental per week	around 60,000 dh for a big 4WD

The price of diesel in 'mainland' Morocco (see also p66) is currently about the same as it is in the two Spanish coastal enclaves of Ceuta and Melilla, though unleaded may work out less here. In Western Sahara fuel is discounted by some 30% compared to the north.

BARGAINING FOR SOUVENIRS

Despite what some may assume, bartering over regular daily purchases and services is not the norm. Haggling over a **souvenir** in a *souk* or market is another game altogether.

You may read about cunning equations such as: offer a third of the initial price and settle on half, but if you don't want to feel you've been cheated or made a fool of, the simplest advice is:

- take your time (take *days* to think it over if you have the chance) and
- pay what you think it's worth.

Ask yourself would you really pay €50 for a studded leather camel skull ash tray back home? Moroccan vendors are world-class masters in the art of selling overpriced handicrafts to tourists. But so-called 'Moroccan chic' and design are world class too, and many of the products you'll admire in the souks would proudly be seen adorning the homes of locals.

My own tactic on seeing something I like but don't need is this: first, mull it over for days. If possible, ask a local what it's worth. Then fix a fair price in your head, stick to it **with good humour** through all the spiel and the 'buy two get one half price', and be prepared to walk away if you don't get it.

The back of the current *Lonely Planet Morocco* guide allocates a full page of sound advice for the wary buyer.

Eating

Bread	from 0.3 dh
Bottled water 1.5 lt	around 5–7 dh
Soft drink	around 4–6 dh
Cup of coffee or tea	from 5 dh
Salad	around 10 dh
Brochette (kebab)	from 50 dh
Omelette and chips	from 30 dh
Tajine	from 40–70 dh

Accommodation

Morocco has a huge range of inexpensive, unclassified hotels as well as basic tourist-oriented *auberges*. In the bigger cities they're often in the charismatic but also run-down and noisy old quarter or *medina* with attendant parking limitations and, away from the tourist axis in the south, basic hotels like this may be all you'll find. At these places booking ahead is unnecessary; very often you'll be the only person staying there.

In the cities or in the countryside you'll not get much more, pound for pound, by paying over 250dh for a hotel room unless you've been roughing it for days and are looking for some sort of lavish treat. Anything with 'kasbah' in the name will usually be in this category. The better guidebooks (see p23-4) can fill you in on other costs and practicalities of accommodation and this book's website has a link to a growing thread of recommendations.

Basic hotel (shared bathroom)	from 70 dh – half board from 110 dh
Moderate (en suite)	from 120 dh – half board from 170 dh
Kasbah-auberge	from 180 dh – half board from 250 dh

BUSINESS HOURS, RAMADAN & TIME ZONE

Morocco is an Islamic country but follows the Western model for business hours.

Things may change in the annual month-long festival of **Ramadan**, when the devout don't eat, drink or even smoke during daylight hours. Shops are still open but in general business becomes dormant, with long siestas to allow people to rest. Many restaurants and cafés close in the daytime, when it can be hard to get a meal.

It's not correct to call Ramadan a **fast**, as a whole lot of eating and drinking goes on once the *muezzins* (prayer callers) or sirens have signalled sunset. The fast is often broken with a light snack of dates and milk, with a big feed late at night and another an hour or two before dawn.

For the non-Muslim traveller, Ramadan in Morocco can be an inconvenience in the daytime, at which time it's good form not to eat or drink publicly. Be discreet; most people are tolerant of non-Muslim foreigners.

Although it's fun to get caught up in the evening's anticipation as the daily fast is broken, perhaps the biggest factor to travellers is that by the end of Ramadan people are pretty exhausted and can get ratty. At this time it should be you who exercises some tolerance.

Every year Ramadan falls about 11 days earlier and currently it's coinciding with the longer, hotter days of summer. The exact timings are governed by the moon sightings in Mecca. Future predictions are as follows:

2014	28 June	27 July
2015	18 June	16 July
2016	6 June	5 July
2017	27 May	25 June

Time
Morocco follows **GMT**. This means in winter it's an hour behind Spanish time (ie: the same as the UK) and in summer is two hours behind Spain. Remember that the Spanish enclaves and ferry ports of Ceuta and Melilla will run on Spanish time. Don't miss the boat!

PLANNING YOUR TRIP

MOBILE PHONES AND INTERNET

Bring your mobile to Morocco, whether or not you plan to even turn it on. Disregarding its day-to-day utility, a mobile is a useful tool in case of emergency. As with many North African countries, the market penetration of mobiles is among the highest in the world and far exceeds landlines. Your mobile will work in any sizeable town and these days there's a good chance of getting a 3G signal too.

The two main mobile service providers are *Maroc Telecom* and *Méditel*, and both have pretty much saturated coverage north of the former Western Sahara border around Tan-Tan. The biggest gaps are the barely populated Rekkam plateau, the crests of the High Atlas and the desert along the border south of what I call the 'Desert Highway' (MS10; see p114). Even then, on the piste it's best not to assume you'll have uninterrupted coverage to keep up with the cricket scores. If you're desperate to get a signal, besides setting your phone to re-scan manually for local providers, it's worth walking around, getting on high ground or on a line-of-sight towards where you think a mast or town might be. As for who you're going to call when you're up the creek? See p65.

If you plan to use your mobile a lot, a much cheaper alternative to paying for roaming charges is to **buy a local SIM card** from the many outlets for the above providers. To do this your mobile phone may need unlocking or 'jailbreaking', but if that's not yet been done, chances are the shop that sells you the SIM can do this for you for a few dirhams. Moroccan mobile numbers begin 06.

Landlines

Public phones do exist but as elsewhere in the world, they are heading in the same direction as the venerable stegosaurus. More prolific and reliable are 'taxi phone' boutiques; private enterprises with a bank of phone booths for those who can't afford a mobile. The **international country code** for Morocco is 212.

Wi-fi and 3G internet access

Although it's not free like wi-fi (where you find it and where it's worth using) and most towns will have an inexpensive internet café (usable speeds can vary), the best way to get online is to buy something like a **Maroc Telecom 3G dongle** and SIM card to plug into your laptop or slot into an unlocked smartphone/tablet. The package currently costs around 200dh for a month's unlimited usage which is less than 50p a day.

You'll need to show your passport as identification on purchase, and if you exceed a certain daily allowance (currently 400mb), the connection speed drops to a still usable level. Once installed and connected, if you're sat in a vehicle you may find it's worth using a USB extension cord to get the dongle out in the open. Where there's reception, 3G speeds around Morocco are good enough to do Skype video calls.

Maroc Telecom 3G SIM for just £15 a month.

Maps

You'll find one of the following maps indispensable but remember the reviews below only relate to a map's utility on the pistes south of the Atlas. **Online resources** for overlanding in Morocco include the Moroccan forum on the HUBB (💻 www.horizonsunlimited.com/hubb/morocco) as well as contributor Tim Cullis' 💻 www.morocco-knowledgebase.net.

PAPER COUNTRY MAPS

Although the medium is moving away from print towards digital, there's still much to be said for travelling with an inexpensive paper map.

Satnavs and the like are brilliant in doing what they do, but until they can project their information holographically, they're never going to be as useful as an unfolded map in showing you **the big picture**. This can be especially useful in the planning stage as well as reminding you that Morocco is bigger than you think.

There are up to a dozen paper maps of Morocco in print. Taking into account scale, price, clarity, availability, date of publication and presence of a longitude/latitude grid to enable rough positioning with a roamer (see picture on p21), only a couple are worthwhile for independent overland travel in the area covered by this book.

Once the available maps are closely scrutinised and compared they're soon shown to be inaccurate when it comes to verifying or differentiating a road from a track and even a track from a footpath. They also tend to copy each other's mistakes which hints at how some get updated. While this book will be no better in keeping up with the programme of sealing backcountry tracks, on some maps minor routes shown as sealed are in fact little-used pistes not likely to be sealed anytime soon, and some tracks depicted identically on several maps don't exist or match the depicted orientation.

In other words, for navigating along the main 'N' or *route nationale* highways in an RV most maps are fine, but using them on southern Moroccan tracks is likely to be a hit-and-miss affair. But as Moroccan tracks are short this uncertainty isn't so much a problem as a potential for adventure!

What also becomes evident is how many interesting and easily navigable pistes there are in Morocco which never appear on modern maps. The same can

> **using these maps ... is likely to be a hit-and-miss affair. But as Moroccan tracks are short this uncertainty isn't so much a problem as a potential for adventure!**

be said for villages; many established settlements on a par with other locally-depicted places are missing while some towns are given inconsistent prominence. So having evaluated them all for the prospective users of this book I can save you some time by recommending the following two paper maps.

Michelin 742

1:1 million

The best thing about Michelin's Morocco map is the intuitive 1:1m scale (a millimetre = a kilometre) as well as the great Michelin design and the fact that the main map goes right down to Laayoune which means you can view all the routes in this book at once (apart from the lower halves of Routes MO2 and MW6). As far as accuracy goes it's no worse than the rest, but what **is** worse is the thin paper which doesn't lend itself to regular use. This isn't helped by the fact that at over 1.5m wide, the 742 is a big map. Discounted online from £8 to around a fiver in the UK, while it lasts it's also the cheapest of the Morocco maps.

Roads and pistes wind around with believable intricacy (unlike the lazier RKH map, see opposite) and you get Michelin's much imitated scenic 'green road' feature which is rather inconsistent, even by the broadest interpretation of what is scenic. In the mountains depictions of forest cover aren't to be relied on too closely either, while further south, dunes get the same vague interpretation. This is the sort of core detail you feel will never get updated.

As for the accuracy of secondary roads and pistes – a common failing on all Morocco maps – look carefully at the map's key (in five languages including Arabic). Unconventionally, uncoloured (white) roads with solid borders on both edges signify 'Road surfaced' (*route revêtue* or 'covered', as opposed to *goudronée*; tarred) but **one dashed edge** means an all-out piste. Surfaced with what you wonder? It's a usefully ambiguous way of saying they could be surfaced with steaming asphalt, gravel or Nutella and some of these 'white roads' happen to be major two-lane highways. As on other maps, a few pistes and even white roads don't exist, while of course many more are missing. In places this data is up to a decade out of date.

Conspicuous by its absence is a longitude/latitude grid for use with a roamer (see picture opposite) or a GPS. A possible reason becomes apparent once you try and hand draw a grid on it yourself, which can work with other maps. It soon transpires the map is actually aligned quite a few degrees east of north, most probably because it's based on the top left corner of their 'North and West Africa' 953 map which is north-centred on E16°. Without presumably expensive correction, printing a grid over a 742 would expose this lean all the more clearly and might put customers off. Baffled? Don't worry, it's not that important.

Overall, you can forgive the out-of-date detail because of the classic, clear design, but instead of banging out so-called 'new editions' with the legal minimum of alterations, Michelin should take a bold step and print double-sided on plastic paper with grid lines – or at least use better paper. That is never going to happen so in my experience the 742 is not significantly better for back-country or piste driving than a more robust and gridded RKH.

Reise Know-How

1:1 million

When you recognise all these maps are flawed, the RKH is the most practical because, unlike the better Michelin, it won't fall apart after less than an hour's accumulated use. Cartographically the RKH isn't the clearest design but the double-sided printing makes it compact and easy to use inside a car, tent or on a bike or out in a gale. Again, the 1:1m scale is intuitive for quick distance estimates and the grid lines work well with a roamer, pictured right. They even manage to squeeze an index round the edges.

The RKH's biggest flaw is the vague alignment of roads and tracks and unprofessional assumptions about which pistes have been sealed.

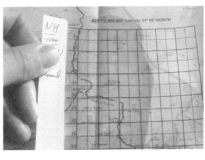

In the sense used here (as opposed to the commercial examples found online) **roamers** are one-degree-square grids printed on clear acetate (pictured above) to help approximate your position on a 1:1m scale map with a long/lat grid.

They're only accurate on a particular band of latitude which for most of the routes in this book is 'NH'. You can download roamers to print off from the *Morocco Overland* website.

Heading for a sealed road on the map that's actually still a piste and will never be a road is more irritating and time-wasting than merely not knowing the full extent of asphalting. But if necessary you can eat your lunch off an RKH, use it as an umbrella and generally treat it roughly without it ending up like Michelin's self-shredding example.

You can also download a pre-calibrated digital version of this map from ⌨ www.reise-know-how.de to import into a computer and should you wish, track your movements using GPS software.

DIGITAL MAPS AND IMAGERY

You'll want a paper map, but below are some other mapping resources. For reviews of older paper maps including IGN one millions, American 500,000 TPCs and Soviet-era topos in three scales, see the website.

Whether riding a moto or in a car, if you take this option get a satnav with a usefully sized screen – typically a 5-inch diagonal widescreen – as well as with the ability to import non-propriety mapping, usually via a mini-SD card.

Morocco satnav mapping

There are a few maps available to import into your satnav to make it much more useful than whatever base map it has for Morocco. Most are free while Garmin will sell you a CD for some £130 that's little better than the free offerings to which it bears a suspicious similarity in places. Open Street Map (OSM; ⌨ wiki.openstreetmap.org) is one source, the Portuguese ⌨ www.viagens 4x4.com/mapas is another, while 'Olaf' is the adopted abbreviation for Marokko Topo GPS vector map (⌨ www.island-olaf.de/travel/marokko /gps.html). This is the original free downloadable Morocco GPS map produced by a German, Olaf Kähler, using tracklogs and other data supplied by contributors.

You can buy a Garmin Nuvi or similar TomTom used for around £70. Both can import and display maps like 'Olaf' via their mini-SD cards. Garmin's bulkier, bike-based Zumo model is about twice as much but on a motorcycle a Nuvi will survive downpours if tucked behind a screen. Otherwise, buy an inexpensive waterproof housing. The Nuvi's suction mount may work in a car but on a motorcycle put the unit in a tankbag or use RAM mounts with short arms.

First a word of warning. Even if you're computer savvy you can spend hours trying to get digital maps to display on your satnav while battling operating system incompatibilities. I tried to install all the maps listed above except the Garmin, but only Olaf worked and it was all the satnav mapping I needed in Morocco.

For the first edition of this book my appreciation of 'Olaf' was rather limited. Using Macs I was unable to view the routes on a computer and the matchbox-sized screen of my handheld GPS unit displayed the secondary 'thin' Olaf routes so faintly as to be invisible. Since then I've been able to see the full potential of Olaf using Garmin's long overdue Mac-friendly BaseCamp software and found that full detail was available on a Nuvi satnav screen. Even though the last update was in 2009, by that time enough pistes in Morocco had been included to make this a comprehensive GPS map. With Olaf you won't run out of tracks to follow any time soon.

With an Olaf track you can zoom right in and follow a path accurately through a village instead of blundering around and frightening the mules. Sometimes the track is out by several metres, and other tracks finish up as dead ends – but that's probably down to the quality and 'authenticity' of track-logs sent in by contributors. Either way, stick Olaf in your GPS unit and, along with a Michelin and RKH map, you'll have an excellent, peer-proven map of many pistes in Morocco and pretty good highway and city information too. Using it in 2012 on a Garmin Nuvi, by merely keeping an eye on my orientation, I was able to confidently skirt the periphery of Marrakech and get on the N8 heading east. Without it, or depending on satnav routability (where available) or referring to a paper map, I'd have gotten in a right muddle.

Google and Bing Maps

Even though they're free, used as a pre-planning reference map Google or Bing Maps are misleading on southern Morocco compared to the maps described above. Click between 'map' to 'satellite' or 'aerial' and you'll often see how inaccurate the highway overlay is compared to the true satellite image, although the 'terrain' screen can be illuminating. Pistes and roads are out-of-date, incomplete, not labelled with the standard Moroccan N- or R- road/track designations, inaccurate in hierarchy (closed piste and two-lane blacktop shown as the same) or are non-existent, just like the worst paper maps. Furthermore, on Google many town and village names are unrecognisable, presumably gleaned from non-standard US sources. Zoomed in, you can look at the Google map of Morocco a long time before you find a name you recognise or work out where you are.

THE DIFFERENCE BETWEEN SATNAVS AND GPS

Satellite navigators such as a TomTom, Garmin Nuvi or their weatherproof Zumo have come to be known as **satnavs** (below centre). They feature a touch screen and built-in street-level vector mapping that moves continuously, showing your position. Among many other features, satnavs are routeable but I'd suggest this 'turn left in 500 metres' feature is more useful on backroads in mainland Europe than in Morocco. On the road in Morocco you'll probably be following well signed major routes between the north and the south so won't need your hand held.

Except when used on a bicycle, a traditional **GPS unit** (on the left) will do the job but is less well suited to motoring in Morocco. The built-in map is usually basic and by the time you get to Morocco will be

pretty poor, but as with satnavs, better maps can be imported. The good thing is that with these units batteries are replaceable and even then will last much longer than a typical car-type satnav, and as such are more suited to cyclists.

Especially on a moto you may find the usual cigarette lighter power plugs will lose contact on rough tracks so consider either hard-wiring them or converting the ends to take more secure **DIN plugs**. If contact is lost for a second your unit reverts to batteries and may switch off to save it going flat.

Now **smart phones** (on the right) have a GPS and vector mapping facility just like a satnav, though operating full time in GPS mode will drain the battery, so you'll need to plug it into a vehicle's power source.

Google satellite (or Google Earth) or Bing Aerial are much more useful and particularly effective in vividly dramatising the arid topography of southern Morocco, even if resolution on the 10-mile-square quadrants is hit-and miss. Bing or Google, some sectors seem to have been shot through the bottom of a Coke bottle, while others appear as crisp as hanging out of a hot air balloon. In Erg Chebbi or Erg Chegaga you can even spot the tourist bivouacs in the dunes. It's well worth looking at both: Bing, for example, is much clearer in the Lac Iriki (MS8) region than occluded Google. At best all three of the aerial platforms can give you a 'map' that cannot lie. With them you can preview your route or cook up new links between pistes, discover new areas and generally be amazed at the bird's eye view of your planet.

Guidebooks

Morocco Overland covers southern Morocco off the beaten track and as such will be indispensable for tracking down wells along the Jebel Ouarkaziz or routes in the vicinity of Jebel Sirwa. By and large it doesn't get bogged down in hotel and restaurant listings and accounts of 'Things to See and Do'.

For the big picture get a proper travel guidebook for Morocco; it'll greatly enhance your experience and background knowledge of the country. For all their minor faults, only *Lonely Planet* or *Rough Guide* do a good job in this respect, while regularly releasing new editions. *Morocco Overland* does cover the often overlooked 'places in between' down south, making an effort to provide information where accounts in the two guidebooks are either out of date or missing. Therefore, in this book you'll get a GPS point for the little-known hotel in a key town missed by both guidebooks, as well as fuller personal reviews of places I've actually stayed in; choices which are often based on Rough Guide or LP suggestions. This has now become part of a sticky thread for **recommended accommodation** at the top of the HUBB Morocco forum (see p19).

Note that the reviews of the two guidebooks below relate both to the region and the type of travelling covered by *this* book. There is little doubt that accounts of the history of the Almoravids or the fine architecture of Fes are as good as it gets because once written, they don't change much. It's the practical details of accommodation, eating and getting around which can go out of date in any triennial publication, but are what most travellers depend on. In this respect the active LP Thorn Tree forum is a bonus in keeping up to date.

Rough Guide Morocco

In common with many Rough Guides which gradually acquired a middle-aged spread, falling sales and rising production costs saw the ninth edition of Morocco go on a drastic diet and lose some 200 pages. Tellingly though, the south of the country which we're concerned with was barely touched and the page count remained the same as the previous edition. That tells you a lot about where they think readers go in Morocco.

Although it tries here and there, the Rough Guide is still not especially well aimed at 'motoring' as they sometimes call it. Regional maps are mutually inconsistent as well as inaccurate (a common flaw with guidebooks), but this is only on the same 'road or track' level as the paper maps.

Should you get sick or laid up with repairs, there's some great background material on Moroccan history, culture, books, music and language, but that changes little from edition to edition. When it comes to finite, precise practicalities and directions it can all get a bit woolly, although there's no escaping the fact that you've twice as many pages in the south as the LP. For this reason alone, the current edition must be more useful. By the time you read this the comprehensively redesigned colour 10th edition will be out, but hopefully won't have lost too many more pages. See the website for a full review.

Lonely Planet Morocco

By far the better selling guide, the LP has a younger, snappier tone but lacks the authority and coverage as well as the budget accommodation options from LP's pre-flashpacking heyday. Just 70 pages cover the *Morocco Overland* area. Many accounts of not so out-of-the-way towns are so skimpy they seem merely index name checks while greatly easing the updating process by not being too specific. That's not so good for the reader but you do get many well thought out boxes advising on the tours and other activities, little use though that is to exploring the south independently.

VEHICLE CHOICE & PREPARATION

2

Chances are you'll already know whether you want to tour the Moroccan outback with a motorcycle, a 4WD or a mountain bike; the appeal and practicality of each is quite distinct. It's worth noting that most of the routes in this book can also be managed in a **regular car** or van, as you'll discover when you get there. By the same token, only some well-watered and less rough routes are do-able on a self-sufficient mountain bike (see the list on p47) or even a regular touring motorcycle.

Realistically though, driving regular road cars or motorcycles, as well as scooters and bicycles on the piste is an unconventional choice – unless of course you live in Morocco! Most visitors are looking for a genuine reason to explore the off-road capabilities of their 4WDs or trail bikes and Morocco has plenty of great places to do just that.

In case it's not obvious, the motorcycle and bicycle travel addressed here is unsupported and self-sufficient with the concomitant results in handling and effort when riding off-road. Both forms of two-wheel travel become much more light-hearted, as well as less risky, when supported by a load-carrying van or 4WD – see p31.

If you have a long-term overland journey in mind or lined up, particularly across Africa, for Western European-based travellers Morocco also happens to be a geographically-convenient location for testing both yourself in a significantly alien culture and your vehicle in an off-road setting. Car or bike, there's a whole lot more about that in my other books: *Adventure Motorcycling Handbook* and *Overlanders' Handbook*.

Motorcycles

These days 'adventure bikes' are all the rage, with manufacturers jumping over each other to produce a machine which looks like it could take on the world. It is in fact the second wave of a trend of potentially overland-ready motorcycles that kicked off in the early 1980s with Dakar Rally look-alikes like Yamaha's Ténéré. The ever-

Little and large: TTR250 and an F650GS.

popular BMW GS twins and singles are less obviously rally-derived, but you're sure to see them in Morocco too.

Little or large?

That is the question that can torment a Morocco-bound biker. Will the chore of riding the typical 3000-mile European leg from the UK on a sub-400cc single be worth the responsive ride at the sharp end of the trip? Or does the smooth, cruising comfort of a big flat-, parallel- or V-twin add up to the nagging regret of doing less off-road exploring than you'd hoped? Up to a point it depends on your attitude, your off-road-riding and overseas-biking background, and how committed you are to exploring off-road. Do you just want to get a feel for your abilities and your machine on a couple of routes and lap up the many other wonderful aspects of the Morocco experience? Riding the pistes doesn't have to be about nailing each berm in a shower of rocks or getting some serious air. Older riders or those on heavier machines are satisfied to simply slow down – which you have to do off-road anyway – and find pleasure in gently exploring the back tracks on a capable machine.

... the popularity of big adventure bikes can exceed the abilities of many Moroccan novices...

The good thing is that sand – the bane of fully-loaded big bikes on *faux*-knobbly tyres – is rare or mostly avoidable in Morocco. What you get instead are rocks and stones that'll work your suspension into a lather and ask much more of your tyres' toughness than their tread pattern, but that otherwise make for reasonably predictable riding. As I found updating this edition on a GS650 twin, ridden with a steady and experienced hand it's amazing how far you can get with a machine that exceeds a quarter of a ton by the time you get on it. That's until the going gets especially muddy, sandy or the bike falls over.

Because the popularity of big adventure bikes can exceed the abilities of many Moroccan novices, each route in this book addresses the suitability on such machines. All you have to do is pick the right route, take it easy and, if conditions become too much for you, have the wisdom to turn back.

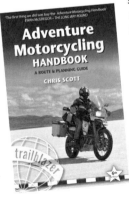

PREPARING A BIKE

For the whole nine yards on outfitting anything to go anywhere, see *Adventure Motorcycling Handbook*. There you'll find advice on everything from ways of carrying baggage to tyre choice. This section will focus just on Morocco because the good thing is that riding here requires comparatively little adaptation to most bikes and not that much in payload.

The problem is that at the very least you're taking on a road trip across Western Europe in probably a less-than-ideal season and following it with off-road riding in some remote desert and mountains. In a car these issues merely add up to more stuff in the back; on a bike bound for the piste any payload is the enemy of responsive handling and therefore riding confidence, so you need to ascertain your priorities.

Much depends on what sort of trip you plan to have in Morocco. Is it primarily a road ride, two-up, with the odd dabble along a piste just to say you've done it? In that case something like the two shortest MW routes, MS1 and maybe MS9 and the popular MH4 are good tasters with as little as 39km or 25 miles of piste (MW4) in a typical Moroccan setting. If you've never ridden off-road before or wonder whether your do-it-all adventure bike lives up to the hype, one of these routes in good weather would require nothing more than a carefully-ridden road tourer and the patience to take it easy as you get a feel for the machine. Others will want nothing less than to pack each day with dirt-track excursions where a light, well-adapted machine with the right tyres and minimal payload will respond much better to the hammering.

MOTORCYCLING IN MOROCCO

Moroccans have, by and large, inherited a continental attitude towards bikes, one that is positive and sees them as cool and exciting. Part of this is because swingeing import taxes mean that motorcycles of the type you'll be riding are unknown in the south of Morocco and are therefore exotic. Four-wheel drives are two a penny down there, but now that the Dakar Rally is finished with Morocco, anything much bigger or faster than a clapped-out Mobylette is rarely seen.

Road riding

It's probable that many riders of big adventure bikes without experience in off-road riding come to Morocco with grand plans to carve through the pistes until they discover two things: how heavy a bike can feel when a track gets tough; and what great roads there are for riding in the south.

Compared to the north, the riding here can be pure heaven. The weather is drier and warmer, the traffic is lighter, there are no big cities to deal with, the scenery's spectacular, the little-used tarmac is in great shape, the relief makes for some great mountain roads and basic, inexpensive accommodation is plentiful. Did I miss anything? So don't be disappointed if you find your well-meant plans to star in your own mini-Dakar get a little truncated. You'll have learned about how your bike handles in the dirt which will be good for next time – and you'll have a great road ride.

Spares and repairs

This exclusivity of riding a cool bike in Morocco backfires when it comes to needing parts or mechanical assistance. Down south you'll be pretty much on your own and even something as simple as an inner tube will be almost impossible to find. (There's a list of recommended parts on p29.) Other riders can be a help and BMW dealers SMEIA in Casablanca can service or repair the very latest models, but at a fraction of UK prices.

If you need a part, often your best bet is to get something brought out to you by other tourists. Mechanics down south will only have a general moped- and car-based understanding of motorcycle engines and electrics, although steel welding can be done in any town or village with the right gear.

Other than that, ask for help on the usual forums or get to Spain for what you need. It will require some messing about with Customs as you'll be leaving your machine in Morocco unexported, but it can be done.

Bikershome Off Road Centre, ideally positioned on the south side of Ouarzazate, is the rare beacon shining in the gloom and where, along with half-board accommodation, a well-equipped garage comes with the price of the room. The other UK bike tour operators in town have enough work maintaining their own big fleets of KTMs and Yamahas and are less likely to help or even sell parts which they themselves must import.

Heidenau K60; a great performing tyre on road and dry dirt. Lasts for ages too.

Essentials

With **tyres**, whether full knobbly, or trail tread pattern such as a Tourance, newer covers will give you fewer problems with punctures. The best compromise tyres are something like Heidenau K60s (left), Pirelli's MT21, Michelin's T63 or Continental's classic TKC80. All these, and a few others besides, make both the ride across Europe and off-roading in Morocco predictable by using a shallow and relatively dense pattern of knobs that gives a good footprint and profile on the tarmac with enough space in-between to get a bite on the dirt. Using these sorts of tyres also means you don't need to mess around dropping air pressures on the dirt to get the most out of them which means less risk of punctures when you inadvertently hit a rock step too hard. Unfortunately something like a TKC80 will probably be all but finished by the time you get back whereas something like an admittedly less aggressive K60 won't even be half worn.

Chain and sprockets will also wear faster with a full payload and on the dirt so make sure they have at least 5000 miles left in them.

Chances are your bike will fall over, most probably at speeds little greater than walking pace on mud or in sand. The best trail bikes are designed for this with foot controls that fold rather than bend as well as proper **hand guards** with a metal frame on the end of the handlebars. With the latter you can forget about the need for spare levers which can easily bend or snap, even in a simple fall.

The underside of the engine is also vulnerable and the rocky nature of most Moroccan tracks means some sort of protection is essential, whatever you ride. Many new trail or adventure bikes come with a skimpy plastic guard that alone will not be adequate; something like a full width **bashplate** of 2mm steel or twice that in alloy is what you want, curving up round the lower sides of the engine protecting water pumps and other vulnerable components. **Crash bars** of course are a good idea, especially if your bike's radiator

Between them, a proper bash plate and handguards are no-brainers for Morocco.

BASIC EQUIPMENT CHECKLIST

Documents
- Passport
- Driver's licence
- Vehicle ownership document
- Cash, debit and credit cards
- Travel tickets
- European roadside recovery card
- Motor insurance
- D16 (see p58-9)
- Bike manual
- Maps
- Guidebook

Camping and cooking (optional)
- Tent
- Sleeping mat
- Sleeping bag
- Stove – plus fuel if not regular petrol
- Tea towel and pan scrubber
- Spoon and fork
- Cooking pot(s) and pot gripper
- Washing-up liquid
- Mug
- Water bag/bottle

Toiletries
- Soap (can be used as clothes detergent)
- Toothbrush and toothpaste
- Toilet paper
- Universal basin plug

Clothing
- Riding boots plus light shoes
- Fleece jacket
- Riding jacket
- Waterproofs
- Gloves for highway and piste
- Socks and underpants
- Thermals and shirt
- Trousers or riding pants
- Cap or hat
- Crash helmet (and goggles)

Bike spares and tools
- Spare key on the bike
- Wire, duct tape and cable ties
- Spare fuses, connectors and bulbs
- Spare nuts and bolts for rack fittings
- Jump leads
- Front and rear inner tubes
- Tyre levers
- Puncture repair kit: mini 12-volt compressor, handpump, tubeless plugs
- Clutch cable if not hydraulic
- Radiator sealant, epoxy & metal repair glue
- Diaphragm for CV carbs
- Hose clips
- Small tub of grease and small WD40/GT85
- Spark plug(s)
- Petrol pipe
- Spare bungees and straps
- Spanners, sockets and hex keys
- Small adjustable spanner
- Cross- and flat-bladed screwdrivers
- Pliers with wire cutters (or multitool)
- Spoke key
- Junior hacksaw with spare blades
- Top-up oil, chain oil or lube and rag

Miscellaneous
- GPS unit with 12V power cable
- Camera, memory cards, charger
- Moroccan plug adaptor (same as Europe)
- Pen, notebook
- Spare batteries for electrical gadgets
- Mobile phone and charger
- Tablet or smartphone with contact list
- Waterproof bags
- String or rope
- Multitool or Swiss Army knife
- Head torch
- Lighters
- Ear plugs
- First Aid kit

VEHICLE CHOICE & PREPARATION

GEARING

The gearing on bigger, chain-driven road-oriented trail bikes is usually too high and too wide for off-roading with a self-sufficient payload. There's nothing you can do about wide ratios but you can easily **lower the gearing** by fitting a smaller engine sprocket, a job that with the right tools can take 10-15 minutes.

A front sprocket with 1 or 2 fewer teeth (12 is a minimum) gives better control at low speeds, such as doing U-turns, negotiating rough slopes and especially uphill hairpins.

With standard gearing you tend to slip the clutch which doesn't do it any good if you're carrying a heavy load or it's hot.

I calculated my 660 Ténéré did 8mph at tick over in first gear which was too fast for loose or rocky hairpin climbs and some descents. Five mph or less would be better.

Shaft-drive bikes are of course stuck with the gearing they're given, but while being at least 20kg heavier, BMW's 'Adventure' version of the 1200GS has lower gearing, making it more suited to slow, off-road riding.

protrudes, as well as a **wider foot** welded or bolted on the end of the side stand to stop it sinking on soft surfaces. And with a long ride in the cool season, any sort of **screen** is also a good idea to reduce the blast of wind and rain.

Fuel and water range

In my Sahara book I observe, 'water = time, fuel = distance'. In Morocco on a bike this pithy aphorism need not be pushed to the limit as it usually is on a bike in the central Sahara. With the exception of MW6 to Smara, among the longest routes in this book is MS8 at just over **300km** or nearly 200 miles – a good fuel range to aim for in Morocco. Two-thirds of the off-road routes in this book are under 250km or 165 miles and many can be strung together in a near-continuous trail. A range of 300km should be possible on any bike with an 18-litre tank returning 17kpl or 48.5mpg (5.9l/100km). These days many fuel-injected bikes will struggle to drop below 21kpl (60mpg or 4.8l/100km) and so will need only a 14.2-litre tank to cover 300km. If that's a stretch or you want to try the longer routes, an inexpensive five-litre plastic can from a motor factor gives you at least another 85-105km or 55-70 miles. In Morocco there should be no need for bulky and awkward jerricans.

Keeping close tabs on your fuel consumption rather than knowing 'it'll do 200 miles on a tenner' is an important aspect of overlanding. By becoming familiar with your bike's range of consumption figures you're able to predict how far you'll get in given conditions or how fast you can do so. Making these calculations these days can be tricky if you've been brought up to think in miles per gallon (mpg) because UK vehicles still come with mph speedos but we all buy fuel in litres. One of the best features of my Ténéré's digital display (and doubtless many other bikes like this) was the ability to change the speed and distance read-out to kilometres. This meant a bit less brain work to convert a kpl figure to mpg which I can relate to. On p67 (and also on the website under Getting there) is a converter from mpg to kpl as well as an equation to calculate the more precise European-style l/100km. With this conversion UK riders with imperial instruments can quickly convert a fill-up in litres against the miles on the bike's odometer to get a comprehensible mpg figure.

Water

Between spring and the early autumn **water** too can become an issue, particularly if you've bitten off more than you can chew and the weather in the desert turns on you. Each route lists GPS points for all known **wells** and you should be prepared to use these; they're there particularly for motorcyclists and those mountain bikers who'll use this book to the full.

The well at KM37 on Route MA9.

At the warmer ends of the season at the very least carry **5 litres** on a day route, double that if you plan to overnight in the wilds. In every village shop you can buy 1.5-litre bottles of water.

Carrying the load

People imagine the Sahara as a sea of dunes but in mountain or desert, Moroccan pistes are generally rough, stony tracks. In a car you sometimes have to crawl along for hours in first and second gear, on a bike you can fly along at twice the speed without any undue hardship to the bike or your backbone. However, the elegant, often plastic, click-on baggage for the likes of European road touring which are often listed as a manufacturer's official accessory are in most cases not built to

Enduristan Monsoon throwovers.

endure the beating you'll give them on Routes MS5 or MS7. Much of course depends on how you ride, how light the load and the mounting mechanism. Such boxes will survive much longer if you load heavy items across the back of the seat and also consider some added support such as strapping them up.

It's one reason why **aluminium boxes** from the likes of Metal Mule or Touratech are so popular. While some are tough and will take crashing better than most plastic touring cases, they can get in the way when you need to take a precautionary dab with your foot to steady yourself. Indeed the very fear of damaging your legs can lead to a loss of nerve and de-optimised technique.

For this edition I used Enduristan's Monsoon throwovers and a waterproof Watershed bag. There's a detailed review of the Monsoons as well as other similar fabric panniers on ⌨ adventure-motorcyclingh.com.

4WD

As you'll find out for yourself, with care it's possible to explore the back tracks of Morocco in a regular car but let's face it, you have a 4WD and you want to use it before some eco-terrorist sets it on fire. Morocco is a relatively undemanding destination in terms of payload and range, but in terms of all-terrain ruggedness it can get challenging, not least because of the variety of conditions you can expect, from sub-alpine snow to mud, flooded tracks and dunes.

If you're new to genuine off-roading in 4WDs it's important to know how to operate your machine correctly to avoid damaging your car as well as getting stuck and unnecessarily chewing up the landscape. Modern, cutting edge 4WDs such as Land Rover's Discovery have an impressive electronically-controlled array of suspension-, traction- and throttle-controlling systems to enable this, but in the real world driver input still requires more than turning a dial from 'grass' to 'sand'. Learning how to do this well is part of the satisfaction of driving on southern Morocco's pistes. There's more on off-roading in Morocco on p76. For a whole lot more on choosing, preparing and using 4WDs, see my *Overlanders' Handbook.*

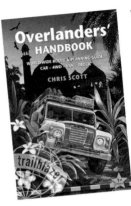

WHICH 4WD?

Petrol or diesel, long- or short-wheelbase, manual or auto and even models without 'Land' in the title will all work fine in Morocco where distances are relatively short and so vehicle recovery – and repatriation where necessary – is comparatively simple. You don't need the full-on, all-terrain ruggedness of a Land Cruiser or Defender but these are among the most common vehicles out there. Other popular models include Toyota's Prado, the Land Rover Discovery, Mitsubishi Pajero, Nissan Patrol and Mercedes G-Wagen; all big, heavy 4WDs capable of carrying four people and their gear anywhere in Morocco.

Not all cars with 4WD capability will work on the mountain pistes of Morocco; a good way of distinguishing a potentially functional, all-terrain 4WD from the likes of a Honda CRV, Freelander or a Volvo XC90 is the presence of an additional **low range gearbox**. If the vehicle of your choice has one you can be fairly sure that it's been built to handle genuine off-roading and not just look like it might. There's more on the efficacy of low range on p84-5.

In Morocco the only thing that may limit a vehicle on some mountain tracks is its size. A small truck like a Unimog, MAN or an Iveco will struggle or even not fit on routes like MA1, 3, 6 and 7 and of course MH5. For them the pistes of the High Atlas, the desert and the east or far west will save too much inching around hairpins with wheels hanging over the edge.

Unusually in an overland setting, a short-wheelbase 4x4 with just two people would work very well on Moroccan pistes. Fuel stages are short and food stops frequent so there's no need to carry post-apocalyptic payloads. Camping gear can be for occasional use only as there's usually a hotel to be found. More significantly there'll be many occasions on washed-out pistes where a SWB's minimal body overhangs would help you get through without resorting to longer detours or mashing your bumpers. A Defender 90 fits the bill of course, as do the 73-series Land Cruisers common in France as well as the venerable Lada Niva. Any of the double cab pickups popular in the UK like the Mitsubishi L200, the Nissan Navara or Toyota Hilux will manage fine

Double cab pickup; a good compromise.

too. The Mazda B2500 I used to research the first edition of this book gave me no lasting regrets (the full story is on the website: click 'Mercedes' then 'Mazda') – where it couldn't go I wasn't so keen to follow anyway.

Other factors

Although the available range in 4WDs can be limited (VX Land Cruisers are an exception), an **automatic gearbox** is a great choice for some of Morocco's steep, rocky tracks. Very often in the mountains it's difficult to be smooth with manual transmission as you lurch between first and second gears with the steering turning from lock to lock; on some routes you'll be driving like this for hours. Automatics make this

'Camel Trophy' style accessories may give an appearance of rugged intent but are not essential.

sort of off-roading much smoother on the transmission and tyres as well as the vehicle occupants, allowing you to concentrate on positioning the car and its tyres carefully and, heck, even have a chance to look around!

Traditionalists often comment that it's impossible to push start an automatic with a flat battery, but for any overlander, manual or auto and especially if travelling alone, a **second battery** as well as a set of jump start cables are an inexpensive and very wise precaution (see p41). If the starter's gone and you're alone, you'd be lucky to bump start any car, manual or otherwise unless you happened to park on a nice, firm slope.

Within reason, **wheel and tyre size** and rim metal are not critical. The norm for 4WD rim sizes is either 15- or 16-inch and both tyre sizes will be found in Morocco, though not necessarily in your exact width or profile. What is important is a relatively tall tyre wall rather than a wide tread. Tall tyres give more ground clearance at the axle, maintain that clearance at lower pressures while also creating a longer tyre print for better traction, and they add suspension (albeit undamped and so not ideal for road cornering). Tyres in the larger, 16-inch rim size as found on Defenders usually have these bouncy characteristics – ie: oriented towards off-roading.

These days alloy rims are the norm on modern vehicles including 4WDs because they're lighter than steel and so perform better. Dents in alloy rims (with the potential for losing the air seal) cannot be knocked out as easily as on steel, but short of some sort of crash, tall tyres, firm tyre pressures and moderate speeds all make such damage unlikely in Morocco.

The **suspension systems** on the types of vehicles listed will all work well in Morocco, be they leaf springs, coil or torsion bar on solid axles (as on Defenders, older Discoverys and 80-series Land Cruisers) or with the now more prevalent independent front suspension (IFS) or even fully independent, cross-linked air suspension. The reason modern 4WDs are adapting to independent suspension, that has been the norm on road cars for decades, is for the fairly obvious reason that it gives a much-improved ride and handling on the road where most of them stay. In my experience, providing you fit firmer springs, the much vaunted ground clearance issues of IFS do not exist.

4WD PREPARATION AND EQUIPMENT

The great thing with driving off-road in Morocco is that, as long as the machine is in good shape and well-equipped, you barely need more gear than going on a regular holiday. That's the way I approached one of the research trips for this book. I took a jerrican for fuel, an air bag jack, a shovel and some sand mats and didn't use any of them. But along with the air-con, I was certainly glad of the additions of a new clutch, a second battery, a compressor and, last but not least, uprated suspension. 'Camel Trophy' style accessories

VEHICLE CHOICE & PREPARATION

may give an appearance of rugged intent but are not essential. A first timer need only make sure the car is in good shape and take appropriate equipment.

Look in a 4WD magazine and you may be overwhelmed by the amount of preparation and gear your 4WD needs. The fact is, it's only Morocco where routes are short and help is never that far away. This is what you actually need:

- Five good tyres (or six old ones) and tyre-repairing equipment
- Uprated suspension
- Air compressor or foot pump
- Back-up battery
- Tow strap, a shovel, tall hydraulic jack and a base plate
- Thick pair of gloves
- Secure, chassis-mounted towing points front and rear
- Tool kit and some spares
- 20-litre fuel can
- Jump start cables

Unless you buy five new tyres, that lot above will cost well under £1000 for a car that'll be ready for anything in Morocco. Broadly speaking it can all be divided into improving some of your car's current systems (most notably tyres and suspension) and adding equipment to make it more effective off-road (including recoveries) and comfortable to live out of. There is plenty more on this subject in my *Desert Driving II* DVD. See the website.

General vehicle check

While it helps to have an aptitude and sympathy for mechanical things, you don't need an in-depth knowledge of your car's functions. Most drivers have little interest in how their car works and increasingly complex, electronically-managed vehicles don't make roadside fault diagnosis by the owner so easy anyway. It's one reason why older and simpler vehicles are preferred for long-range overlanding but for Morocco, as long as it doesn't have a disastrous record for reliability, it's safe to take as complex and modern a vehicle as you like.

When checking over your vehicle, focus your efforts on what counts: the basics of engine, transmission and suspension. At times all will be working hard on Moroccan pistes so make sure they're in good shape before you start buying extra equipment. At the very least, the vehicle should be serviced well in advance of your departure with fresh oil, coolant and air, oil and fuel filters and with any serious faults addressed. You can save a lot of effort and time by either fitting new consumable items like tyres, fan belts and radiator hoses or taking them as spares and hoping for the best. They may well be available locally but getting hold of them may take a few days.

Be warned though, simply buying these bits and throwing them in the back is not the same as fitting them and taking the partly-worn items as spares. That way you avoid the sinking feeling on discovering that your spare fan belt is the wrong size when you need it most. With show-stopping items like belts, it's a good idea to **fit new** and **take the used but still usable item as a backup**.

Air filters

Raised air-intakes or 'snorkels' breathe at roof level where there are fewer air-borne sand particles and also have the benefit of greatly increasing a vehicle's potential wading ability. They also look cool and up to a point can lengthen maintenance periods by keeping a filter cleaner for longer.

Most 4WDs have air-intakes somewhere in the wing and some manage to pre-clean air better than others. I've found on 60- and 80-series Toyotas a raised air-intake makes little difference; whatever 'cyclone' arrangement they have to spin out the particles before they reach the air filter element worked fine. The Mazda's pre-cleaning was not so good and the air filter element was relatively small, but even

Greasing the inside of the airbox keeps the element cleaner for longer.

then, for the cost of fitting a snorkel I could have bought 20 air filter elements – enough for 250,000 miles.

Corrugated paper elements can be cleaned by carefully tapping out the dust or by using compressed air, but eventually they'll need replacing. Because you're probably only visiting Morocco rather than emigrating there, a new standard paper element will be sufficient for a typical month's trip. Use your air compressor to blow it clean after a particularly dusty run and consider taking a spare if you expect to be driving in convoy where rear vehicles can catch bronchitis. Greasing the inside surfaces of an airbox is a useful dirt-biking practice which catches still more dust and sand before it clogs the filter.

Transmission

Even with a lightly loaded vehicle your transmission will work hard in Morocco, crawling up steep, rocky slopes and out of creeks. If there's any undue slack in the drive or if gears jump out or are hard to engage (including low-range selection), you can be sure that a week in the Anti Atlas won't be a miracle cure. Prop shafts in particular have a hard time on rough tracks. Check there's grease in the telescoping section, fit a gaiter to keep out dust and also check for play in the four or more universal joints ('UJs'). They frequently wear unnoticed or lose retaining bolts so should be regreased or better still replaced on an older vehicle. They're not expensive.

With any manual 4WD, the many unseen components of the vehicle's transmission benefit most from a smooth, gentle driving style. Know the correct use of low range as well as the importance of not using locked diffs on grippy surfaces (see p36).

Suspension

Along with good tyres, the single item that will benefit most Morocco-bound 4WDs is uprated suspension. As is widely recognised, most 4WDs do not lead true 4WD lives and are sprung at the factory accordingly. This is fine around town, but when bouncing along a track on a hot day with a large payload, original equipment ('OE') springs will show their limitations. Soft suspension means continuous bottoming out against the axle stops and having to slow down for the mildest bumps. It's harder on the tyres too, and of course it reduces your ground clearance which leads to other problems.

On 4WDs with coil-sprung suspension like Defenders, Discoverys and 80-series Cruisers, firmer coils are widely available, relatively inexpensive and

READ THIS FIRST: TRANSMISSION WIND-UP

Imagine having each limb twisted in a different direction. That's what's happening to your 4WD's transmission components when you use locked-out four-wheel drive on a hard surface. On a loose surface such as sand, this tension (brought about by left or right wheels covering varying arcs through bends) dissipates as undetectable wheel spin, but on a grippy surface such as bare rock, **wind-up** soon becomes apparent. Steering stiffens, your transmission clicks and groans, and then a suddenly spinning wheel unloads the tension, or something in the tortured transmission breaks.

Particularly on bare rocky hairpins such as Route MH4, you should avoid driving a selectable 4WD in four-wheel drive, or a full-time 4WD with centre diff locked for long periods. In dry conditions with good traction it shouldn't be necessary. Even on a wet road, driving locked-out in four-wheel drive is a bad idea. A wheel suddenly unloading the wind-up in a fast wet bend could bring on a disastrous skid. To release any wind up in the transmission only requires momentarily unlocking a central diff or releasing freewheeling diffs or hubs. But if there's a lot of tension in the system these actions may not work instantly; it may take a few bends and a minute or two.

Only engage selectable four-wheel drive or lock the central diff on loose surfaces where you think you'll need the extra traction. Away from the dunes in Morocco (what few there are) this only includes crossing steep, washed-out creek banks or muddy/sandy creek crossings; in other words no more than a few hundred metres on the average route in good conditions.

On snow, mud, sand and gravel staying locked-out in four-wheel drive is OK (though not always necessary) as any tension spins out before it reaches damaging levels. It is only on bare rock or concrete (as well as the tarmac highway of course) that staying locked out can be bad for the transmission.

If you're now wringing your hands wondering if you can use your 4WD safely on the dirt, don't worry about it too much. Whatever system your car runs, most of the time you can simply leave the road and follow a track without doing anything until the going gets tricky. Lock in the 4WD with the central diff or engage the front axle when you must, unlock it all when you can. After a few hours on the piste you'll get the feel for what's needed and within a few days you'll know exactly when to bring locked-in four-wheel drive into action.

This must be understood clearly. Full-time 4WD with the central diff locked provides near-optimum traction but will also wind up the transmission. Therefore the same limitations to driving on hard surfaces must be observed: lock the central diff only when you really need to and never engage it with the power on, with wheels possibly spinning; it won't like it.

There is more on off-road driving techniques on p84-5.

easy to fit. Resist the urge to go over the top with raising suspension; a vehicle's stability is compromised by just an extra couple of inches above standard. Use the 'looks normal and level when fully loaded' rule as a guide.

Old-fashioned semi-elliptic leaf springs can be uprated, but are more expensive and harder to replace than coils. Adding a leaf or two to the pack and re-bending the current set (not such a bodge as it sounds) are some things you can do with leaves. Theoretically, a good leaf-spring manufacturer will be able to dial in exactly how much lift you want or the desired height when loaded.

The secondary leaf springs, ie: the ones which have loose ends and do not wrap around the mounting points, have a habit of cracking in tough conditions but this is no great drama compared to a main leaf breakage, and is one thing any Moroccan mechanic is familiar with. I fully expected this problem with the OE rear leaves on my Mazda in Morocco and sure enough I got it, although it took me days to notice as the Air Lift bags masked any sag.

Shock absorbers – more correctly described as dampers – are vulnerable to damage on some leaf-sprung vehicles, but work a lot harder with coil springs which lack the friction-damping element of leaves. If you're fitting new units take the old ones as spares; problems are common and even new ones can break, bend, seize, leak or get crushed by rocks. A car is driveable with a missing damper but a spare unit takes up little space.

Air Lift bags. The pressure can be modified for heavy payloads or even broken springs and they work with coils springs too.

TYRES

In Morocco, tyre choice is not as critical as it can be in other off-road environments, but because of the hammering they'll get, good-quality items are advisable. Remember that along with suspension, your tyres will carry the brunt of the shock loads over rough terrain for weeks on end, not just weekends away and if anything stops you on the piste, it will be a puncture. Don't take chances with tyres just because they'll wear out anyway. Save money elsewhere but replace old or inappropriate tyres with the best you can afford.

Ordinary drivers distinguish tyres by their tread pattern, today as much a factor of marketing as function. What matters much more is the integrity of the tyre design and the quality of the construction – something that is hard to see and is why people choose cheaper brands which look just as 'black and round' as more expensive tyres.

These days most 4WDs are fitted with tubeless tyres on 15-inch rims; 16s appear on more functional off-roaders like Defenders where the taller sidewall increases clearance. Because most piste surfaces are predominantly gravel or stone, in Morocco the finer points of tread design aren't that crucial.

In general choose AT (all terrain) designated tyres from quality manufacturers over cheap MT (mud terrain) or M&S (mud and snow) designated tyres (205 x 16 M&S tyres are particularly hopeless in sand). Providing they're a good brand in good shape, your current tyres might well be adequate and will certainly do in rocky Morocco.

As with many things, you get what you pay for. An expensive Michelin (who also own BF Goodrich) may last twice as long as other brands. There are

VEHICLE CHOICE & PREPARATION

TALL TYRES, NOT WIDE TYRES

A 'tall' tyre, that is one with a high sidewall, is desirable off-road as it gives more protection to the rim and so the seal of a tubeless tyre. You can tell this just by looking at a tyre size or aspect ratio, the second number in the tyre size moulded on the side. For example 185/75 15" decoded means 185 tread width in millimetres, '75' is the sidewall height as a percentage of width; so about 139mm – and 15" indicates the rim diameter.

A high aspect ratio of 65 or more is better for off-roading because, like a thick-soled boot, it provides added suspension over bumps and gives enough scope to partially deflate the tyre for traction in soft sand while still cushioning the rim.

no absolute rules; much depends on rim types, driving style, experience and engine power characteristics. One thing is certain though: drive a heavy car fast on any tyre in an under-inflated condition and you risk overheating which damages the structure of the tyre and will cause problems down the track.

Pumps and compressors

For tyre repairs as well as for altering tyre pressures over varying terrain, some kind of pump is essential and a powerful air compressor is one of the most useful items you can fit to an off-roader. Besides saving time and effort, it means you're never reluctant to drop pressures (which means fewer boggings) or to reinflate again – so avoiding premature tyre wear and damage.

Viair 2.5cfm compressor in the engine bay.

Manual foot pumps take about 300 strokes to gain 1 bar (14.5 psi) and realistically are too slow for off-road use. Your engine generates electricity so it makes sense to utilise that energy to power an electric air compressor. Prices range from £20 – for something not designed for the sustained loads of big 4WD tyres – to over £400. Plan to spend at least £100 for a model that will last the trip. What counts is not that they can inflate a bicycle tyre to 180psi, but how many cubic feet per minute (cfm) they can push out, especially as pressure builds up. For something that pumps out at around 2 cfm or more, expect to pay £140. To avoid flattening the battery **keep the engine running** if reinflating all four tyres.

RECOVERY EQUIPMENT

In Morocco you could get stuck in sand, mud and snow in just one eventful day. In most cases simply **backing up** and finding another way round or turning back is the answer. There's always somewhere else to go in Morocco. Nevertheless, it's wise to be equipped for getting stuck.

Standard recovery items include a jack, a shovel, a compressor and a long recovery strap. This latter item, along with another car to pull you out, is the single most useful item. Unless you're planning to play around on Erg Chebbi or Chegaga, sand plates or mats are not necessary in Morocco. In fact, outside of storm conditions, it's hard to imagine getting stuck on any of the desert routes in this book.

Your car's standard jack (ideally an extra-height hydraulic bottle-jack as opposed to inferior pillar- or scissor-jacks) will be good enough to make wheel repairs but not if you manage to get deeply bogged down.

Bottle-jacks are designed be placed directly under the axle or a wishbone, not on a chassis rail or a sill. This way the jack lifts the wheel directly off the ground and not the compressed weight on the suspension... and then the wheel. It's only this placement which makes them awkward to use off road and is why high-lift jacks or airbags are preferred.

SUMMERTIME IN THE MOROCCAN SAHARA

Although I could think of better holidays, within reason it's possible to do southern Morocco in summer (May to September) in a car without taking too many chances. You'll experience the same temperatures as the central Sahara at this time, but not the exposure in terms of distance.

Air-con helps of course, as does the ability to carry lots of water and setting off at dawn. Forty-five-degree days will also put a strain on your vehicle. Working hard in these conditions, any weakness in the cooling system can become apparent at a time when your safety margins are already slim.

In August 2008 a French couple suffered two punctures in a rental 4WD while on Route MS6. The man wandered off to try and get a mobile phone signal and eventually came upon a village. By the time he returned to his car later that day his wife had died from the heat. In June 2012 a similar event befell two Portuguese bikers around the back of Erg Chebbi. Their heavy bikes got stuck in the sand and within an hour of a third coming back with help, the others had died from the heat, exacerbated by the preceding exertion.

Sand dunes, where a 4WD will work hardest, are few in Morocco and easily avoided, but in soft sand in summer the temperature needle may get close to the red zone, especially when crawling along slowly in a tailwind. Because it's hard to know just how your vehicle will respond in such heat, play it safe and consider a new or reconditioned radiator (especially if it's ever been repaired), along with new or spare hoses and belts.

Old desert lore advises only fresh water should be used in the radiator in case of a survival situation (antifreeze being poisonous). It sounds prudent but overall you're much better off with the slightly higher boiling point and corrosion-inhibiting properties of antifreeze and putting another 20 litres of water in the back.

In my experience big, four-litre 4WDs are fitted with huge radiators and powerful fans that rarely overheat. Smaller engines work a bit harder and along with older engines, may benefit from a 'tropical' fan with extra blades (available for Land Rovers). Aftermarket intercoolers also raise engine bay temperatures; you'll feel it in the cab alongside the gearbox tunnel and the floor of the cubby box, though it won't necessarily register on the temperature gauge.

If your vehicle runs hot consider supplementary (as opposed to replacement) electric fans such as those made in the UK by Kenlowe or Pacet. Not built for off-road, frames or feeble zip-tie mountings supplied can work loose on corrugations and damage the radiator, so make sure it's solid and that the retaining bolts are secured with locking compounds – and check them regularly.

Running thicker engine oil is another way of keeping things cool. In Europe 15W-40 has become the norm but 'old-fashioned' 20W-50 increases your cooling range at the upper end. If things get desperate, straight 40W can be used, but let the engine warm up gently on cold mornings.

If the engine gets very hot point into the wind and open the lid. Keep the engine running until the needle drops back to normal. Switching off a hot engine makes things temporarily worse and can crack a cylinder head or blow a gasket.

VEHICLE CHOICE & PREPARATION

Hi-lift and airbag jacks

In Morocco the number of occasions when you actually need to jack the car right up are fewer than you think. Hi-lift jacks are well known to pukka off-roaders and though heavy and awkward to stow (and dangerous if used carelessly) their ability to lift a two-ton car quickly makes them very useful and they cost from just £50. The problem is a hi-lift needs a solid, chassis-mounted metal bumper, as on the front of a Defender, to lift up the weight of a car.

An airbag jack can easily lift one side of a 2.5 ton 4WD to speed up recovery in sand.

Although adaptors are available, most 4WDs these days have rounded plastic bumpers to limit injuries to pedestrians and in the UK at least, bull bars rigid enough to take the weight of a car are outlawed.

It's possible to get wheel adaptors to enable a hi-lift to quickly raise a wheel – either straps that hook into the spokes or clamps for the free-wheel drive housing (see the *Desert Driving* DVD). It's a useful facility when bogged down to perform a simple lift and recovery, but it's definitely not a stable way of lifting a car to get underneath – used alone a hi-lift jack never is.

Airbag jacks are tough vinyl balloons the size of a small dustbin which are inflated by the car's exhaust and can easily lift one side of a 4WD. For something like an older Hilux an air jack rated at two tons will do the trick; for a heavier Toyota 80-series four tons is a better bet.

Air jacks are a rare sight but for effortless sand recovery or even righting overturned vehicles they're ideal, spreading the weight over a large area and requiring no strenuous or dangerous jacking. The bag needs less than 1 bar to lift a car so no engine damage from the exhaust pressure can occur, although the exhaust system must be sound if it's to survive as well as fill the bag efficiently. They won't work on vehicles with twin exhaust pipes unless you seal one pipe (something like a potato works – until it shoots you in the face...).

Under the car, choose the position carefully to spread the load; remember you'll be putting half the weight of the car on the lifting area. At the very least a footwell mat should be used between the undercarriage and the bag – and something similar on the ground if thorns or rocks are present.

Shovels and tow straps

A shovel has many uses: burying waste as well as digging the car out. The best type to choose is one with not too large a blade – so anyone can use it without straining their back – and a full 'D' handle that you can grip and angle firmly rather than the cheaper 'T' handles as found on the ex-Army shovels available in the UK. The long-handled shovels recommended by some to dig sand away from under the car are in fact very awkward to use. If you're that stuck just get down in there and scoop away with your hands.

Along with solid, chassis-mounted towing points, a tow strap (more compactly stored than a rope) is an essential part of any overlander's equipment. Nine metres is a standard length and the minimum necessary for towing or righting an overturned vehicle; 20 metres is much more useful for recovering a vehicle from deep sand, dune crests, a wet chott or mud. Two straps can easily be joined with nothing more than a tightly rolled-up magazine or a stick (right).

Both are less dangerous than shackles which are lethal if something breaks, although a couple of shackles rated at four tons or more are useful accessories if one car has closed towing rings, rather than more useful hooks which avoid the need for shackles altogether.

Joining a rope and a strap with a rolled up magazine. It doesn't have to be the latest issue of *Hello*. © longroadtripsouth.com

Auxiliary batteries

Because the primary battery is such a vital component, especially with a diesel, a second battery is a good idea, and essential if you're running things like fridges. For the cost involved, a spare car battery gives peace of mind, especially if you're travelling alone. I've heard of cheapo no-name batteries lasting for years and expensive sealed 'space shuttle' items mysteriously pack up in a few months. For any sort of remote driving where you can't readily flag down a passing car, a second battery can be considered as indispensable as a spare tyre.

When camping, a second battery also allows you to run electrical ancillaries with the engine turned off but, if correctly isolated, won't flatten the main battery on a freezing High Atlas morning when it provides a back-up should the main battery fail. Jump-starting from another car is the simple answer (or tow-starting if no jump leads are available), but this assumes another vehicle is around.

Avoid expensive and specialised 'leisure' batteries as used by caravaners. These are designed for long, slow discharging and regular flattening, not to provide the short powerful burst of 'cranking' amps needed to start a cold engine and then quickly recover. In Morocco starting the engine is more important than keeping the milk from going off, so a second SLI ('starting, lighting, ignition') battery, either identical or a bit smaller, is best. There's more on running auxiliary batteries in the *Overlanders' Handbook*.

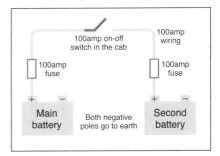

The simplest way to wire up a second battery is in series with a cut off switch fitted inside the cab. Starting on one flat and one good battery will instantly average out below 12 volts: it won't work. With the above set up, if the auxiliary battery goes flat through use, *isolate it* before starting the engine on the main battery. Then once running switch on the second battery to charge it up.

VEHICLE CHOICE & PREPARATION

2WD

Just about all cars bound for the Moroccan pistes will be 4x4s; naturally enough as these vehicles can carry the load across rough terrain without complaint. But nearly all the pistes in this book can be done much more cheaply and with as much fun in a suitably prepared regular 2WD car or van. Morocco has very little sand (seasonal snow and mud may be another matter) and ground clearance rather than all-wheel drive is the critical issue and is something that some 2WD cars have enough of.

DO YOU NEED 4WD?

Many of the pistes in this book are regularly traversed by locals in 2WD vans or cars. Certainly they come from a limited selection with an often coincidental design, or with suspension modifications to provide better clearance, because with the good traction of dry conditions, four-wheel drive is hardly ever necessary on tracks. After all, motorbikes manage fine and up to the point where Unimogs and the like come into their own, bikes can skip across gnarlier terrain with less discomfort than most regular 4WDs.

In all but the softest sand it's primarily **decent ground clearance** and not all-wheel drive that enables a vehicle to keep moving; 99% of the time your 4WD won't require all-wheel drive in Morocco. But it takes just one rock to crack a low-slung sump, one steep ascent or creek bank to fry a clutch, or a series of corrugations to have rusty engine mounts fail. That remaining one per cent can finish off an old machine.

Choosing to explore Morocco in a regular car is not as foolhardy as it sounds. It's commonly tried by experienced four-wheel drivers who've 'been there and done that', have nothing more to prove and so are looking for something new. There is more coverage of overlanding with regular cars in the *Overlanders' Handbook*.

Citroën C15 van. Up to 2-litre engine, great economy and ground clearance.

Limitations of a regular car

Low ground clearance and long overhangs (the front or back of a car that sticks out beyond the wheels) are what initially limit a road car in an off-road setting, followed by a lack of a supplementary 'low range' gearbox. In the thousands of kilometres I covered for this book in the Mazda pickup, I usually engaged 4WD for less than a minute at a time and for a total distance of just a few kilometres. On most pistes I never engaged 4WD, but when

I did, it was almost always when in low range (which automatically selects 4WD) to crawl slowly over a ditch, rocks or through soft sand so as not to strain the clutch or transmission.

Finally, not all regular cars have the **build quality** to take an off-road beating so breakdowns and other problems are simplified by choosing a model which is commonly found in Morocco – see p44.

> **In all but the softest sand it's primarily decent ground clearance and not all-wheel drive that enables a vehicle to keep moving...**

Road cars: what to look for

Part of the appeal of a road car is keeping it simple and doing it on a budget, as well as having a more pleasant vehicle to drive on normal roads (unless you can afford top of the range Land Cruisers and Rovers). Without the need to carry huge amounts of fuel and water, a hatchback or a small van makes an ideal choice for one or two people because of its relatively short wheelbase and limited body overhangs compared to a sedan (a car with a boot). When it comes to rear body overhangs many hatchbacks are in fact better than most 4WDs; they can take extreme angles before tailpipes, spare tyres and, less commonly, fuel tanks get scraped. On the front end, spoilers, steering components and particularly the radiator's low position are the vulnerable points.

Because most road cars feature independent suspension the underside is generally smooth, with no beam axle casings protruding, as on a 4WD. They therefore lend themselves well to the fitting of a long sump guard. Shorter cars also have a better ramp breakover angle which means they won't belly out so easily when driving over a hump or a sharp crest. Saloons and estates generally have longer back-end overhangs and some have overhanging fronts too.

Try to anticipate what will ground out and whether it matters. Most importantly, consider the bottom edge of the **radiator** behind that spoiler. Will it get mashed and pushed into the fan following a nose dive into a narrow ditch?

Larger wheels are preferable as they roll over rough ground more smoothly while marginally increasing clearance on suspension components. Larger tyres (see box on p37) also produce a longer 'footprint' when deflated which helps traction in soft sand. Fifteen-inch rims are found on some Mercedes, bigger Peugeots and the like, but hatchback rims are usually fourteen inches or less.

Recommending marques and models is trickier but naturally some have better reputations than others. Mercedes and the three main French

Thirty-year-old Mercedes in Akka Ighern; adequate ground clearance once the front bumper conforms.

VEHICLE CHOICE & PREPARATION

marques of Peugeot, Citroën and Renault are most common on Moroccan roads, the former because of the superior build-quality of older models, while the French marques exist most probably because of nothing more than long-established trade connections.

With no 4WDs to speak of, French car manufacturers have long produced 2WD utilities suited to off-road use; the 2CV being the original example. Many hatchbacks still fit in this category: Peugeot 106s and 205s, Citroen AXs and C15D or Kangoo vans. French marques derived from the original 2CV concept are popular, even if they don't necessarily have the build-quality and reliability of German and Japanese equivalents. These models feature independent suspension with rear wheels attached on high-mounted arms offering excellent clearance as long as the payload is modest. During research trips, besides several old French and German hatchbacks, I saw many newer small, so-called 'car-derived' and 'high-cube' vans out in Morocco like the Citroen Berlingo/Peugeot Partner or the Renault Kangoo.

Modifying a road car

Most Moroccan locals won't undertake any of these modifications; they'll just drive slowly and make repairs as necessary. This is really the best way to go as half the point of using a 2WD is not to spend extra money and time adapting it. As long as the general mechanical condition is good, particularly the tyres, you'll manage most of the time.

If you want to push a 2WD towards its limits, some underbody protection of the engine and gearbox, as well as steering and suspension links, exhaust pipe, fuel and brake lines and fuel tanks, is a good idea.

The simplest way to achieve this is to fix on a big metal plate: 3mm steel will do, or alloy twice as thick. This bash plate will earn its keep so it needs to be fixed on well. If you're doing this just as you're about to start a piste, wiring on an old oven door with a coat hanger is better than nothing, but a bash plate bolted solidly onto whatever points are available is best, as they often come adrift. Leave a small gap between the plate and whatever it's protecting; it may help to stuff in some thick, shock-absorbing material like a bit of old tyre, so a severe impact is not transmitted directly through the plate.

Raising ground clearance is most easily done on cars with coil suspension all round. The cheapest solution is a spacer above or beneath the coil: the car instantly sits higher. Mercedes offer these 'spring pads' in a variety of thicknesses (see the website) but anything will do. Extreme lifts will stress steering- and final-drive components, so don't go too far. It's another reason why it's better to buy a car with relatively good ground clearance in the first place.

Remember too that the coil spring sits more or less halfway between the pivoting point of the wishbone and the tyre, so a spacer or longer spring of 20mm will raise the car by 40mm at the

...the easiest way of maintaining your car's ground clearance is by driving slowly and not overloading it.

wheel. It's not uncommon for coil springs to break but it's also usual not to notice this for months; another advantage of coil suspension.

Torsion bar suspension is also adjustable by repositioning the pivots in the spline. This increases the pre-tension (so raising the car) but on a hard hit can also twist it beyond the point it was designed to go which can lead to failure and a complicated repair.

It's worth reiterating that, just as with 4WDs, the easiest way of maintaining your car's ground clearance (and reducing stresses overall) is by **driving slowly and not overloading** it. Position any heavy loads centrally, between the axles.

Once you've made the best of your ground clearance and underbody protection, all that really remains is to ensure things like the exhaust pipe and fuel tank fittings are solid as they commonly come loose or fall off on corrugated pistes.

OFF-ROADING IN A 2WD

You may have made the most of your ground clearance but in a 2WD you're still missing two 4WD attributes: all-wheel drive and a low-range gearbox. What this means is that when you hit rough ground you must rely on **momentum** – also known as 'speed' – to get you through. Knowing exactly when to accelerate and when to back off is crucial to successful off-roading in a 2WD, as are a pair of **bridging planks** to smooth out the creases in the Moroccan landscape.

The problem is that sometimes you have to drive a 2WD fast across sandy creek beds or up the banks just to maintain that momentum to avoid getting stuck. Crawling steadily in full control, as you can do with a 4WD in low range, won't always work and the faster you go the more the suspension compresses – and there goes your ground clearance. It's at times like this that a bash plate earns its keep.

Reducing tyre pressures to gain traction gives you a bit more leeway before you get stuck and is essential when you're stuck in sand. As with 4WDs, one bar or 14.5 psi is the optimum 'get-out-of-jail' pressure, but in stony Morocco it's best to leave tyres at road pressures until there's no choice.

Note that regular cars may not have **towing points** strong enough to withstand dragging a car out of mud or sand. The loops or rings you often see protruding on the back are for locating a car on a car transporter. Pick attachment points carefully; close to a suspension pivot is a good idea, but certainly not bumpers. For more advice see p84-5.

An alloy sand plate cut long ways to make two thin ones will do near Erg Chebbi, but thick wooden planks have the added advantage of also bridging ditches.

Bicycle touring in Morocco

Within the limits of season and range Morocco offers self-sufficient off-road tourers some fantastic opportunities for adventuring. Distances are not too great, services (including transportation over dull stages) are close at hand and there's enough variety of landscape to find something you like.

Linking the pistes of the south are also some great **road rides**, not least Route MS10, the 1500km 'Desert Highway' (see p114), nearly all of it on comparatively good surfaces and with very little traffic. If you're more into travel than off-road riding you may find the pistes give you and your bike simply too much of a beating. Take to the roads with the odd off-road excursion and you'll still have a great time in Morocco.

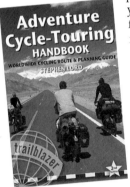

As it is, not all the off-road routes in this book are suitable for cycling. Some are simply too long, too rough, too arid and too remote. A few have a combination of surfaces that won't shake your bike to bits all the time and have wells at regular intervals to avoid carrying masses of heavy water; the crux to making off-road riding fun. And would you believe it, Trailblazer Guides have a book for this too.

Check out the *Adventure Cycle-Touring Handbook* for the full story on long-range bike touring.

Like ACTH, this book assumes you're **self-sufficient**, but with a support vehicle carrying the gear, either following you or better still meeting you at the end of the day, all the routes in this book open up and riding becomes still more fun.

Whatever direction a route is described in, consider accessing the higher end by road where possible, so giving you a mostly downhill run on the dirt.

The great thing with bikes is that you can sling them onto a car when you get tired or bored, and that you can get over rockfalls and other terrain which will stop everything bar a mule.

VEHICLE CHOICE & PREPARATION

Pick of the pistes

Cycling in Morocco doesn't have to mean heading south into the fringes of the Sahara, though this is often the initial motivation. Down here the sealed roads are quieter, the people can be less hassle and all in all it's what you've come here for. Taking the train from Tangier to Marrakech, or flying to these cities (or Ouarzazate) saves days cycling across the busier and less interesting north.

Road riding most of the time will still give you a great time in the south of Morocco.
© Raf Verbeelen (and top of p50).

East of Marrakech picking up the two long trans-Atlas routes: MH1 and the sealed MH2 diverting onto MH13 make a great way of getting down south. Other highway alternatives include the less-used R203 road over 2092-metre Tizi-n-Test south-west of Marrakech, or the busier N9 Marrakech–Ouarzazate highway over the 2260m Tizi-n-Tichka pass. Turning west over the top at Aguim you can head down Routes MH6, MH8 in reverse or eventually MH7. Alternatively you can take the barely-used road from Demnate to Ouarzazate; Route MH12. All these high routes may have their share of rough tracks or mud and even snow from November to March.

Once south of the High Atlas the Jebel Sarhro routes: MH4, MH5, MH10 and MH14 would be fun on a mountain bike. The only self-sufficient MTBs I've seen in Morocco were coming down MH4 to Nekob. Once down in the warmer Anti Atlas, early spring or late autumn would be best on the longer pistes. Just about all the routes in the 'MA' Anti Atlas region are do-able on a bike, but they're stony and rough so better stick to the shorter ones like MA2, 4, and 5 which will tire you out less, as will MW4 and 5 and at a push MW3.

Over on the east side the riding is bleaker in the ME region although ME1 is a great road into an area of short but fun routes, and ME9 via Debdou is another great road stage with a good stiff climb up past the tree line. Routes MS1, 2 and 5 are all short but the latter especially will be rough, as will MS7, even if it's only 163km. The longer routes have been done by bike but will require some commitment.

A bike for Morocco

While you could manage some of the *Morocco Overland* routes in an old 2WD car (as many locals do), with a fully-autonomous payload it's hard to imagine a cheap MTB not disintegrating fairly quickly after a couple of routes. For Morocco you'll have a better ride with fewer problems on a solid machine with quality front suspension and equipment to match: a mountain bike with tough wheels and tyres.

Down south what bike shops you'll find will cater for heavy Chinese clunkers or blinged-out 40lb MTBs. A five-star Shimano dealer will be a mirage so, as with motorbikes, expect to be self-sufficient for spares, special tools and repairs.

Frames and other components

These days it doesn't really matter whether your frame is made from widely-used aluminium or less fashionable steel. Die-hard tourers prefer Cro-Mo steel's feel and small-town weldability, but aluminium frames have advanced enough to be reliable in the short term and suspension helps disguise alloy's inherent harshness. Your bike should have a **long rear triangle** so there's room enough to accommodate a rack and panniers that won't snag your heels. It's worth knowing that higher end MTBs may be designed for climbing, with a short rear triangle, ie: the front of the back wheel is very close to the seat down tube. Aim for a handlebar set-up that doesn't put too much weight on your wrists; a common failing with racier MTBs – easily fixed by a more upright or adjustable stem. Select simple, solid, well-proven components which are easy to repair and use Loctite on all bolts that fix important components like racks.

Eight gears on the freewheel mean the chain can be wider and so stronger; don't expect to be cycling every last inch of the routes. I've found 24-speed gearing composed of a 12–32 cassette with 22/32/44 chainrings, was ideally matched for a 16-kg light payload on thin 26" tyres. By the time I was panting up steep tracks in 32–22 I could barely balance anyway. Walking is much less effort and only about half as slow.

Tyres and wheels

Large 2.2" tyres will absorb shocks and so spare your rims and spokes (the weak link on all bikes carrying a load off-road) – especially important if you're not running suspension on the front. They may slow you on the highway, especially if they're less than smooth like the XR Marathon below left, but will give you more comfort on the tracks. Use robust touring tyres rather than lightweight off-road racing items: anything by Schwalbe is good as they seem immune to punctures; you can pretty much leave a spare tyre and even a spare inner tube at home. The Marathon series are the heavy tourers' choice; elsewhere I've run skinny Schwalbe City Jets which rode with less effort and coasted faster down the hills compared to the fully-loaded Marathon-shod bike I travelled with, but they gave harsh riding on the dry tracks by the time the front fork had all but seized.

Left: Schwalbe XR Marathons may be relatively heavy and expensive but will last for thousands of kilometres with barely a puncture, as will the narrower and smoother City Jet, with less rolling resistance on the road. **Right**; spoke breakages on the cassette side require the removal of the cassette, something made much easier with : a 'Next Best Thing' ('NBT') 2.

It may not look so off-road purposeful but I'd use such relatively slim and plain-treaded road tyres again because the highways in the south can easily be as satisfying as hammering along a piste for two or three days, focussed intently on a patch of dirt 15ft ahead. Only in mud (or at the speeds and agility only attainable without any baggage at all) would a knobbly tyre have a distinct advantage.

You may find that your **spokes** need regular attention. In the early days you can expect some loosening or

Setting off from Foum Zguid back to Agadir on a couple of inexpensive Decathlon bikes.

even breakages (especially on the rear wheel) after which they should settle down as long as you keep on top of the dark art of spoke tensioning. The key I'm told is to turn a little at a time so you don't end up with Pringle-profiled rims. Carry spare spokes and the nifty 'NBT' gadget pictured opposite to remove the cassette. Biking lore states that the spokes always break on the cassette side where they cannot be replaced without removing it.

Suspension

Prolonged riding over stones and corrugations with a full payload is extremely tiring. Add a headwind and you'll wonder if the Samaritans have an 0800 number. Along with fitness and a good attitude, up to a point fat tyres at medium pressures reduce the shock, but front suspension will relieve shocks from both your arms and the bike's components and improve traction on fast and loose downhill bends. Suspension forks are the norm nowadays, but as with so many trends, cheaper coil-sprung front forks are rather crude and heavy. You don't need the full 160mm of a downhill racer; 100mm will take the sting out of the trail. Something like Rockshox's Reba juggles performance, weight and cost well.

The ability to fully **lock-out** the front fork is very useful, eliminating the energy-sapping bobbing effect on long climbs. **Full suspension** bikes have drawbacks for carrying a rack securely, but without a load (ie: with a support vehicle) one would of course make for a brilliant downhill ride.

Racks and panniers

It's only Morocco, even on a bike, so you could get by without a full touring set up on the front and thereby enjoy a lighter, more manageable bike on the dirt. The trick is to plan your routes to make the most of the towns, villages, cafés and if necessary any streams or wells. Each route description details wells and other water sources.

OMM rack. The lower mount (unseen) is the wheel spindle, not a drop out – a longer skewer is supplied.

VEHICLE CHOICE & PREPARATION

As with motorbikes, the rattle of Moroccan tracks stresses a rack and its mountings – breakages are not unusual, especially on cheaper aluminium racks. A loaded rack will flex from side to side as well as taking direct vertical shock loads, so quality racks in aluminium or steel from, among others, Blackburn, Old Man Mountain or Tubus are preferable.

Use chunky clip-on/easily detachable panniers such as Ortlieb Classics and something like a kayak bag with a similar roll-up closure for light sleeping gear on the top of the rack. I've found this bag handy to quickly remove at rest stops giving something soft to sit on.

Avoid carrying anything more than a small rucksack **on your back** – it puts extra weight on your already stressed backside and makes you even sweatier. Something light with a hydrator of a couple of litres of water should be OK. Handlebar bags are very convenient for storing light, fragile and precious things such as a camera, tools, diary, maps, GPS and so on. They should have a quickly detachable fastener that allows you to remove them when away from the bike without even thinking about it.

Water

It's essential to plan your routes wisely – both by season as well as time of day as your margin for error can be very slim. Depending on the weather and effort, a rider will require up to **six litres** of drinking water a day; if you're drinking much more than this it's really the wrong time of year or you have a leak. With the sustained physical effort of cycling, **clean drinking water** is all the more important – you don't want to get too sick to cycle on to your next water supply, so be extra careful about local water. Fit two or more water bottle cages with at least one to take a large 1.5-litre soft drink bottle (fizzy drink bottles are more robust).

Bottled water is easily bought in any village with a store, but quality filtration equipment greatly increases your autonomy and helps you avoid burying the planet in empty plastic bottles. In Morocco it's not essential to purify

Cooling off; south of Alnif near Route MS4.
©Raf Verbeelen.

water from desert wells but sources near settlements are better treated. Some wells have a bucket and rope but take up to 40m of cord and a suitable container to enable you to draw up water anywhere. All the wells described in the routes in this book, with an estimated depth, were visually checked, though like investments, water levels can fall as well as rise. On some sections you may be able to depend on passing vehicles, but this is a bad habit to acquire.

Mixing in an **isotonic drink** powder like *High5* or *Nuun* makes sense in warm conditions, but also carry some pharmaceutical **rehydration sachets** like Dioralyte or Rehydrat and take them pre-emptively as you feel yourself getting weak. You must be vigilant about your water consumption because the wind dries sweat so quickly you'll barely notice you're losing fluids.

Clothing

Clothes have to be functional and comfortable, keeping you protected from the elements. Moroccans are used to European tourists walking about in skimpy clothing and can appreciate that cycling in a goat-hair chador gets itchy. But respecting local customs in the traditional south will pay off in the hospitality you'll encounter – something that's much more likely on a slow-moving bicycle. Male or female, avoid body-hugging clothing as well as too much exposed skin.

Overall, a *cheche* works well on a bike. Easy to buy locally, but make sure you get cotton, not brighter-coloured synthetics. If in doubt, scrunch the end in your fist; cotton stays creased, synthetics spring back.

Your face, hands, neck and eyes are permanently exposed to the sun so should be covered whenever possible. I've found that a baseball hat caught the wind on downhills, a hankie tied on my head was better but my face got burnt, while a wide-brimmed hat (lacking a neck strap) also caught the wind and obscured the mountain scenery all around while riding. A traditional *cheche* (turban) would have worked best, protecting you from sun, and dehydration as well as the cold, while not blowing away, but of course can't be worn with a helmet. I learned that you don't want the distraction of a hat that's about to blow off, especially when hammering downhill, but you definitely need to protect your head, neck and face with something.

When to ride

Overall October to March is the most pleasant time as long as you avoid the High Atlas above 2000m in mid-winter. At this time the desert will be as cool as it gets. At warmer times, set off in the early morning when the air is still cool, the wind is light and so water consumption is less. Have a long relaxing siesta or better still end the day's cycling by early afternoon and let the day cook away unnoticed. Riding at this pace, depending on your fitness and the wind, you could expect to cover up to 80km a day on the easiest tracks. On steeper routes with lots of pushing 30–50km a day may be all you can manage.

The wind not only slows you down, it also dehydrates you if you don't protect yourself properly, so your water consumption will increase. Remember, you're unlikely to be carrying more than a day's supply of water at any time so plan the route within your capabilities and around dependable watering points.

VEHICLE CHOICE & PREPARATION

3 GETTING THERE

If you leave the UK on a Friday night, by Monday afternoon you could be in Morocco and a day later south of the Atlas. Depending on where you start, you'll have covered nearly 2000 miles across up to four countries, taken two sea crossings and may well feel a bit frazzled. In bad weather a solo driver in a 25-year-old Land Rover, or the rider of an XR400 will feel very frazzled indeed.

ACROSS THE CHANNEL OR THE BAY OF BISCAY

Most visits to Morocco take place outside of summer, if not in the dead of winter, making for a possibly grim continental transit through southern Spain. These short, cold and possibly wet days may not wrinkle the composure of a big BMW motorcycle, but they'll still add up to two very full days on the road including quite a bill for road tolls. With a car full of people sharing the driving and costs, driving all the way is less expensive. Otherwise you can halve the minimum 1400-mile stage from the Channel ports to southern Spain by ferrying across the Bay of Biscay from Portsmouth or Plymouth to Santander or Bilbao in northern Spain. It's not all about saving the pennies though; the Biscay ferries may be a more restful option in mid-winter. Operators may offer promotional fares, as does membership of some organisations or reading the right magazine at the right time.

On the overnight crossings such as those to Le Havre or northern Spain, a 'reclining seat' can be translated as 'sleeping on the floor' in much greater comfort. Bring a sleeping mat, sleeping bag or a blanket, blindfold and earplugs.

It's said the Bay of Biscay is notorious for rough ferry crossings, but having taken this route at all times of year, I've never experienced any discomfort in what were predicted as Force 8 gales.

FRENCH AND SPANISH TOLL ROADS

From somewhere like Dover, the French stage down to the Spanish border costs around €80 in tolls (*péage*), possibly more for a 4WD and about half that on a bike. Spain has a less dense network of toll roads or *autopistas*: (see 🖥 www.viat.es) but those it has are expensive. On a typical transit from northern Spain to Algeciras only about 20% of the road is tolled (*peaje*) and of course avoidable: they include autopista stages from the French border to Burgos; leaving Madrid for Toledo; and from Seville to Madrid. At a guess the cost is nearly as much as all of France.

Note: Not all cross-channel ferry routes shown

4hrs

6-8hrs

2-4/week on both routes 24hrs

2-4/week 20hrs

Distance	miles/km
Dover-Sète	704/1133
Dover-Irun (Spanish frontier)	688/1108
Dover-Almería	1250/2010
Dover-Algeciras	1400/2256
Le Havre-Irun	562/904
Le Havre-Sète	565/910
Le Havre-Almería	1200/1930
Le Havre-Algeciras	1274/2050
Bilbao-Almería	596/960
Bilbao-Algeciras	665/1010
Santander-Almería (via Madrid)	627/1010
Santander-Algeciras (via Salamanca)	627/1010
Irun-Algeciras	715/1151
Irun-Almería	680/1094

The port of Tarifa is 14 miles/22km south-west of Algeciras

To Genoa

1-3/week from 26hrs

1/week 31hrs Nador 33hrs Tangier Med

See Spain–Morocco ferry routes map, p55

Mediterranean Sea

GETTING THERE

European ferry routes

CROSSING SPAIN

Even in a fairly gutless car and avoiding toll motorways, crossing Spain from north to south is possible in one long day, although circumnavigating Madrid at rush hour can cost you some time. From Santander the A67, A62 and A66 via Salamanca and Seville for Algeciras is well signed and effortless. Spain doesn't have the dense network of toll motorways (*autopistas*) as found in France but it's clear that in the good years a lot of money was spent on superbly engineered but near-empty highways.

Almería may be a little nearer than Algeciras, but has less frequent ferry services and longer crossings to Melilla or adjacent Nador. If you're in a blind rush, head for Algeciras any way you like because whatever time you arrive, a ferry will be leaving for Tangier Med port soon.

CROSSING TO MOROCCO

Car ferries are run by half a dozen companies across the Straits of Gibraltar as well as other ports on the south-east Spanish coast, plus Sète just west of Montpellier, and even Genoa (via Barcelona). If heading for Sète it's worth knowing the hilly la Méridienne A75 autoroute is free for 340km south of Clermont Ferrand to Montpellier (excepting the spectacular Millau Viaduct which you won't mind paying for). Driving from Le Havre via Orleans to Sète adds up to around €50 in tolls.

The simplest way to cross to Morocco is a ferry from Algeciras to **Tangier Med port**, 42km east of Tangier city and about 24km west of Fnideq (among other names), the Moroccan border with the Spanish enclave of **Ceuta** which is also served from Algeciras. The crossing to either port takes just 40 minutes but prices are high for the tiny distance involved. Technically still in Spain, from Ceuta you proceed a couple of kilometres to Fnideq and the sometimes intimidating Moroccan frontier. From the much more modern and efficient facility at Tangier Med you drive straight out onto a motorway.

Algeciras attracts touts who can try little scams like tricking you into paying 'parking fees' while legitimately queuing to board a boat, for example.

TRANSPORTING A BIKE TO SOUTHERN SPAIN

Getting a bike transported to southern Spain and flying in after it is a time saving alternative if someone in your group has a van or trailer and the time. It must be Spain not Morocco because the vehicle owner must be present at a Moroccan port of entry. There are ways round this (it helps if you do it regularly). Entering Morocco with say, a van and a bike *both in your name* can be done but don't do the TVIP online (see p58-9), do the triplicate version at the port and **put both vehicles on the one form**.

With Easyjet flights from Stansted, **Málaga** is the favoured option, just 140 sunny kilometres from Algeciras or 200km from Almería in the other direction. This inexpensive option can also work for car passengers wanting to miss out the European stage. Bikers can try and stash a van in Spain and ride to the ferry port and Morocco.

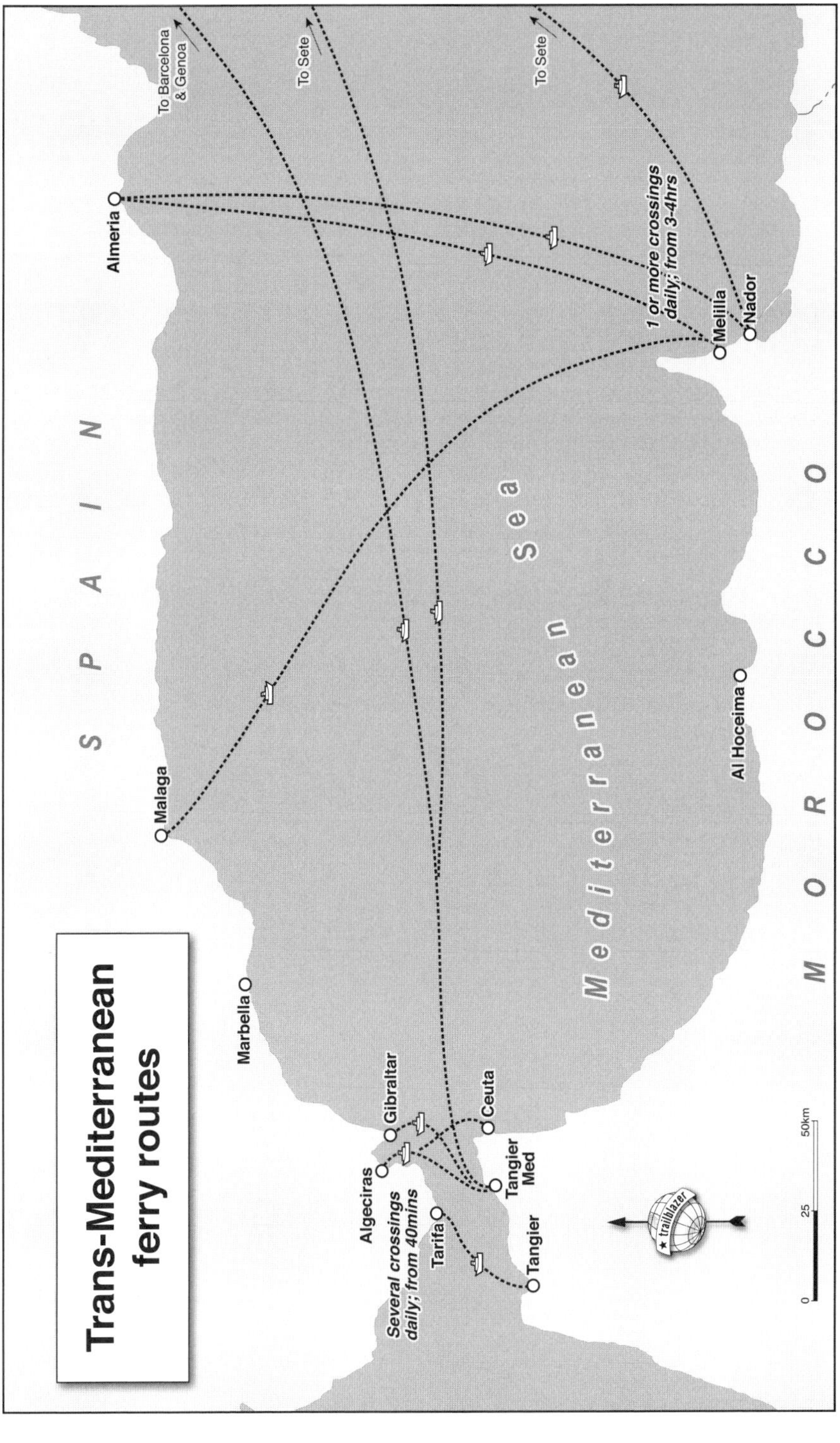

Trans-Mediterranean ferry routes

To Barcelona & Genoa

To Sete

To Sete

Almeria

Melilla
Nador

1 or more crossings daily; from 3-4hrs

S P A I N

Malaga

Marbella

Gibraltar
Ceuta

Algeciras
Tangier Med

Tarifa

Tangier

Several crossings daily; from 40mins

M O R O C C O

Al Hoceima

Mediterranean Sea

GETTING THERE

0   25   50km

FLYING TO MOROCCO

At the moment, from the UK, Morocco is served by budget airlines Easyjet and Ryanair flying from their usual UK airports to Marrakech, Fes or Agadir. Royal Air Maroc (RAM) serves many more cities and RAM also owns Atlas Blue, a charter operator similar to Thompson Fly who cover Agadir and Marrakech from several UK airports.

Marrakech, Fes or Agadir are by far the cheapest places to get to from the UK with single fares from just £35, and Marrakech is well positioned for getting over the High Atlas. Ouarzazate is even closer to the action but flying direct from the UK you can expect to pay at least £200 in winter and much more in summer.

Brace yourself; Morocco is coming to get you and this can lead to a tense few hours for a first-timer until you're well past Fnideq and wired up for action. Long before you approach Algeciras you'll see countless places selling ferry tickets. The price is pretty much the same wherever you go and all will be kosher, but you've not much to lose driving right up to the port and wandering from office to office seeing what they offer. See the website 'Getting there' page for a link to 🖳 www.viajesnormandie.net agency near Algeciras, where Carlos charges around €200 for a 4WD or €100 for a motorcycle with an open return to **Tangier Med**.

For a couple of years Tangier Med was normal but touts and chancers have encroached there too on occasions. Much depends on how you handle yourself, but there's something to be said for taking crossings to the quieter ports of **Nador** or the adjacent Spanish enclave of **Melilla**. They cost more and take longer, but if you've just set a land speed record across France and Spain you'll be due for a rest. With negligible queues and barely two touts to rub together, at Nador you can be on your way in 30 minutes.

Unless you're an old Moroccan hand, it's hard to come up with a good reason to ferry to the old **Tangier city port** once you've read stories about the 'antics' befalling drivers unfamiliar to that city. Even on a good day getting through the port can be very slow, and then you have to battle your way out of the city. Although most find the whole Moroccan arrival procedure nowhere near as bad as imagined, Tangier Med is as easy as it gets.

AT THE BORDER   4

For most first-timers entry into Morocco can add up to a tense hour or two as their nose gets pushed right into the crack between Europe and Africa. Coming via Ceuta, Tangier city or less so Melilla merely prolongs it, but it's this requirement that puts many people off driving to Morocco. Your xenophobia meter swings into the red as your vehicle becomes a conspicuous emblem of your separateness. At busier crossings it's hard to tell who's in authority as guys wave you down to 'guide' you into a parking space 40 feet wide, or sell you an immigration card you already have or which are piled up free, just ahead.

This attention can disorient you as you worry about wasting time in the wrong queue, having someone run off with your passport, or leaving without the correct papers. As always, at these sorts of borders it pays to be prepared, put on a brave face, keep your cool and be polite – but also to stand your ground. While there's nothing to pay for apart from motor insurance (where available), it's not the end of the world to get a helper to submit your forms for you. He'll know where to go and what to do and even if you don't stick with him, he'll be back soon and all for a couple of euros tip.

The good news is the border is better than it used to be, if for no other reason than strict EU regulations trying to stem the northbound flow of migrants. Here in Africa these informal helpers are commonplace and are tolerated as merely trying to grab a few crumbs falling from the big cake. In some North African ports like Tunis these guys appear to work with the authorities to share the spoils of scamming you; in Morocco it's much more informal and small-time. Africa's reputation for bribery is much exaggerated and here it's rare for a uniformed official to demand or expect a tip from a tourist (local chancers may be another matter).

> **For most first-timers entry into Morocco can add up to a tense hour or two as their nose gets pushed right into the crack between Europe and Africa**

Joining the queue

If you arrive at Ceuta or Melilla from Spain you're still in Spain with no formalities to go through as you leave the boat. In both cases the actual Moroccan border, Fnideq or Beni Enzar near Nador respectively, is a couple of miles down the road (see map on p60).

YOUR CIN NUMBER

If you've been to Morocco you'll have a 'CIN' number (**national identity card number**) in your passport composed of about 5 numbers and 2 letters (right). It corresponds to your details on the immigration service database. If you don't have one they'll allocate you one and stamp it in your passport on arrival.

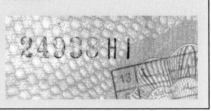

On the ferry try and pick up an A6-sized immigration card in French and English. Under 'going to' write any big Moroccan town; for 'coming from' put the European port you've just arrived from (Algeciras, etc). For 'address in Morocco' make something up if you don't know: a *Hotel Fes* in Fes will do.

Temporary vehicle importation document: TVIP or 'D16'

Aboard the ferry (on longer crossings) or in the Moroccan port of arrival you need to find the Customs desk and get the triplicate white, green and yellow A5-sized 'TVIP' form titled in French: *Declaration D'Admission Temporaire de Moyens de Transport* ('Temporary Importation Declaration of [means of] Transport). This is a welcome alternative to the dreaded Carnet de Passage which Morocco doesn't require, and declares you'll re-export your vehicle once you leave Morocco. The TVIP form is valid for six months.

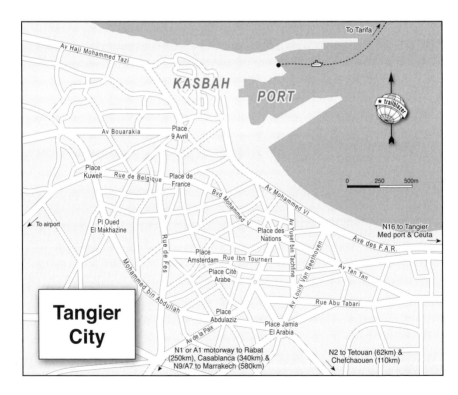

Tangier City

At home you can fill out a TVIP or 'D16' online in advance at the Moroccan Customs' website 🖳 http://www.douane.gov.ma/d16ter. It saves a little stress on arrival, but isn't vital. On the webpage click the second green tab top left: '*Saisie et Edition*'; an online form appears with drop down menus.

- *Bureau d'entree*   Choose your port of entry
- *Date d'entree*   Add your date of entry
- *Prénom et Nom*   Your forename and surname
- *Identifiant*   If you have a CIN from a previous visit (see box opposite) choose the third, '*deja visite*' option and add the number on the right. If not click the fourth '*première visite*' option and get your CIN stamped in on arrival
- *Immatriculation*   Your vehicle's registration number with no spaces
- *Marque*   Select one. If not listed choose 'autre'. For Land Rover select 'Rover'
- *Type*   For example 'Defender 300Tdi' or 'F800GS' for a bike
- *Genre*   Select *Motocycle*, *Vehicle de Tourisme* or *Camping Car*
- *Pays*   Select your country
- *Date 1ère mise...*   Your vehicle's date of registration appears on your ownership document
- *Numero châssis*   Your VIN (vehicle identity number), also on your ownership document

Then press *Imprimer* (print). Your D16 appears with all your information formatted between French and Arabic translations, as well as a couple of bar codes. If it all looks correct (see next page) print the page. Don't forget to **sign each one** in the bottom left-hand corner. Whether you fill out a D16 in advance online, or the triplicate version while queuing in a Moroccan port doesn't matter, the former is one less thing to worry about, but do the latter if you have **two vehicles in your name**.

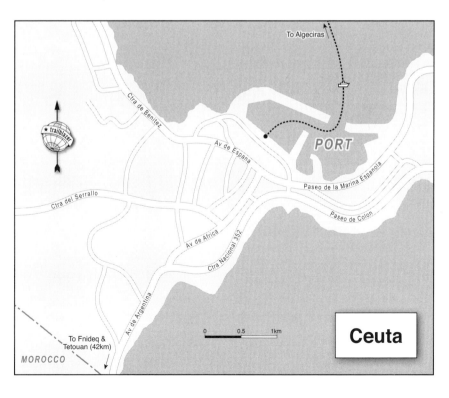

Entry procedure at the port

If you're not sure where to go or what to do, hang back and follow someone. You'll need your **passport**, **vehicle ownership document** and a **pen**. A rudimentary knowledge of French helps. Ideally all your ducks will be in a row and you'll have filled out the immigration card on the ferry (having grabbed a blank spare should you have made a mistake), your temporary vehicle importation permit ('TVIP') was printed off online back home (as opposite), and you may even have valid motor insurance for Morocco.

- Hand in your filled out immigration card to the police – they might come to your car at Tangier Med – or park up and hand it in at a booth at Fnideq or walk into the big embarkation hall in Nador. Your passport is stamped and if necessary a CIN is issued
- If you haven't got a D16, Customs will fill the triplicate A5-sized form in white, green and yellow. They'll need your vehicle ownership document. Whether a D16 or a TVIP the guy will stamp them and hand two copies back which you'll show when you leave the country
- Possibly submit to a perfunctory search of your vehicle
- Change money at a kiosk or find an ATM in town
- Buy motor insurance if available at the port (see p14)

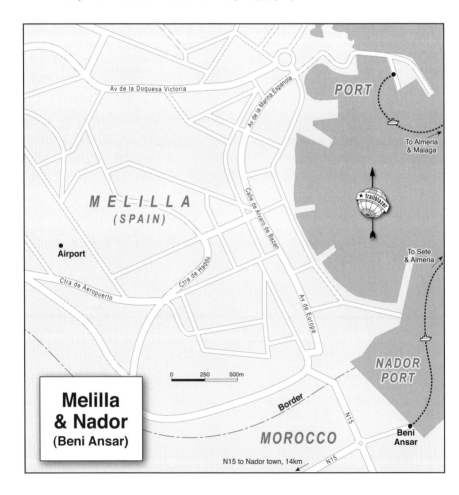

Melilla & Nador (Beni Ansar)

Left: a printed out D16. You'll need three copies. **Right:** immigration card. Grab some spares.

To complete these few steps can take as little as 30 minutes at Nador, or up to two hours or more at the busier ports when fuller ferries all arrive at once.

Leaving the port and heading into Morocco

You can now head out into the wilds of Morocco. Take it easy through towns; bored policemen sometimes want to check your documents. All four major ports have fuel stations within a couple of miles. With your papers stamped and your tank full, a stressful episode is now behind you and you're ready to cut loose and see what Morocco has to offer.

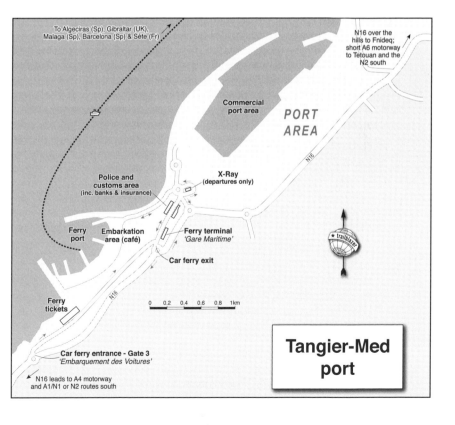

To Algeciras (Sp), Gibraltar (UK), Malaga (Sp), Barcelona (Sp) & Sète (Fr)

N16 over the hills to Fnideq; short A6 motorway to Tetouan and the N2 south

Commercial port area

PORT AREA

N16

Police and customs area (inc. banks & insurance)

X-Ray (departures only)

Ferry port

Embarkation area (café)

Ferry terminal 'Gare Maritime'

Car ferry exit

★ trailblazer

Ferry tickets

0   0.2   0.4   0.6   0.8   1km

N16

Car ferry entrance - Gate 3 'Embarquement des Voitures'

N16 leads to A4 motorway and A1/N1 or N2 routes south

Tangier-Med port

5   **ON THE ROAD**

Various subjects are covered under this heading and add up to elements of driving or riding around Morocco that are not always well covered in the guidebooks recommended on p23-4.

First days

Your first day or two in Morocco may be critical. After getting out of the port some travellers wonder what all the fuss was about, others get off on the wrong foot, get ripped off or intimidated in some way and flee back to Spain before they give the place a chance.

Experience, attitude and expectations add up to much of it, but so does your planning. Getting off the boat at somewhere like Tangier city and blundering into the medina looking for a cheap hotel with secure parking and being taken in by the first 'good Samaritan' you meet can end in tears. On this side of Morocco (as opposed to Melilla/Nador), for your first night it's best to head for somewhere **specific**, **recommended** and **easy to get to**. Plan to arrive in Morocco early, factor in a couple of hours to get out of the port and have most of the rest of the day to get to somewhere more manageable such as Asilah or Chefchaouen well before dark, or an out-of-town campsite or motel with fewer parking issues. Knowing where you're going that first night is one less thing to worry about at a time when you may have enough on your plate.

DANGERS ON THE ROAD

Local **driving standards** in Morocco are no worse than in southern or eastern Europe, adding up to a certain macho flair that can sometimes be interpreted as aggression. In the east and south of Morocco traffic is very light with few big trucks and well-surfaced roads passing sometimes fantastic scenery and with fuel, food and lodging never too far away.

Along with beaten-up cars, you'll see many **pedestrians**, **cyclists** and **animals** on the rural roads, usually near towns and villages. Schoolchildren released from class seem to wander right across the road without a care in the world. Slow right down as you pass through these villages or any crowd.

On the road the most intimidating encounters will be with the **intercity coaches** which seem to run to a timetable that the driver can barely maintain but which will cost him his job. Give way to these coaches and other similarly pushy drivers. Don't be angered by flashing or hooting as they pass; this is a local custom for 'attention, coming through' rather then 'get out of my way', though edging right to let them know you know they're there is a good idea. Drivers will also flash you as they come towards you, day and night; it's hard to know why unless they want confirmation you're awake. The most dangerous places at **night** are rural towns, especially around dusk when a place becomes mobilised by the evening *promenade*. At this time a tractor or a bicycle with lights is as rare as a moped rider with a helmet and a high-viz vest. The best advice is again, to slow down.

Single-width roads that vary from definitely one-car wide to two-cars-at-a-push can also be tense. Ideally, converging vehicles drive their nearside wheels off the asphalt onto the dirt as they pass each other, but such cooperation is rare. Usually, a game of chicken ensues with drivers waiting until the very last minute before edging slightly towards the shoulder, their mirrors whooshing just inches apart. In a right-hand drive car judging this distance can be tricky so it's best to just head for the dirt to be sure you won't get whacked; chances are you're in a 4WD that can handle a few metres of rubble. Bikes have a better time of it; oncoming vehicles often pull to the right, but just as you get used to this there's always one who won't and gives you a fright. Always be ready to brake hard and take to the shoulder.

Next are single-width **mountain roads** which, if sealed, have obviously a higher chance of traffic. The Tizi-n-Test and Route MH12 is like this in places and, along with the landslides, roadside rubble and steep drops, you really must approach each bend with the possibility that someone is doing the same from the other side.

Checkpoints and police

At most temporary checkpoints it's common for a tourist vehicle to be waved through, but don't always assume this. Slow down and watch the guy until he invariably gives you a signal to move on. Occasionally they may stop you (more so in the deep south), but chances are it'll only be for a chat. In the north it's rare to have to show your papers, but be ready and amenable to this. Despite many people's anxieties, unprompted **bribery** is unknown; that all starts from Mauritania onwards, but even then much less than is assumed. If you've broken a law such as overtaking on a solid line, that's another matter.

Only in **Western Sahara**, south of Tan-Tan, will the **permanent check-points**, very often on each side of a town, require full details right down to your mother's name. Here it speeds things up to hand over a home-made, pre-filled out form (*fiche* in French) with all your details in French. A Word template is available on the website at 🖥 **www.morocco-overland.com/fiche.doc**. This form can also be handed over at hotels which like to keep your passport to copy its details. It's always better to hand over a fiche than a passport and down south basic hotels don't bother with your details at all.

Police **speed traps** are common in the north, especially on the N1 along the Atlantic coast and even minor coastal routes. If the car ahead seems to be dawdling and isn't just a clapped-out Renault 4, chances are they know what could be around the bend. On the N1 and parallel A1 motorway speed limits are high enough to make good progress, but if you get caught fair and square you'll have to pay an on-the-spot fine of at least 700dh or try and talk your way out of it.

ELEMENTARY VEHICLE TROUBLESHOOTING

If you don't know how engines work, try to solve problems logically: will it start; will it run; will it go, steer and stop? Engines won't start for two reasons: a lack of electrical power or fuel. More rarely some mechanical issue like a broken starter motor may be the problem or more commonly these days, a relatively insignificant electronic malfunction like a blown brake light fuse may disable your modern engine by default.

Should an error code appear somewhere on the dash, getting on the internet (for cars, for example, try ⌨ www.obd-codes.com) to find out what it means may help track down the problem. Generally, they're classified with prefixes relating to 'P' (powertrain), 'B' (body), 'C' (chassis) and 'U' (network); hopefully you're a little the wiser.

It's not uncommon for non-terminal error codes – to do with emissions, for example – to flash up even if the vehicle seems to be running fine. You can ignore these.

Once running, engines that perform badly or intermittently are usually due to the air/fuel 'mixture', though again on modern, electronically-managed engines, a loose connection, faulty battery, or some electronic sensor may be the cause.

Assuming the engine started and is running sweetly, only some element of the transmission can be a show stopper – brakes and steering usually leave you something to get by with. A clutch should not go without warning unless it's been flogged to death. In a car, if you're lucky, it's the master or slave cylinder seals (one is by the clutch pedal, the other by the clutch housing under the car) if you're not, it's the plate. With a bike it's usually the cable; wet clutches rarely just give out. On bikes or cars, gearboxes too give plenty of warning, often thousands of miles, before they pack up entirely. Which leaves only tyres; the most likely cause of a breakdown and the most easily fixed.

Accidents and breakdowns

For most overland travellers, dealing with **minor vehicle problems** – or for bikers, minor injuries as well – will be as bad as things can get in Morocco. For a much smaller minority a road traffic accident or a heavy fall while riding may also involve injury.

If you've had an accident involving local drivers or pedestrians, it's best to get the police involved. Assuming you're not blatantly in the wrong and a government minister's son is not involved, in Morocco there's little to fear from the police setting you up. If you're clearly in the wrong then hold on, it could be a rough ride. Amicably exchanging details, kicking your bumper straight and expecting the other party's insurance to eventually cover the costs of your damage is unlikely to happen. Because of this, in Morocco it's best to drive around as if you're effectively uninsured, in other words with great care. You may not be in the depths of sub-Saharan Africa, but you're certainly not in the EU out here. It's this lack of certainty in how things pan out when they go wrong which puts people off driving in Morocco with their own vehicle.

Many tourists feel nervous about accepting medical care in Africa, but while it may not always be reassuringly close at hand in the south, for regular injuries emergency healthcare in Morocco is reliable and efficient. All you have to do is reach it. Nevertheless, **travel insurance** which includes repatriation in the event of a medical emergency is worthwhile, inexpensive and can put your mind at rest. Ascertain that you're covered while driving or riding off sealed roads (a common exemption), familiarise yourself with the procedure in reporting a claim or just make note of the **emergency phone number** you'll need to call to get things moving.

Breakdowns

Where an accident or breakdown happens and whether you're **alone** has a lot to do with how easily it gets resolved. On a sealed road and assuming no one else is involved, either your travel companion can tow you to somewhere useful or it won't be long before someone stops and offers to help. In southern Morocco, away from the tourist axis, chances are this'll be a genuine offer of assistance and not necessarily anything to be suspicious of. People may well become mobilised to help you, but any over-hasty claims of 'my brother has garage/is Rally mechanic' need some consideration. On the piste the same scenario may take a bit longer to solve but one thing is certain, **not travelling alone** certainly makes a tense situation easier and less expensive to fix.

It's most likely any spares for your vehicle will be miles away in a northern city or may not be available in Morocco at all. In this case many travellers have relied on others coming down to bring the needed part, as getting them sent by air courier can slow things down in Customs. Having access to the **internet** and a **mobile phone** (see p18) speeds things up greatly. At the very worst, nip back to Europe to get what you need, although if you are the one who brought the vehicle into the country, that may require leaving it with Customs which may not be practical.

Roadside recovery

When your vehicle is immobilised for any reason, it'll either be something you know how to fix sooner or later – or something you don't. Particularly on the piste, it can be a panic-inducing situation to suddenly have your Moroccan adventure stalled with a dead vehicle. Don't worry and rely on your ingenuity. It's only Morocco and eventually it'll get fixed at the cost of some time and some money. Your objective is to minimise both by thinking rationally so it's best get to a town with a hotel and a phone signal.

In Morocco there's no national **roadside recovery service** as there is in Europe; certainly not in the south where roadside recovery is a local affair dealt with by a cut-down van or 4WD with a hook on the back. Just as back home, these freelance operators have you at their mercy and can charge whatever they can get away with. Some European nationals are able to cover these costs by being members of their national roadside organisations, but Brits are not so well supported. It's well worth asking your insurance company whether they offer an add-on to cover the cost of recovery and repair in Morocco. Chances are they won't, although certain UK motorhome specialist insurers like Comfort (who also insure cars) do offer this as long as you're insured with them. They'll farm out the recovery side of things to the RAC who then subcontract to a local Moroccan service. By the time this reaches you halfway between Assa and Akka, you may well have sorted it out yourself, but with such cover, if you decide to sit it out you could get your costs repaid.

Bush mechanics

'Knowing about engines' can help speed things up still further, but with mobile phones and internet someone, somewhere will have an idea of what's wrong or what to do, even if you don't. Having a vehicle manual either in paper form or on a laptop is useful. Even if it makes no sense to you, someone else may get it.

Relying on local mechanics is a lottery. In a simple case of an obvious mechanical fault that requires garage facilities, they can manage as well as any mechanic. Simple electrical and fuelling issues can also probably be dealt with, especially with older vehicles or models with which they are familiar. Remember, these guys have seen it all before and are accustomed to problems caused by local conditions. Turning up at a dusty hole-in the-wall garage in a spluttering Porsche Cayenne with error codes flashing across the dashboard will be less successful, as will any form of electronic diagnosis (see box on p64). This is the gamble of using modern, electronically-managed machines south of the Atlas.

DAY BY DAY

In most southern towns and villages you won't find supermarkets or clearly designated **shops** selling certain products. Instead, lots of small, general stores sell the same selection of items: tinned, dried, jarred or other preserved foods, soft drinks and juice, dried milk, processed cheese, sweets, fresh bread and some fruit and vegetables. With a bit of creativity and improvisation there's everything you need here.

Bakers are usually pretty basic hole-in-the wall places rather than glittering *patisseries* – that's more of a coffee shop. Moroccan bread is either a flat brown bap or less commonly, a white baguette. The Arabic word for bread is *khobz*. The other place to shop is of course the **souk**, sometimes a weekly event and a big part of the fun of being in Morocco, even in a touristy town like Zagora. Fresh meat is another matter and not one I've ever bothered to investigate. It may be easier to track down a piece of lamb or chicken from a restaurant if you can't locate a butcher. For advice on souvenir buying see p16.

Dress codes

You may well range from sipping cocktails in sophisticated urban nightspots to slurping tea with desert nomads where the more conservative and traditional pace of life will require more appropriate dress. Local values differ greatly between Casablanca's trendy Aïn Diab district and Labouirat, halfway to Smara. While Morocco is much less strict than other Islamic countries, it's good form and less crass to dress in long trousers or skirts down south. Women are not obliged to cover their hair or bare arms, but may feel less conspicuous in towns if they do the latter. There's more on Islamic customs on p12.

Moroccan fuel

You can now get diesel as well as **unleaded petrol** just about everywhere and it is as clean and reliable as anything you'll find in Europe. The two main service station chains you'll see down south are *AFRIQUIA* and *ZIZ*, identified at the start of many of this book's routes. These are spacious, modern-looking service stations often with a shop, restaurant, car wash and mechanic as well as toilets that won't give you nightmares. At these places the attendant fills you up, you pay him cash and he dispenses change from his satchel. I've never had a problem getting change (or short-changed), but I don't quibble over every last dirham because neither do they if it's a few dirhams over.

Smaller garages in the south (basic places, often under a *SHELL* banner) may still only serve two-star leaded and diesel and have no other facilities. For

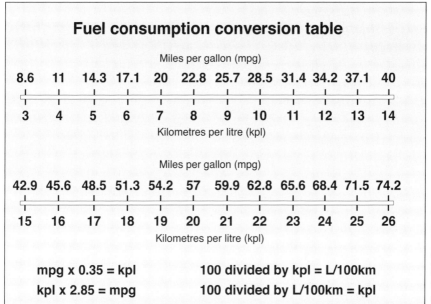

Fuel consumption conversion table

Miles per gallon (mpg)

8.6	11	14.3	17.1	20	22.8	25.7	28.5	31.4	34.2	37.1	40
3	4	5	6	7	8	9	10	11	12	13	14

Kilometres per litre (kpl)

Miles per gallon (mpg)

42.9	45.6	48.5	51.3	54.2	57	59.9	62.8	65.6	68.4	71.5	74.2
15	16	17	18	19	20	21	22	23	24	25	26

Kilometres per litre (kpl)

mpg x 0.35 = kpl   **100 divided by kpl = L/100km**
kpl x 2.85 = mpg   **100 divided by L/100km = kpl**

ON THE ROAD

modern petrol vehicles, using **leaded fuel** will coat the catalytic converter which may affect emissions, but it's not something you'll notice until your next emissions test and in my experience on the Yamaha didn't affect performance. Overall, it's best to fill up with unleaded where possible.

A few years ago near some tourist places like Tinerhir, a **scam** operated in some fuel stations where the numbers kept rolling on the bowser but no fuel was actually pumped. It's something that's easier to do to a car than a bike, but certainly in a car, if you bother to get out and open the cap you may find that these days the pump attendants will often point out the fuel bubbling up to the brim, presumably to prove you've not been tricked. It's another good reason to **always fill up a tank** rather than put in say, 100 dirhams worth.

Roadside food
In Morocco it pays to learn the difference between a **café** and a **restaurant**. In towns the former serves coffee and tea, cakes, soft drinks and cigarettes; a place for young men to hang out. Out in the countryside a café will serve tea or instant black coffee, whatever long-life snacks they stock and at best, could do you an omelette with bread.

For a more substantial meal you'll need a restaurant, which besides the main roads in towns, are often found adjacent to AFRIQUIA and ZIZ fuel stations. At all these basic places it's best

Roadside brochetterie.

Full Moroccan breakfast for 25 dirhams in a non-tourist town.

Lunch in more touristy Foum Zguid where at some 80 dirhams this was overpriced.

to ask what's available (in French: *qu'est qu'il y'a à manger*?) rather than wait politely for a menu and a napkin to be draped over your lap. In a town hotel or auberge, you'll simply be asked what time you want to eat which is fine if you're not fussy or a vegetarian.

Away from the posh, kasbah-hotels, authentic **Moroccan cuisine** is composed of a limited range of dishes. For starters there may be a soup (*shorba* is the Arabic word); a meat-based broth and rarely disappointing, or salad. A *salade marocaine* is a finely-chopped combination of tomatoes, onions, green pepper, olives, cucumber, seasoning and olive oil, all of which you can be sure won't have been flown in from Tanzania, but came into town on a cart.

For the main course **tajine** is a word you'll hear regularly, actually the name of the cooking vessel (much like the Indian 'balti'), in this case a thick ceramic plate with a conical top in which any number of stew-like dishes can be cooked, or even an omelette. In roadside restos they'll have half a dozen two-ring stoves round the back, all merrily bubbling away and waiting for the lunchtime rush. Tajines will vary from delicious, huge, overpriced and 'is that it?', but can be as good as authentic Moroccan cuisine gets down south.

Other more familiar staples include lamb *brochettes* served on a skewer with chips (*frites*), chicken (*poulette*) and chips, and of course **cous-cous**, which is commonly served as part of a bigger, communal meal and will be what you'll get fed by nomads or country folk. Cous-cous is a big bowl of fine-grained semolina, cooked by simply pouring on boiling water. Depending on what's piled on top (a tajine of some sort), it can be a bit bland compared to the above dishes, but is easily prepared with only vegetables for vegetarians. Dessert will usually be an orange, possibly sliced and sprinkled with cinnamon, and a few dates. For some typical prices of meals see p17.

Health and water

Intestinal fortitude varies from person to person, but Morocco has a comparatively good reputation for avoiding stomach upsets compared to somewhere like Egypt. There's more chance of a package tourist getting sick from an expensive hotel's stagnating buffet than by eating a brochette cooked before your eyes at a road-side stall, although such a snack was the likely cause of a spell of food poisoning on my last ride.

WHEN GOOD HOLIDAYS TURN BAD: SURVIVAL STRATEGIES

Some readers may now be licking their lips at the prospect of learning cunning tips like pointing the hour hand of your watch at the sun or rubbing Bear Grylls and Ray Mears together to make a fire. Within a week of writing this, both these presenters had prime-time TV shows about desert survival but watching them made you wonder what these guys have against lighters?

'Survival' in the wilderness sense has become a glamorous subject but, one should ask, is there any practical value in chancing upon a dead camel and gutting it to sleep inside the cadaver, or more seriously, taking the time to arrange a solar still? To a wilderness hiker possibly, but with a vehicle much less so because your bike or car is carrying all the elements you need to survive and only when it – or possibly you – are incapacitated might you be in trouble.

The worst possible scenario might involve a lone biker in the middle of summer straying off a little-used piste or falling down a deep ravine and breaking a leg or more. Badly injured, unseen and dehydrating

rapidly, the situation is indeed grave. The advice is simply to avoid putting yourself in such a situation in the first place by adopting the following guidelines:

Choose your season
The shelter and carrying capacity of your car makes this less critical but even then, ill-equipped tourists have died in summer in the desert (see p39). Solo biking is much more perilous at this time, as it might also be in a mid-winter cold spell in the High Atlas.

Communications
Mobile phone coverage extends yearly across Morocco. It could be a lifeline. Renting an inexpensive satellite phone can fill the gaps.

Company
At any time of year, if you prefer to travel alone be prepared to face the consequences.

Equipment and provisions
Be sure you have the equipment to both recover and repair your vehicle and sustain yourself or again, be prepared to face the consequences and expense.

Bottled water is widely available and it's best to stick with it unless you're here long term or have good water filtration gear. Almost certainly tap water anywhere is fine, but on a short holiday it's not worth the risk. In a car, if you're reluctant to use **wells** and other natural sources, bring up to 60 litres from home and save on discarding 40 locally-bought plastic bottles.

Stomach trouble strategy
Getting sick takes two forms. Most common but even then, rare in Morocco, is an onset of turbulent bowel activity requiring the need to be close to a toilet or a toilet roll. This could follow a meal you weren't sure about anyway.

More severe is full-on food poisoning when your whole body feels weak and sore and you need the toilet even when there's little to give from either end. You're much more susceptible to the latter south of the Sahara or in the Moroccan summer at which time it's easy to get run down from the heat.

For both such ailments the best advice is to stop eating solids, drink plenty of clean water and most essentially, dose yourself with rehydrating powders like Dioralyte, as well as 'blockers' such as Imodium (in the event of diarrhoea) until normal service resumes. With proper food poisoning this may take a few days by which time you'll be feeling quite weak, while vomiting tends to purge the toxins more quickly and the recovery is speedier. Some say dairy products, rice, Coke or toast are OK to eat or drink while recovering. It's best just to manage with salty soups and sweet drinks.

Vaccinations are no more necessary for Morocco than they are for Spain. There may be mosquitoes in some oases but there is no malaria.

HASSLE

Time to address the elephant in the room; the reason why many swear never, ever to return to Morocco. Incessant and seemingly opportunistic begging, persistent hassle from touts which can turn nasty; being treated as a dumb, gullible tourist or worse still, the terrible feeling of discovering you've just acted like one.

Your mission is not to allow this notorious side of Morocco to get to you, and one of the best ways is to **head south** where, apart from a few well-known towns and places along the 'axis of tourism', people are more chilled and there's generally more space to relax. Then, when you feel you've got the hang of Morocco, you might be ready to march boldly across the Djemma el Fna in Marrakech, or burrow deep into Fes's souk.

Some Moroccans involved with tourism – or even any sly individual encountering a tourist in need – have devised countless strategies of relieving you of your dirhams, and if you take the short stories of the late, Tangier-based Paul Bowels at face value, they've been practising among themselves for centuries and trust each other even less than a paranoid tourist. You don't necessarily have to be a worldly, streetwise traveller to be able to recognise whether a person is genuine or not because, just as back home, any stranger who approaches you out of the blue when you are clearly not in need, probably isn't. The balance you then need to acquire is to be able to deal with these people on your terms, but also not to assume or treat every last Moroccan who says 'Salaam' as a potential invader of your much prized personal space.

More hassle

Broadly speaking, the hassle you get in Morocco falls into two categories: the harmless if at times irritating kids whose chants of 'Donnez moi…' resonate off the valley walls like a deleted scene from The Sound of Music – and the more relentless and polished pestering from touts in the popular resorts and cities. In between, you may get taken in by your share of roadside chancers waving you down for a cigarette or a lift, even if they don't smoke or are headed in the opposite direction.

'Donnez moi…' to give or not to give?

Chances are, over a stay of a few weeks, you'll be asked scores of times for bon bons or stylos (sweets, pens) or even just dirhams or cigarettes; whatever they see on your dashboard. Received opinion suggests that blindly handing stuff out is bad form, however good your intentions. By doing so you further engender a begging mentality that stops people – if not whole African nations – from standing on their own two feet.

An urban myth resurfaces now and again, claiming the origin of such widespread begging comes from successive rallies or expeditions who threw out branded pens and hats at the delirious throng, so as to bask in the afterglow of a job well done. It's convenient and politically acceptable to

…in most cases it's not the need for the object so much as the desire to receive it.

blame big expeditions or rallies, but the reality is probably far more prosaic as it's easy enough to feel good by handing out whatever falls to hand. I've seen or heard of travellers becoming so intimidated by the kids that they think they must throw out a 'sacrifice' or decoy lest they get stoned or torn limb from limb.

Detractors would say we have a lot of old junk we'd otherwise throw away so why not make someone's life a little better by passing on what you don't need? I've read accounts of travels in Morocco where the tourists unabashedly handed out expired domestic goods all over the country and saw it as a benevolent service. Locals hear of this and so equate 'tourist' with free goods. This is all very well as long as you accept that what you hand out may be taken swiftly to a souk and sold for something they actually want or need. And as anyone who's tried will know, you can never give away enough because in most cases it's not the need for the object so much as the desire to receive it. Of course one must distinguish between handouts and giving a tip in return for some service, however slight, or offering to cover the cost of genuine hospitality or a meal laid on by a poor peasant or desert dweller.

By African standards Morocco is not a poor country and these days begging is more of a genetic national reflex spawned from a long history of tourism rather than one of genuine need. But just as people claim to have travelled the world without paying a single bribe, so it's possible to get fixated on not giving anything ever, under any circumstances whatsoever. This disregards the element of human compassion, especially when you pass through some bedraggled, windblown village with your mouth clamped around a succulent chicken, pesto and avocado bap.

Once we stopped in such a place on a baking hot day and a little girl came up to say hello. The lack of the usual clamour made the exchange much more equable and after we asked her name I gave her an orange that was lying around and which she took happily. 'Bad move' claimed my passenger. Now the little girl will associate car with free gift, just like the rest of Morocco and so the disease of indolence spreads. My only retort, other than being sympathetic for a poor child on a hot day in the desert, was when was the last time she may have seen a fresh orange? The injection of Vitamin 'C' will do her a world of good and was certainly better than some bubble gum or a *Morocco Overland* branded baseball cap. The debate continued for days.

Compassionate responses clearly depend on the manner in which you're approached. It's hard to respond warmly to a horde of yelling brats banging on your windows, but a peasant woman with babes in arms sitting quietly under a tree watching you eat is another. The rules aren't black and white.

What it seems these kids crave above all is attention which is easy to dish out in spades and takes up no room in your baggage. Ignoring people, be they Moroccan kids or the in-laws, is an excellent way of proffering disrespect and getting people's backs up. Crawling through a village at a safe speed, you can't outrun them so make eye contact, smile and wave. Sometimes approaching yet another such village you'll feel like Alvin Stardust bracing himself to head out on stage drowned in teenybopper wails. Wave, nod, open your windows or lift your visor or goggles and have a few choice phrases like *rien ne va plus* (no more). By doing so you're disarming the crowd (in some cases, literally).

> **What it seems these kids crave above all is attention which is easy to dish out in spades and takes up no room in your baggage**

'Hello my friend'

With these three chilling words you know your cover is blown and once again you'll have to Play the Game. Hustlers, *faux guides* (false guides), touts, plucky entrepreneurs, call them what you will, from their nests in doorways or on street corners they swoop down on their prey to see if they can get a bite. While far from unique to this country, these people are the bane of Morocco and are as despised by honest, hardworking locals. They can be responsible for many miserable experiences and vows never to return.

While on the move, village kids are easy to deal with. Not so harmless in some tourist towns are the more malicious, misguiding and mischief-making touts, or the incessant pestering for any number of services from mechanics to guides, camel rides and accommodation. Some of course could be genuine, but with experience it's easy to read from the tone used, appearance or dress which ones are not, just as they too can probably spot a gullible target. Across the world these hustlers are attracted to places where tourists congregate and the best are extremely adept at persuading the credulous, in five major languages, that a carpet is *ancienne*, a bargain and for the right price will probably fly itself home. Morocco is no different and, hard though you may think it to believe, thirty years ago was even worse. Attempts at outlawing the practice have worked to an extent, but with current levels of unemployment, working with or on tourists is seen as a short cut to riches.

As bad as getting had can be, the danger is of becoming suspicious of all encounters, so that you stomp about in a snarl in every town. When on foot, shuffling around slack jawed and purposelessly while clutching a map upside down is bound to attract the wrong sort of attention. Even if you don't quite know where you're going, look as if you do; adopt the same sort of advice given back home to lone women walking anywhere at night.

My **advice** is this: pursue engagements beyond a quick smile, a shake of the head and a *'non merci'* at your peril. Don't even return a greeting, just smile and keep moving without provoking any antagonism. Leave them to focus on another target. Once you verbally engage in answering inane enquiries about your name or provenance, a relationship, however slight, has been established and it's much harder to break away – at worst requiring rudeness which is something you don't want to resort to. Ignoring them totally is mildly antagonistic – they will keep at you until you respond in some way – while gamely playing along eventually sees you drawn into a pitch.

Under pressure, or after too many instances of unremitting hassle, you might be tempted to shame or ridicule your tormentors. Don't waste your time; they've heard it all before and have skins as thick as the city walls of Taroudant. And even then, acting like this usually leaves a bad taste. Far better not to let things get that far.

These hot spots are well known in Morocco and without trying to tell you where not to go, are alluded to in this book: in the south it's pretty much the line between Marrakech and Merzouga.

> **... are extremely adept at persuading the credulous, in five major languages, that a carpet is *ancienne*, a bargain and for the right price will probably fly itself home.**

If you find you don't have the temperament to deal with it, there's much to be said for avoiding these places and spending your money and time elsewhere. There's more chance of interacting with 'normal' people which adds up to the vast mass of the population. Your memory of Morocco will be all the sweeter.

WILD CAMPING

Wild camping is part of the appeal of overlanding in southern Morocco. In the north, if you're considering camping on arable land or in orchards, either ask permission first or be discreet. Even down south, wild camping in total solitude is not to be assumed. It's not uncommon to think you're alone under the stars only to have a nomad come out of nowhere to sit and watch you, or hang around to see if anything's going spare. As often as not they'll invite you back to the family tent, which can be a night to remember.

For your own peace of mind it's good practice to camp **out of sight** of the highway or at least a kilometre from the tarmac, as well as a good distance from any settlement or encampment unless you're looking for interaction. This will dissuade chancers from stopping and coming over to nose around. Alone, your first night out off the road or out by the piste can be rather unnerving. It's common to feel vulnerable and exposed, but after a few nights you'll have the feel for finding a good spot (many are recommended in the route descriptions) and have organised your gear efficiently to make the whole process easier.

Desert lore suggests you should **never camp in a river bed** for fear of flash floods. In fact the soft sand, vegetation, windbreaks and possible tree shade make creeks great places to camp compared to an exposed, stony plain. Use your common sense if the weather looks stormy and you're in the mountains.

In the back of a car, in a roof tent or on the ground by your bike, before you go to sleep it's good practice to tidy up and put things away; more against the possibility of a dust storm or rain shower than any chance of pilfering. And of course, in the morning don't leave anything other than tracks and footprints. **Burn** what will reduce to ash, throw out or bury organic matter and pack anything else like empty jars or tins to dispose of in the next town. This can be more easily said than done in some places, but at the very least it's better to centralise refuse in one place rather than leave it all over the desert.

When not using roadside lavatories, bury your toilet waste in sand or under a rock where it'll dry harmlessly and above all, get into the habit of **burning your toilet paper** (keep a lighter with the toilet paper). Many tourist sites in the Sahara have been despoiled by little white tufts of used Andrex.

RENTING VEHICLES LOCALLY

In Morocco there are a few places offering motorcycles and many more offering 4WDs to rent, all of which are capable of doing most of the routes in this book. Combined with budget airline flights from under €100 (see p56), rental fees can work out low enough to make a week or two's exploring viable when compared to the time and expense of driving or riding down.

The drawbacks are that you don't quite know what you'll get and whatever it is, it'll have no camping gear, adequate tools or recovery equipment. Unless you know what you're getting into or are renting from the internationally-known rental agencies like Avis, it would be best not to plan too much of your holiday in Morocco around it.

You should be fine with a Toyota Prado (a 3.5 TD that's also known as a 'Land Cruiser') or a 'real' Land Cruiser (a 4.2, six cylinder), especially if there are a few of you. Even with standard suspension, a Land Cruiser will manage most of the routes in this book. Of the cities close to the routes in this book, cars are most commonly found in Agadir, Marrakech and Ouarzazate, with bikes in Marrakech. The prices shown below are of course bound to change, but give an idea of what's available and where.

Motorcycle	Location	Price per week
XR250R	Marrakech	3500 dh
BMW G650 GS	Marrakech	6000 dh
BMW R1200GS	Marrakech	10,000 dh

4WD		
Old model Toyota Prado	Marrakech	€560
Land Rover/Land Cruiser	Marrakech	€770

Using a rental

It must be understood that most rental agencies would not expect you to head off with a copy of *Morocco Overland*, a pick-axe and dynamite to see how many routes you can knock out before handing the vehicle back. While out of the factory some 4WDs perform better than others on the dirt, the lack of off-road **preparation and related equipment** makes it clear that this isn't encouraged.

Be aware of the expense that could be incurred if damaging a marginally suitable vehicle while negotiating rocky tracks, and attempt to unravel the small print in the contract while reading between the lines. With a car at least, renting with one of the international agencies should come with some security. Ask what will happen if the vehicle breaks down and you can't fix it? Who pays for the repair?

With a car or bike, it may be best to come clean and fully explain your intentions and enquire about the state of the tyres (and on a bike, the chain as well). It might encourage the agent to check and renew such items. It's also worth noting that, as is the norm elsewhere in the world, insurance for damage and possibly even third parties is **not valid off sealed roads**, even if these tracks are designated as recognised rights of way (as are most routes in this book). The typically low speeds off road mean that the chances of having a **collision** or running someone over are small, but if nothing else, this ought to be a reminder to keep speeds down, especially when passing through villages where throngs of kids can swarm towards you.

For a **rented motorcycle** check for a spanner to remove the wheels and bring some of the tools listed opposite, plus tyre levers, a hand pump or mini compressor and a puncture repair kit, if not a spare tube. Hauling adequate **camping gear** on a plane or sourcing it locally is asking a bit much, so it's best to settle with using local lodgings which, with a bit of judicious route planning, are plentiful and inexpensive in the south.

TWO-DAY 4WD EXCURSIONS FROM THE MAIN MOROCCAN RESORTS

Marrakech

From this city the High Atlas MH routes are right on your southern doorstep. A good two days would add up to heading out of town via Asni and the Tizi-n-Test pass towards **Aoulouz**. From here you can consider tackling routes MH6 or the more impressive MH7, taking the option to follow MH8 north at Askaoun. Or you can carry on to overnight in **Taliouine** at one of the many auberges there and then follow MH8 or the eastern half of MH7 from Askaoun. Once you're down at **Anezal**, Marrakech is about three hours away.

The 'Route of the Kasbahs' between Telouet and Aït Benhaddou is also easy to follow and a popular way of getting over the Atlas.

Ouarzazate

Ouarzazate is close to some of the best routes in this book. With the High Atlas to the north, Jebel Sirwa to the west and Jebel Sarhro to the east, it'll take some self-discipline to decide what to pack into two days of rental. If you want to get high, head east out to **Dades** and up the gorge. Don't spend time crawling along Route MH3. Instead head up MH1 in reverse over the highest track in this book to **Agoudal** for an overnight auberge, then come back down the all-sealed MH2 to Tinerhir for an easy drive back west to Ouarzazate.

Alternatively, at Dades or Tinerhir head up along MH10 (or MH4 from Tinerhir) and over the Jebel Sarhro for the amazing drive down to Nekob. From there you can return via Agdz to Ouarzazate by road or try and pack in MH14 back over the massif.

Besides the Jebel Sirwa routes outlined under Marrakech, the other good loop from Ouarzazate would be to head down towards Foum Zguid via Tazenacht, a great drive in itself, and then pick up MA7 to Issil and the N10 where you turn east back to Tazenacht for a spot of carpet shopping and so on to Ouarzazate. MA7 is slow and tough on cars – make sure your vehicle is up to it.

When collecting a car, don't leave the parking lot until you've checked the location and state of the **spare tyre** as well as all the necessary tools: jack with handle, wheel brace and crank (see below). Locals may have a fatalistic attitude towards punctures but you could easily waste the best part of a day when you find the spare is missing or the jack has no handle. (If you've never changed a tyre on the likes of a Land Cruiser before, the spare winches down on a chain from the back, using a rod as a crank slotted through a tiny hole near the rear number plate.) It's also important to be aware of the possible instability and inadequate lift of a standard supplied bottle-jack when lifting a car on soft ground (see p38).

Rental vehicles are unlikely to be supplied with any useful items for heading off-road, so the items listed below are recommended on a trip of a week or more of full-on piste bashing, either bought locally or brought from home.

- Portable compressor
- Tow strap
- Multi-tool
- Spanners adding up to at least 10, 12, 13, 14 and 17mm
- Adjustable spanner
- Zip ties and duct tape

6 OFF THE ROAD

Off-highway riding

Many bikers dream of riding the desert sands but in Morocco tracks are predominantly **rocky** with sand filling some creek-crossings; for most riders that'll be more than enough sand. To an experienced dirt biker, rocky terrain doesn't hold too many surprises but to a beginner far from home on a loaded bike, inching off the blacktop for the first time can be unnerving.

In Morocco's mountains and desert it's not so much the actual riding as the relentless concentration demanded by riding and navigating that'll wear you out. Although you'll often be riding through spectacular scenery, the only chance you'll get to appreciate this splendour is by stopping, either by choice or by accident.

Your goal is to conserve energy, keep track of your position and preserve your machine from damage and yourself from injury; most biking trips to Morocco will include one and possibly the other. Having all this dropped in your lap after days of tranquil highway cruising can be quite daunting, especially if you're alone. Suddenly your sure-footed sled skitters about from rock to rock and feels as heavy as it really is.

Expect to fall off in the early days when you're still getting the feel for your machine off-road, and then later to fall off harder should you become over-confident. Only then will you have acquired the right balance of caution and confidence. In the inverse of a rodeo rider, your bike breaks you in after a few hard days and within a week you finally loosen up. But push your luck and get too tired and you'll simply fall off through fatigue. You need to judge and pace it right.

Fifty miles an hour or **80kph** is the safe maximum speed on any dirt surface. Faster than that, it's not possible to react quickly enough to the ever-changing terrain and even half that speed will feel way too fast on some exposed mountain routes.

Ride light

First-timers on the dirt tend to tense up and grip the bars. Try to relax your body because, as with suspension, when too rigid it has a detrimental effect on handling. On rough terrain try to hold the bars loosely, guiding the front end while allowing the bars to bounce around loosely in your palms.

By being relaxed and responding fluidly to the knocks, you'll preserve yourself and your bike from sudden and ultimately tiring shocks. Riding light includes weighting the footrests or standing up (see below) over any cross ridges or V-shaped dips, and using your body rather than the handlebars to steer.

In a nutshell: stand when you must – sit down when you can. The key is to preserve energy with smooth, efficient riding.

Your body needs to be relaxed, but the mind must be alert and at times ready to mobilise the body into assertive action. Anticipate and react to the changing surface just as you do with dozy car drivers and other hazards in a busy city. During the course of a long day on the dirt you'll find this kind of responsive riding saves both physical and mental energy. Alert, smooth riding is the key and learning to do so is part of the satisfaction of dirt riding in Morocco.

Stand up on the footrests

One thing that transforms the control of a bike on rough or loose surfaces is standing up on the footrests. When you stand up and grip the bike between your knees:

- Suspension shocks are absorbed through your slightly-bent legs and not directly through your back
- Your bike is much easier to control as the weight is borne lower through the footrests, not the seat
- Your forward visibility improves a little

It's one reason why the more purposeful enduro bikes have such narrow seats and why trials bikes have no seat to speak of. You may never have stood up on your bike's footrests for long, but now is the time to try it and find out if it's a posture you can comfortably sustain for a while. Chances are taller riders may stoop so they should consider taller bars or installing bar risers. When standing up for more than a few seconds – for example to get a good look ahead – it's OK to lock your knees out to save fatigue, but as you approach a hit, always **bend your knees**, just as you would when making a jump.

When standing up it also helps to press in on the tank or seat lightly with your knees to brace the bike. With three points of contact – feet, knees and hands – the rigid bike is effectively triangulated to your flexible body and gives you much better control over rough surfaces. You may want to make sure your standing up knee-bike interface is comfortable. Inner kneepads may help. You may also find that non-motocross riding boots lacking a tough, steel shank are uncomfortable on your instep after a short period of standing, and that normal rubber footrests are fine until they get wet.

Standing up enables smoother progress, providing it's not a crouch.

BIG BIKES

can be tricky without resorting to paddling. Slipping the clutch to raise the revs and so smooth out the pulses may help, but risks the back end stepping out as the clutch or traction alternate from grippy rock to gravel.

Any stylish motocross moves like sliding the back end while leaning forward, and sticking the inside leg forward to steady the machine takes some nerve on a machine nearly three times your weight.

In deep loose gravel or on sand it's easy to bury a heavy, powerful machine up to the crankcase until it can stand up by itself. A good trick to know in this situation (one that works on any bike) is to simply lay the bike on its side, fill in the hole excavated by the back wheel and then – the hard bit – pick the bike up again. With the engine now off the deck, start the bike and walk it out under power to firm ground.

You can get a long way in Morocco on a big bike as long as you accept the off-road limitations which come at the cost of highway cruising panache. If a slope up or down looks gnarly and loose, get off and walk alongside the machine, assuming you want to continue at all. Or at least stop and have a think about your line over an obstacle. Not all the routes in this book are suited to big bike pilots with limited off-roading experience. Give yourself a couple of weeks and all that could change.

Big heavy bikes have their own set of rules for off-roading. The mass and inertia that comes with all that weight means you're best off plodding along steadily and avoiding the need to make any sudden moves. Despite its daunting bulk the stability of something like a flat-twin GS responds amazingly well to this sort of riding. Just concentrate on the path of least resistance and allow the suspension to do its job while relieving it of excessive loads by keeping the speed down and standing up when necessary.

The high gearing and massive torque put out by such big-capacity machines (not helped by a Boxer's shaft drive characteristics) can be a bit of a liability on loose and rocky hairpins or deep gravel and sand. Trying to balance round a tight bend in first gear as the engine's power pulses thud away

Weighting the footrests

It's not always necessary to stand right up; sometimes just leaning forward, pulling on the bars and taking the weight from your backside and onto the footrests for a moment will be enough to reduce an impact. As you get the hang of riding on the dirt, standing up, just like sticking your leg out on a slithery bend, will soon become instinctive, as will briefly unloading the saddle to lessen an impact. In a nutshell: **stand when you must – sit down when you can**. The key is to preserve energy with smooth, efficient riding.

ROCKY MOUNTAIN TRACKS

Some of the best routes in Morocco will be the mountain tracks in the High- and especially the Anti-Atlas. In a car you plod along at little more than walking pace and watch the scenery inch by. A bike is faster and more fun on this sort of all-engrossing terrain, but too much speed on loose hairpin bends could all end badly. Some of the routes in this book demand reduced speed for no other reason than uncertainty about what's around the next corner or over the brow of the hill. Keep your hands over the handlebar levers and be ready for anything: grazing goats, landslides, other vehicles.

Again, in the mountains as much as anywhere, you must ride within the limits of your visibility and the terrain. Read the ground constantly. A steep descent will probably end at a sandy creek or ditch, while a steep ascent rarely continues down the other side of the crest in the same direction.

On some very stony tracks, like the entry into the Cirque de Jaffar or the two MA routes over the Jebel Timkouka, or even coming down to Igmir (MA2) from the north, excessively wide alloy panniers will be a liability. With the wall of rock rising to one side of the track you'll be forced to take the more exposed drop-side rut where putting a wheel wrong does not bear thinking about. On a bike some of these ascents and descents are very challenging, requiring clearing rocks or even walking the bike up. On all these kinds of routes keep tyre pressures firm and check your rims and spokes (if you have them), sometimes nightly.

Riding in sand

Morocco has very few sandy pistes but occasionally you can't avoid riding in a sandy rut, usually across a dry riverbed. Here you must be ready to stand up and gas it to maintain front end stability. Momentum and acceleration are often the only things that will get you through a particularly soft stretch of sand, so don't be afraid to stand up and accelerate hard at the right time, revving your engine as hard as necessary. A quick snap of the throttle gives the drive and stability to blast assuredly across a short, sandy oued. No matter how much your bike weaves and bucks around, keep the power on and your backside off the seat for as long as it takes. So long as the front wheel remains on course (or even if it doesn't) you're moving and so remain mostly in control. Decelerate, and sand builds up in front of the front wheel, the geometry of the front end's self-centring 'caster effect' is lost and down you go. Keep off the brakes, especially the front. Reduce speed through the gears not the brakes – or lock the brakes hard, stick your best leg out and hope for the best.

Sand-riding can be hair-raising and you'll often come close to falling off, so much so that at times it'll feel like a relief to actually fall off and get the inevitable over with. The techniques described here are the only way to get through soft sand, short of paddling along at 1mph. As often as not, this is the safest if not so elegant solution.

Knobbly tyres

Trail tyres like Tourances are essentially road tyres with an off-roady appearance and will compromise your off-road experience. The extra grip, control and directional stability of proper knobbly tyres or even just Pirelli MT21s and Continental TKC80s makes dirt riding less unpredictable and so more fun. Unlike on a car where tread block is immaterial to cornering, a motorbike needs knobs to lean over securely on the dirt. With knobbly tyres you can also leave the pressures almost at road levels while still benefiting from the knobbly tread pattern for good grip in the dirt.

Low tyre pressures

Dropping tyre pressures to as little as 0.6 bar (10 psi) lengthens the contact patch with the ground, dramatically increasing traction and reducing wheelspin. It works even with a regular trail or road tyre, but in rocky Morocco is

OFF THE ROAD

not such a good idea, unless you're spending a day in soft sand. In this under-inflated state, even a tubeless tyre gets much hotter, while a conventional tyre can pinch a tube on a sharp-edged hit that can result in a puncture. Ride light, keep your speed down and your tyre pressures as high as possible.

Dune riding

Arriving at **Erg Chebbi** the temptation may be to dump your baggage and head out for a quick blast. On my solo biking trips in the central Sahara the idea of thrashing about in the dunes was always far too risky and, over 30 years later, passing Erg Chebbi I feel no different. Motorcycle accidents are most common in dunes where riding anything heavier than a 100-kilo dirt bike is just too dangerous. If it's briefly part of a piste like MS6, commit your-

CROSSING FLOODED TRACKS

Flash floods are a common phenomenon in the mountains of Morocco where they often peak a few hours after a storm, after which the flow quickly recedes. Waiting overnight or even just a few hours can see an impassable torrent drop to a muddy trickle. All hard running fords should be given at least a moment's thought before diving in. It only takes rushing water a foot deep to push a bike onto some unseen rubble and down it goes.

If in doubt the simplest answer is to **walk** across. By walking you can pick a good line, get a feel of the surface which can include rocks, holes or broken cement. Getting your feet wet is the only sure way of knowing the depth and what lies beneath the surface. Better wet feet than soaked baggage or a water-logged bike. If it can be walked it can probably be ridden and can certainly be crossed by walking alongside the bike under power. If it's too dangerous to walk then chances are walking alongside a running bike will be risky too.

It's said that a rider should walk with a bike on their downstream side so that if the bike falls or the rider stumbles he won't get pinned under it. This may be true at the extreme end of the scale with water rushing over your knees, but in less severe conditions it can be easier to *lean onto* the downstream side of the bike which is being pushed against you by the flow (as below), so making a stable combination. It's also easier to walk a bike on the left side with your right hand resting naturally on the throttle and front brake and your left easing the clutch in and out to stop the engine stalling, something you'd rather not do on a kickstart-only XR400.

Otherwise, pick your spot. Generally where the flow is wider it's less deep and the current less strong; it may look a long way across but it will be shallower. As you ride across, keep your feet ready to drop in and steady yourself, and keep the speed down to give you more time to correct a hit. Except, of course, when taking action shots!

Route MS11. Better wet boots than wet boots and everything else. © Eric De Nadai

self to the task single-mindedly. The sand may appear cushion-soft, but a cart-wheeling bike landing across your backbone is not.

Dunes can be a maze of varying, similarly-coloured slopes, sometimes hard to distinguish and Erg Chebbi is particularly complex. Most accidents happen when the speed you're compelled to maintain sends you over a drop. If you're lucky it'll just be a harmless tumble; if not it's the end of your trip and the beginning of a stressful evacuation.

Approaching dune crests on a bike is tricky compared to a 4WD as you don't have the stability or the traction of a 4WD. It can often be easier to plan to fall over on a crest rather than go over the edge and fall down with your bike behind you. Having fallen on a crest, pick the bike up and walk it down if necessary. In the dunes, never let your concentration drop while riding, attack very soft sections standing up on the footrests and with the power on. Cross other deep tracks as close to right angles as possible and with a short burst of acceleration. You can expect your engine to get very hot in the dunes as you'll be revving it to the limit in the lower gears. Keep an eye out for the temperature and stop to cool it down if necessary, but keep the engine running. There's more on Erg Chebbi on pp162-3.

Day trips for motorcycles

Even if you're not lugging around full camping gear you'll still have brought a certain amount of baggage that you don't need every minute of the day. While these bags may not weigh much, alloy boxes and in particular hard road-touring cases can be a liability off-road, either getting in the way on narrow tracks, getting damaged in a fall, or simply breaking their mounts.

If you want to dabble on some pistes but don't want to mash your Givis, the routes in this book can be chopped up and re-arranged into day trips of varying length and difficulty. Leave most of your gear in a hotel or auberge and enjoy a fun day out on a lighter, slimmer bike with the knowledge of what awaits you at the end of the day. For recommended places to base yourself see the website link or your guidebook.

Distances given include figures taken from maps along non-GPS'd stages (usually highways) so may vary from your readings. Distances in brackets indicate approximately how much of the total distance is tarmac. An 'r' after the route indicates it follows this book's route description in reverse. Many southern loops include a stage along Route MS10: The Desert Highway (see p114), but as it's all road it's not indicated.

Give your bags the day off and it's like having a whole new bike.

L1   Alnif – Tizi-n-Ouli-Ousir – Alnif
(MH5, MH10)   **100km (includes 7km tarmac)**

A hundred kilometres of off-road action up to the heights and back down. On a good day the scenery here is something special. A 600cc trail bike would be on the limit up on the Ousir, while big adventure bikes will see as much, if not a whole lot more, by doing the route below.

L2   Alnif – Iknioun – Nekob – Alnif
(MH10r, MH4)   **228km (97km)**

Incorporates most of the route above, but without the extremes. At twice as long it's twice as good too because any reasonably fit bike can manage it. With fuel in Nekob and no backtracking, it's among the finest loops in the land.

L3   Assa – Aouinet Torkoz – Tadalt – El Borj –Torkoz – Assa
(MW4r, MW5)   **227km (98km)**

A very satisfying day's ride out from Assa up into the hills and canyons, and back again for an Orangina at the roadhouse. With little sand and little chance of mud, a big bike will manage fine.

L4   Tinerhir – Agoudal – Dades – Tinerhir
(MH1, MH2)   **265km (200km)**

Up through the Todra Gorge, past Ait Hani and over the motorable crest of the High Atlas. Have lunch in Agoudal and then dirt back over the Atlas to Msemrir. On a sunny day in dry conditions it's as good as a loop gets in the High Atlas and blizzards excepted, one a big bike with the right tyres will manage.

L5   Foum Zguid – Issil – Agmour – Foum Zguid
(MA7, MA6, MA9)   **213km (50km)**

On a well-shod and light bike this rocky canyon and valley ride with little tarmac will be a blast. The MA9 stage is an easy ride just when you'll need it and is getting slowly sealed, but L5 may still be too much on a big bike.

L6   Foum Zguid – Mrimina – Dakar piste – Lac Iriki – Foum Zguid
(MS8, MS7r)   **237km (78km)**

A full day out of Foum Zguid with a possibility of making your own tracks back to town from around KM170. Otherwise it may be a bit of a reach on fuel and anyway it's best not done alone.

L7   Igmir – Izerbi – Tasserirt – Tizerkine – Afella – Izerbi – Igmir
(MA2, MA1, MA2)   **139km (66km)**

A short day but with great scenery and quite a lot of river bed shingle at the end which may be tricky on big, wide bikes. Head north out of Igmir past Izerbi and along the lovely Tizerkine Gorge to Afella. Here you follow the river bed piste towards Aït Herbil (a short diversion to refuel is possible) before heading back up to Igmir, an amazing ride in itself.

L8   Midelt – Cirque de Jaffar – Midelt
(MH1)   **about 90km**

The classic short, spectacular, all-piste run out of Midelt. The way back to Midelt from KM48.5 is unlogged but will get you back one way or another. Allow three hours; a big bike will manage if the weather's been good.

L9 Ouarzazate – Anezal – Ouarzazate
(MS9) 116km (62km)

This adds up to a fun half-day out of Ouarzazate to get the measure of your abilities and your bike. It can be strung out with lunch at a resto in Tazenacht or Amerzgane, both nice towns, or of course you could simply ride the same route back to Ouarzazate to make a good day out on the piste.

L10 Tafraoute – Tizerkine Gorge – Timkyet – Tazalarhite – Tafraoute
(MA1, MA3r, MA8r) 114km (79km)

A satisfying excursion along the back roads and tracks east of Tafraoute. The loose climb after Timkyet may require some thought on a big machine, but after that, it's an easy ride over the plateau and down the other side. Although not long, this will take more than half a day.

L11 Taliouine – Askaoun – Assarag – Aoulouz – Taliouine
(MH8, MH6) 223km (117km)

Ride up towards the southern flanks of Jebel Toubkal followed by an easy but possibly muddy 'Transit' route back down through the villages to Aoulouz (fuel). If you have the range you can make it all a bit sportier by turning off at MH6/KM79 or so to pick up MH7 heading back up to the heights of Askaoun and back down to Taliouine – about the same distance. Allow a full day.

L12 Tata – Imitek – Tazegzaoute – Timkyet – Afella – Tata
(MA3) 240km (120km)

Another great day out, up onto the plateau and down towards Afella. Includes shingly riverbeds, steep ascents and descents so could be hard work on a big bike and not recommended two-up. Just before Afella you take an unlogged but easy track back east towards Imitek (see MA3/KM140). Allow a full day.

L13 Taliouine – Askaoun – Anezal – Tazenacht – Taliouine
(MH8, MH7) 236km (190km)

Even if it's less than 50km of dirt, you get a great ride up to Askaoun from where you're crossing high dirt passes below Jebel Sirwa summit. Rejoin the road down to Anezal and a great road ride back to Taliouine via Tazenacht.

L14 Tazzarine – Oum Jrane – Alnif – Tazzarine
(MS3, MS4) 177km (58km)

One of the few logged loops you can take out into the Sahara zone in a day, giving over 100km of piste and a good impression of the desert tracks out here. Some short sandy stages. Also possible from Alnif.

L15 Tinerhir – Iknioun – Nekob – Alnif – Tinerhir
(MH4) 254km (100km)

A classic run over Jebel Sarhro that's been done two-up on a 1150GS running Tourances. The rise up to Iknioun can get muddy, but beyond that it's just the rock-step descent that will need concentration, along with distracting views. From Alnif a turn by the radio mast in town leads north to the N10.

L16 Aït Youb – Imitek – Tara tunnel – Amellago – Aït Youb
(MH11) 91km (49km)

Easy half-day ride out through the spectacular Imitek gorge and up onto the escarpment with a great view from the Tizi Tagountsa just before the tunnel.

Off-road driving

In a comfortable four-wheeler with the air-con humming and the Psychedelic Furs on the stereo, it's possible to feel immune to the hammering your vehicle is getting. There is a tendency to assume that 4WDs are indestructible and worse still, for a minority to drive them as if they are.

Unlike bikes, the risk of personal injury in a car is small, but the risk of damaging your two-ton wagon while off-roading is not, and it's this which ought to limit your speed on the tracks of southern Morocco. On many rocky mountain routes you may drive for hours at little more than walking pace; any faster and something may break.

Along with punctures, suspension commonly fails in Moroccan conditions, even when driving at a moderate pace. Flood damaged tracks apart, the need for good axle articulation or 'twisting' is rarely needed, except on routes like MH3 and MH5. Most other routes are passable in a 2WD with care.

Ditches and creeks

What you will be in for is a lot of crawling in and out of ditches and oueds, such as on Route ME3. Here, long body overhangs (usually the rear) combined with low suspension can be a liability. All such obstacles should be taken slowly to avoid compressing the suspension and so reducing ground clearance. Use the low range gearbox to maintain control rather than relying on momentum, as a 2WD or a bike must do. If it looks like the back might dig in and lift the weight off the rear wheels, crawl across the bank **at a 45° angle** very slowly in low first. Know too when to use a central diff lock, if you have this feature; avoid locking it unless stuck in soft sand or mud (more on p36).

If you have to inch around a fallen boulder or rockfall, get someone ahead to guide you with clearly agreed hand signals to spare unnecessary contact with the vulnerable tyre sidewalls or undercarriage.

Getting stuck

At a sensible pace it's all very easy in a 4WD until you become stuck, and in Morocco it could be snow, mud, a landslide, rockfall, flooded creek or sand that brings your wheels spinning to a halt. Unless you're dying to put various items of recovery equipment and techniques into use, the trick is to avoid getting stuck in the first place by knowing **when to turn back**. Along with not damaging their vehicle, it's something a solo driver or a single vehicle will address frequently. With more than one vehicle and the equipment outlined on p40 you can be a bit more adventurous and explore your car's abilities. Initially, there can be a thrill about cracking out the unused hi-lift, shackles or sand plates and early on, until you get a feel for how your machine responds, they may actually be needed.

The skill you want to master is to look ahead and assess the risks, primarily to reduce impacts to the car but at times also to avoid getting stuck. If you're unsure, get out and have a look around on foot. Are there other recent tracks or an alternative route to one side? If you do get stuck will it be an easy recovery? One reason people tend to push their luck and even play around on dunes is that getting unstuck is relatively easy (though so too is rolling a vehicle). Dry sand doesn't stick like mud or waterlogged sand, and doesn't soak like water, hurt like rocks or chill like snow. Scooping with your hands is actually quite pleasant as long as it's not over 40°C.

Particularly in sand, the knack is to **stop before you get deeply bogged**. Recognise that the vehicle is losing speed and soon you'll be sinking quicker than you're going forward. If you do this in time simply reversing out and trying elsewhere will do the trick.

Whatever loose surface you're stuck in, **reducing tyre pressures** is the first step, if it's not been done already. It doesn't have to be much; 70% of normal road pressure is a start and will elongate the tyre's footprint enough to improve traction in all the above scenarios. If you're not being towed out (or if you are because you're deeply bogged) take the time to **clear the wheels** in whichever direction you're going. Now is the time to engage low range. In most vehicles this automatically engages the front axle or locks the central diff, though on bare rock it's not a state you want to be in for long (more on p36).

This tyre is at around 40% of road pressure in preparation to cross a river. Contrary to the impression and the bulging sidewall, the contact area does not become wider but, in this condition, about twice as long, imitating a tracked vehicle. The need to optimise traction by altering tyre pressures is one reason why a powerful compressor is a useful accessory. The tyre is a BFG All Terrain ('A/T'), a good choice for Morocco.
© longroadtripsouth.com

Flooded tracks

Briefly powerful torrents following storms are more dangerous than regular rivers and in Morocco many locals have paid with their lives in underestimating this force. At a flooded road ford there'll often be a queue of regular cars and vans waiting on either side and in your big off-roader there can be pressure to plough in bravely. Resist this and firstly see if others are crossing. Otherwise, walking is advisable, but if the current is flowing hard and rises much above your knees it's too risky even to do that. In a car, that mass quickly builds up on the car's flank and remorselessly pushes it sideways, possibly over an unseen edge and onto its side. Aiming **slightly upstream** deflects this force and can help 'ferry' the car across as the current pushes you forward as well as sideways, but this sort of practice is marginal. It's better to wait a few hours for the flow to recede. If you do this, place a stick or a stone at the flow's edge to see more easily if it's dropping.

Lately, most years the Oued Rheris blocks Route MS6 for a few weeks at Remlia (or MS12 just north). Elsewhere, on clay pans such as the normally dry Lake Iriki near Route MS7, the surface can appear dry, but beneath is a soggy mush which a heavy 4WD will readily sink into and require towing out.

There's more on off-roading in the *Overlanders Handbook* and the DVD.

OFF THE ROAD

Introduction to the routes

Understandably, wanting to make the most of their holiday, many visitors take on too much in Morocco, misjudging the distances involved and the appeal of actually slowing down. Accept that in a typical fortnight's break you won't see it all. It's not all about ticking off routes; they're merely an effective means of unveiling the essence of southern Morocco which doesn't lie between two waypoints. It's not a bad idea to view your first trip as an exploratory tour to find out what you'd like to see or do more of next time.

Additional online content
The '*Description*' introduces the route but will be influenced by whether I rode or drove it and the weather that day. Even then it's well worth reading the entire route description to get a full feel for what lies ahead. '*Off road*' is a

summary of track conditions for vehicles other than a 4WD which can manage anything, namely 2WDs or 'road cars', heavy 'adventure motorcycles' and mountain bikes. Recognise that these conditions **are very reliant on decent weather**. '*Route finding*' assumes that you may not have a GPS or 'Olaf' (see p21) and adds to the route description. If you don't have a metric odometer to record distance, to convert kilometres to miles 'halve it and add a quarter'; 40km = 25 miles.

'*Fuel and Water*'; with the exception of ME5, MH3 and MO2, each route begins and ends at a fuel point. Known water sources are described along the way, but not all may be dependable and others may exist. The '*Suggested Duration*' is based on which vehicle was used to log the route; it's probable the mountain bike estimates are a bit optimistic.

An attempt is made to use cardinal points ('north', 'south-east' or 'SE', etc) rather than 'turn left at...' so that the description needs less interpreting in reverse. Frequently 'the Rains' are referred to, a catastrophic few weeks of rainfall that befell Morocco's north coast and eastern provinces between the two main research trips in 2008. Some tracks logged before the Rains may not be in the same condition, while others logged in the aftermath are bound to be repaired or improved. To help clarity the **route maps** only show the main settlements.

Additional online content – www.morocco-overland.com

Each route has a corresponding online folder with additional content to print off or download onto a laptop, a hand-held image reader or a GPS unit. It varies from route to route but includes a stripped-down list of key waypoints in a .gpx file format to import into any GPS, track logs depicted on small-scale maps and from various angles on Google Earth, photos, corrections and clarifications and anything else that might be useful. Don't get over-excited about the .gpx files – you'll soon learn that most routes are navigable without a GPS, it's merely a good back up when things go awry and can save time if the way ahead is not clear. The website address is also on the back cover.

Leaving Assaragh (Route MA13)

EAST

Outline of the East region

Between the coast and Algeria's desert border sprawls the bleak **Rekkam Plateau** where the Atlas ranges deflate into a barely populated tableland of uncultivatable scrub, low escarpment and shallow creeks. Arriving from Spain or France at the ports Melilla or Nador, this corner of Morocco lacks the drama of imperial cities or palm-fringed kasbahs found elsewhere so travellers usually head for Fes or directly south towards Midelt or Erg Chebbi.

The northern plateau has little going for it although the few sealed roads like ME9 are deserted. It's in the south where the Rekkam crumples into lateral ranges that things can get more interesting. You could string together ME9, 1, 7, 2 and MS11 for a great **back route to Erg Chebbi**, or if the weather's fine just see where some of the many unlogged pistes lead you; it's all part of the adventure.

This region may not be top of the list for first-timers in Morocco looking for the sand, seas and dates but as in the far west, tourist infrastructure is minimal if not non-existent here. This may mean the negative effects of tourism are limited which can be reason enough to spend some time exploring the Moroccan east.

ME Routes

ME – MOROCCO EAST

N

To Guercif

MISSOUR

To Midelt

N15

ME1

Azdad

Anoual

Talsint

ME1

Gourrama

To Rich

ME3

Korima Pass

BENI
TAJITE

ME4

ME5

N13

ME7

ME5

W

Tazouguerte

DESERT HIGHWAY

DESERT HIGHWAY

N10

BOUANANE

To Er Rachidia

N10

ME7

Boudenib

ME2

N10

ME7

ME2

H a m a d a   d u

AOUFOUS

To
Tinerhir

DES H'WAY

ERFOUD

MS11

A L G E R I A

N13

N12

Rissani

To Alnif

Erg
Chebbi

Merzouga

Piste to Zagora

S

To Oujda

N

A L G E R I A

N 33°00'

N17

BOUARFA

N 32°30'

DESERT HIGHWAY

N10

ME4

Mengoûb

N10

DESERT HIGHWAY

N17

ME6

DESERT HIGHWAY

E

FIGUIG

N 32°00'

0 10 20 30 40 50km

W 1°30'

G u i r

A L G E R I A

N 31°30'

★ trailblazer

East Region (ME) Routes Overview

Not all alternative pistes shown

ME1 Missour – Beni Tajite
ME2 Bouanane – Erfoud
ME3 Gourrama – Beni Tajite
ME4 Beni Tajite – Bouarfa
ME5 Korima Pass – Bouanane
ME6 Figuig – Bouarfa
ME7 Beni Tajite – Aoufous
ME8 The track to Bou Redine (not shown)
ME9 Taourirt – Outat Oulad El Haj (not shown)

W 2°30'   N 31°00'   W 2°00'

ME9 TAOURIRT – OUTAT OULAD EL HAJ 184KM
March 2012 ~ BMW F650GS

While the Rekkam may not appear inspiring, coming down from the ferry ports these two satisfying backroad drives bring you to the heart of the ME collection of tracks. Once at Beni Tajite road-bound vehicles need not fear; they can continue on tarmac south-east to Bouanane, or west to Gourrama from where roads lead on to Rich on the N13, or cut back south-east via Tazouguerte to the Guir Bridge on the N10 'Desert Highway'.

With Nador afternoon ferry arrival time it's possible to get to the vicinity of Taourirt a couple of hours after dark on quiet backroads. You can camp and eat at the **roadside rest area** (N34° 24.6' W02° 57.3') just where the N19 joins the N6 and the Fes-Oujda motorway. Or in **Taourirt** you'll find a few cheap hotels around the town centre roundabout.

Route ME9 starts at the fuel station at the west end of Taourirt. At the town centre roundabout (N34° 24.80' W02° 53.63') turn south onto the N19 for Debdou, soon crossing another roundabout and the railway. At a roundabout about 2.5km from the town centre, you're on the edge of town and on your way. There's not much drama until the unexpectedly forested north escarpment of the Rekkam rises over **Debdou** (KM51). Before the town turn left (Olaffed) at a sign for a gîte and commence the 15km ascent to nearly 1600 metres with views down over town through the pines. Soon after the gîte at 1500m you emerge on the exposed plateau top.

Olaf leads off to the west on an obsolete track; you continue directly south crossing a couple of pistes, the second with graves and (possibly) a grassy dip near El Alef village. Then, 40km from Debdou (KM91) you get to the signed crossroads with the Ait Benimathar road (N33° 43.20' W03° 01.60') indicating 115km to Outat. South via Matarka ('66km') leads to pistes to Talsint (KM133, ME1) via Anoual. You go west; around KM163 passing a green-domed mosque on the right with wells and some trees; a nice place for a break, with the snows on Jebel Ayachi near Midelt (MH1) to the west. Soon you join the main N15 coming down from Guercif and after about 20km arrive at the ZIZ on the outskirts of Outat at KM184. That wasn't so bad, was it?

ME1 MISSOUR – BENI TAJITE 163KM
October 2008 ~ Yamaha Ténéré

From the Outat ZIZ it's some 45km to Missour, the biggest town along the N15 before the Midelt junction. There's nothing in the guidebooks but there are signs for at least two hotels in town and a gîte as well as plenty of cafés and restaurants. The motel at the AFRIQUIA roadhouse on the south end of town is easy to find.

A track runs south-east from Missour directly to Talsint via **Taoura**. Look for the sign 'Talsint 98km', cross what since 2008 ought to be the rebuilt bridge over the **Oued Moulouya** and follow your nose. Even then, this route to

Taoura remains a piste, while the less-direct road south of Missour which you're about to follow is sealed, possibly because it usefully connects several villages along the way to Talsint. When this route was originally logged several bridges were out following what may have been an ordinary flash flood. This means vehicles with low, long overhangs such as campervans might want to ask around at Missour or be prepared to turn back. The map is on p107.

Route description

At the **fuel station** in **Missour** town centre head south-west out of town. In a kilometre or so, just before the *AFRIQUIA* with the motel, turn left at the lights and soon cross a concrete ford of a usually-dry tributary of the main oued. You enter an outlying garden suburb and wind along tree-lined lanes; what might be the original villages of Missour.

At KM4 bear left in the village. Soon you emerge from the greenery into the scrub and at KM5.5 turn left at the T-junction (also accessible had you gone straight at the lights and turned left off the N15 a few kilometres from town). The road winds along a shallow, arid valley, even veering west at times and passing small villages. You cross a tributary of the Oued Moulouya at KM36 just before **Ouizret** where you'll pass the old mud-brick ksar. Once the core of every Moroccan town was like this.

There's another rebuilt bridge at KM47 just by the village of Tadmaia and 8km later is a 1400m pass. On the far side, tracks lead south-east to **Tagouast** village but the road then curves west, south and back east to get around an escarpment and a canyon. Note that this is not the sharp turn or crossroads indicated on paper maps. At around KM62 a track heads off south-west through a gap in the range to possibly make a link with Route ME8, a route that would be suitable for off-road vehicles only.

Around here you begin the eastward traverse along the base of the Jebel Asdad. Just north of **Tagentatcha** village is a big bridge and **Boumeryema** (KM92; a name not found on maps) is where the track comes down from **Taoura**. Carry on east and at KM109 crest a 1700m **pass** on the Jebel Tioudersine. A few kilometres later the road turns south and takes a sinuous passage through the Jebel Skindis. South of this pass, the vegetation suddenly changes as the land takes on a much more arid appearance.

Soon after passing a village with a pink mosque you arrive in **Talsint** (KM133) with a *ZIZ* fuel station, a restaurant and a shop or two. A sealed road leads 50km north-east to Anoual village from where little-used pistes continue north towards ME9 or east to Tendrara and the N17. Once through Talsint the road curves south again through a gap and at KM142 a thin track runs off south-east to pick up Route ME4 coming up from Beni Tajite. The main turning left for ME4 is at KM159 as you bend to the right, and 2.5km after this point you pass an *AFRIQUIA* at the junction for the road to Gourrama.

KM163 is the *ZIZ* fuel station at the north end of **Beni Tajite**. This appears to be a garrison and maybe a former mining town with little for the visitor. For a basic **café** in the town centre, head south from the *ZIZ* a couple of hundred metres, turn left and immediately right; it's on the right. Tracks lead from Beni Tajite in all directions and the **tarmac road** continues east and then south to **Bouanane** on the N10 'Desert Highway', about 60km away and where there may still be a basic **hotel** in the town square.

ME – MOROCCO EAST

ME2   BOUANANE – BOUDENIB – ERFOUD   155KM

April 2008 ~ Mazda pickup

Description

A short cut from the east down to Erfoud which won't actually save you any time. After crossing the Oued Guir you traverse a rubbly limestone plateau, crossing several lesser oueds on the way.

Southbound, heading away from the mountains it's not exactly on the shortlist for designation as an Area of Outstanding Natural Beauty; a bleak plain sparsely occupied by hardy nomads on the western limit of the Hamada du Guir. But it's always fun to be off the road, travelling at your own pace and dealing with each oued as it comes. At KM124 you arrive at a cairned junction where MS11 leads east right up to the Algerian border before turning back and dropping down into the sands around Erg Chebbi.

Off road

If the Oued Guir out of Boudenib is flowing and too deep, consider the suggestion at KM66. After that on the northern half there are many splits in the track that can get confusing, but as long as you keep going south and west you'll get to the junction at KM124 from where the way to the Erfoud highway is clear.

On the limestone plateau a car will get a hammering if you go too fast, and rainfall will always affect this route's northern end. **Motos** large and small will manage fine. On a **bicycle** it's at least pretty flat and oued crossings over your knees can be waded. It's unlikely you'll encounter any traffic.

We actually drove this track from Erfoud to Boudenib and the route description has been reversed. Because of this, some obvious landmarks when heading southbound may not have been recorded.

Route finding

As mentioned there are several tracks on this route, sometimes they merely split and rejoin, at other times they may lead off to nomad camps so keep alert. The **map** for this route is on pp98-9.

Fuel and water

There is fuel at Bouanane and Erfoud. The ZIZ at Boudenib still looked abandoned, though there's fuel in town if you ask around. There are a few wells and water in the oueds as well as some big puddles.

Suggested duration

Half a day will do you if the oueds are on form.

0km   N32' 02.20'   W03' 03.10'
Bouanane fuel station. Head west on the N10 for Boudenib.

57 (98)   N31° 57.02'   W03° 36.10'
Boudenib town centre, such as it is. On maps it's marked as a bigger town than Bouanane but it's not. Seven hundred metres up the road is the old ZIZ fuel station looking as dormant as ever.

61.5 (93.5)   N31° 57.11'   W03° 37.85'
Leave the tarmac to the south at kilometre post 'Boudenib 1' near a white bollard. Within a few hundred metres fork left.

63 (92)   N31° 56.86'   W03° 38.75'
You pass a modern *khettara* underground irrigation system.

64 (91)   N31° 56.67'   W03° 39.12'
Cross a small oued.

ME – MOROCCO EAST

65 (90)   N31° 56.39'   W03° 39.57'
A track joins from the left as you turn SW.

66 (89)   N31° 56.04'   W03° 40.03'
Drop into the wide Oued Guir. If it's too deep return to the road and carry on west a few kilometres to the **Oued Guir** bridge. Over the bridge you're effectively 'south' of the river. Head south, cross country to KM77.5. Or better still, give up.

66.5 (88.5)   N31° 55.94'   W03° 40.18'
Exit the oued, turn right and continue west and slightly uphill.

71.5 (83.5)   N31' 55.60'   W03° 43.30'
At this point the track turns south.

75.5 (79.5)   N31° 54.28'   W03° 44.65'
The track curves to the west gradually and then again, after another sharp turn south of here. In 1500m cross a oued.

78 (77)   N31° 53.09'   W03° 45.13'
As the track turns to the SW Olaf forks off to the left, you can keep right on the more direct line.

80.5 (74.5)   N31° 52.28'   W03° 46.54'
Various tracks diverge.

84 (71)
Rejoin Olaf.

91 (64)   N31° 48.11'   W03° 50.76'
Approach a oued from the NE, possibly with water.

94.5 (60.5)   N31° 47.17'   W03° 52.51'
A track comes in directly from the left opposite a cairn on a hillock on the right, and in 500m a track joins from the right.

100 (55)   N31° 45.90'   W03° 55.27'
Cross a small oued and another soon after.

103 (52)   N31° 45.07'   W03° 56.94'
Fork right.

112 (43)   N31° 41.99'   W04° 00.13'
Fork right, but these are possibly parallel tracks. Isolated small dunes appear as you cross the stony limestone plain.

115 (40)   N31° 40.93'   W04° 01.32'
Key point. Find a way to cross the big Oued Rahmoun, possibly running and with a **well** on the far bank. The old cobbled ford is badly damaged. Five hundred metres after the oued a track joins from the left, probably an alternative crossing for the oued.

119 (36)   N31° 39.20'   W04° 02.38'
Cross the smaller Oued Arid with a washed-away cobbled ford.

120 (35)   N31° 38.92'   W04° 02.67'
Fork right. Left is a triangle on the Erg Chebbi junction.

124 (31)   N31° 37.04'   W04° 03.13'
Key junction marked with cairns; KM31.5 of MS11 which goes east to the Algerian border before swinging south off the escarpment and then back west below along the Oued Talrhemt to Erg Chebbi.

For Erfoud turn south and west here and drive down over limestone slabs into the Oued Zerzel valley.

125.5 (29.5)   N31° 37.24'   W04° 03.95'
As you cross a small creek there's a mysterious memorial hidden on the right to Marius-Louis de Bouche ('1898-1933'?) from his friends at Citroën. The explanation is on p170.

126 (29)   N31° 37.33'   W04° 04.23'
Pass a well on the left (30m). The piste then does a loop round a bend in the valley before continuing SW.

131.5 (23.5)   N31° 36.54'   W04° 05.61'
Another well on the left of the piste.

136 (19)   N31° 34.69'   W04° 08.61'
Fork right near some buildings where people may have fossils for sale.

141 (14)   N31° 32.92'   W04° 11.08'
Join the N13 highway and turn south for Erfoud. In about 7km you'll come to an *Afriquia* fuel station.

155   N31° 26.23'   W04° 13.95'
Total fuel in the centre of **Erfoud**. Erfoud is not as touristy as Rissani, so may be an easier place to spend time.

ME3   GOURRAMA – BENI TAJITE   74KM
April 2008 ~ Mazda pickup

Description
With tarmac roads to the north and a good piste from the south, this old track across the Plain of Snab deteriorates year by year as the Jebel Bou Arouss washes away the tracks and carves at the oued banks. It's eastern Morocco's equivalent of Russia's Kolyma Highway only it takes two hours and doesn't hit -70°C in January.

Scenically, there's not much going on; most of your time will be spent focusing on the ground ahead and wondering what the next ditch holds.

Off road
How not to get snagged on the **Plain of Snab**, that is the question. As anywhere in the desert, a track which runs below a ridge gets cut up by the runoff. Old road builders got round this by constructing fords and culverts, but tracks still require maintenance, something which ME3 no longer gets unless you're up for it. A **short 4WD** or a lightly-loaded **trail bike** will manage it all, but big bikes will need to launch rather than finesse over obstacles.

Route finding
East by east it is and fully Olaffed too, although the outdated paper maps can portray a false sense of ease. Expect to make regular deviations to find easier creek crossings. You probably won't see any traffic. The route **map** is on p107.

Fuel and water
Gourrama and Beni Tajite. No wells were seen on the piste.

Suggested duration
A 4WD or dirt bike will take an hour or two, anything less will take longer, although a portable mountain bike is relatively immune to the creek banks.

0km   **N32° 20.28'   W04° 04.27'**
Gourrama ZIZ. Leave town to the east.

5.5 (68.5)
Tarmac junction: turn right for Boudenib towards a distinctive cone hill. Left leads to Beni Tajite from the north; the route normal people take.

17.5 (56.5)
Mud-brick ruins on the edge of Mehalla.

29 (45)
A pylon piste heads off to the left, possibly to meet this route later.

31 (43)   N32° 13.27'   W03° 49.33'
Leave the road to the left just after a oued crossing. 'Boudenib' may be written on the ground in stones. Head north towards the ridge and village there.

The ruins on the south side of the tarmac are **Atchana fort**, built just before WWI. This valley saw several battles with renegade tribes in the last century right up till 1931. There's not that much left at the fort apart from the stone pentagram emblem of the *goumiers* (native troops engaged by the French) which features on the Moroccan flag.

33 (41)   N32° 14.18'   W03° 48.90'
A track joins from left and then another, possibly the pylon piste from KM29. Soon you come to a big oued just south of a village. The bank opposite may be too much for 2WDs or big bikes, but get used to it, this is how things will be. In this case head north up the oued into the village and find a way back to the next waypoint.

ME – MOROCCO EAST

35 (39)   **N32° 14.53'   W03° 47.81'**
A track joins from the north, possibly a regular piste from the village.

37 (37)   **N32° 14.57'   W03° 46.73'**
The track ahead splits off in three directions; straight ahead or left may be best but expect washed-out oued crossings.

39 (35)   **N32° 14.21'   W03° 45.51'**
However you got here, continue directly east. In the next 11km or so there are half a dozen gullies and oued crossings which will take some negotiating.

50 (24)   **N32° 14.95'   W03° 39.12'**
Drop down into a oued, drive along it for a bit and exit on the left where you can.

52.5 (21.5)   **N32° 15.14'   W03° 37.61'**
Cross a wide, stony oued (as opposed to the gullies you've encountered so far). and work your way round to the main piste visible ahead.

54.5 (19.5)   **N32° 15.29'   W03° 36.51'**
Track joins from the left near a few cairns, possibly an easier way round a oued.

58.5 (15.5)   **N32° 15.78'   W03° 34.10'**
A line of cairns runs south. There are no more tricky creek crossings from here on.

65 (9)
Pass three white-painted cairns to the north and an old milepost on the right saying 'Beni Tajite'. The hills to the left have receded and in 1.5km you easily cross a wide oued.

68 (6)   **N32° 16.23'   W03° 31.04'**
At a **concrete block** the Tazouguerte track (Route ME7) joins from the SW. Turn left (NE) for Beni Tajite.

70 (4)   **N32° 16.90'   W03° 30.03'**
A local track joins from the left.

73.5 (500m)   **N32° 17.59'   W03° 28.12'**
Drive among some trees by a wall then turn right **onto a road** to the SE, passing **Beni Tajite** barracks on your right. After approx 200m turn left (NE) for the ZIZ.

74   **N32° 17.59'   W03° 27.91'**
ZIZ fuel. For the café go back to the main road, turn left then right; it's on the right. There was no hotel here. From Beni Tajite roads and tracks lead off in all directions.

ME4   BENI TAJITE – BOUARFA   165KM
May 2008 ~ Mazda pickup

Description
Whether you've got here via Route ME1 or ME3, this is a satisfying run eastwards between the jebels, dodging washed-out creek crossings. The highlights might be a break or a camp at KM36 and the 'Korima Pass' (as I have named it). Soon after this point you can take Route ME5 back down to the N10 highway for Bouanane, or continue on east to Bouarfa. You'll see a couple of nomad tents along the route, especially in the east, but no villages to speak of.

Being the far east of Morocco the scenery won't set your hair ablaze but some of the broad oueds offer a break from the drab, scrubby plains, giving a sense of openness and interest. This is another route we tried from the east end in 2004 in a Mercedes 190, getting as far as KM70 near the Korima Pass. I now know had we continued the car may well have folded in two.

Off road
The original piste built over oueds with small bridges, culverts and fords has disappeared in places, with some concrete fords also mashed by flash floods. As anywhere in the Moroccan East, this adds a challenge and a 4WD will often resort to low range to climb up the steep banks. In many places these

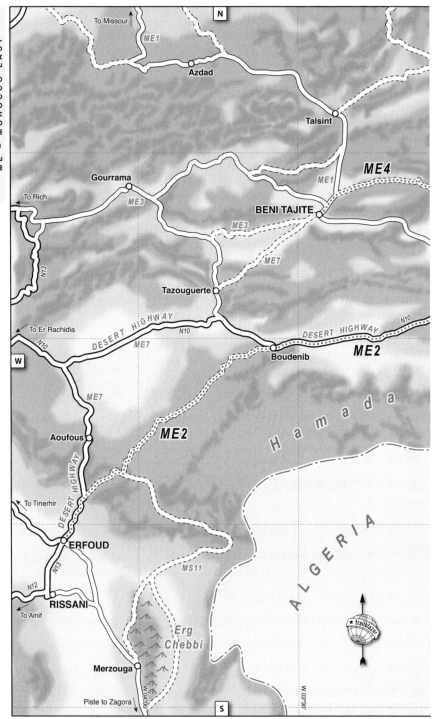

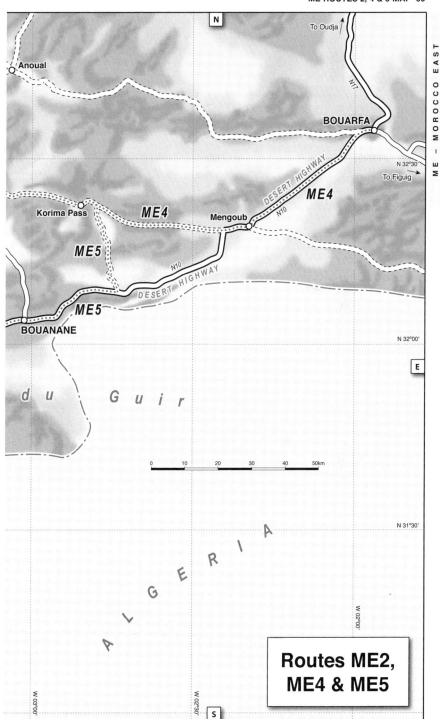

diversions have developed from the original Olaffed route. At KM42 a 2WD wants to be ready to blast across 100m or so of soft sand as it comes out of a big oued crossing, and again 2.5km later over some streambed rocks. These short sandy sections won't cause a **big trail bike** too much concern and they'll manage the ups and downs of this route just fine. The relatively smooth track rolling along between the successive oued crossings makes appreciating it all the easier and so it's a good, if long, route for a **mountain bike**. As always in Morocco the caveat is the weather. If it's raining or has rained recently, things could get a whole lot more difficult.

Route finding

Straightforward enough, notwithstanding keeping track of the deviations around the washed-out original piste. On the bright side, the orientation given on the RKH and Michelin maps is reasonably accurate, except that the RKH has again wrongly guessed tarmac. Unless they discover ready-bagged molybdenum by the trackside, it's not likely to happen.

No **traffic** was seen; don't expect any. This route's **map** is on pp90-1.

Fuel and water

Beni Tajite and Bouarfa have fuel stations. Wells as indicated and in May a few of the bigger oueds were trickling.

Suggested duration

Allow half a day for a 4WD, a 2WD may require longer to deal with the oueds and a slick motorbike might blast through in 3 or 4 hours. As always, overnighting out here would be worthwhile, with a near certainty of privacy.

0km   N32° 17.58' W03° 27.91'
ZIZ fuel at the north end of **Beni Tajite**. In case you miss it, in 1500m you get to an *AFRIQUIA* by the junction west to Gourrama where a sign reads 'Talsint 28, Missour 156km' (near enough; see Route ME1).

4 (161)   N32° 19.39' W03° 26.36'
Buildings and pylons as the road bends to the left. You leave the road to the right, joining a piste alongside cultivation. In 3 or 4km you cross a flood-damaged oued.

11 (154)   N32° 21.06' W03° 22.94'
Go straight, not right which leads to old mines on the jebel. There'll be other tracks leading off south later, also to be ignored.

13 (152)   N32° 21.43' W03° 21.73'
Well on the right near a bridge. At KM26 fork left.

30 (135)   N32° 22.35' W03° 11.06'
Keep straight, not right (which goes to some buildings on the valley side).

31 (134)   N32° 22.37' W03° 10.37'
Fork left. Straight ahead goes to more buildings on hill and the Olaffed route.

33.5 (131.5)   N32° 22.84' W03° 09.32'
Track splits. Go left to get over the Oued Safsaf, the easiest way via N32° 22.96' W03° 09.13', 400m further on. Or try the original crossing to the south at N32° 22.66' W03° 08.75'. From this point cross the oued with ease and continue to KM36.

35 (130)   N32° 23.05' W03° 08.79'
Back on the northern Oued Safsaf crossing, you pass a **well** (15m) at this waypoint. Soon, fork right and head SW back to the original oued crossing above.

36 (129)   N32° 22.67' W03° 08.60'
East side of the Oued Safsaf. Whichever route you took, it's a nice place for a break or even a camp. On the far western bank there were some rubbish-free ruins by a **well** and shady trees where the steep western bank drops into the oued.

In the oued, apart from water running over the remains of the ford, you may see tiny fish and frogs in the pools, and pink oleander on the banks.

39.5 (125.5)   N32° 22.02'   W03° 06.19'
Oued crossing by a broken ford.

41 (124)   N32° 21.77'   W03° 05.34'
Pass a pump house on the right from where a small concrete canal follows the track to buildings. In less than a kilometre (N32° 21.62' W03° 04.83') turn left and cross the wide, shingle bed of the Oued Hallouf just before it joins the Oued Remila. As soon as you exit this oued there's a patch of soft sand worth being ready for, as well as some buildings. Out of the oued, head NE.

43 (122)   N32° 21.78'   W03° 04.50'
You're leaving a village and on a parallel track north of the main washed-out track – it rejoins from the right in about 400m.

44 (121)   N32° 21.98'   W03° 03.42'
You recross the now wide and sandy Oued Remila but with blue-grey rocks to get over on the far side. Once out of this oued there's a tricky crossing of a small side oued. Soon you'll join other tracks looking for a way over these oueds.

50 (115)
Cross W03° as you head east towards a pass – useful to orientate yourself on a gridded paper map. In 700m you cross a stony oued and in 1.5km (N32° 22.07' W02° 59.10') take the northern route alongside the oued.

54.5 (110.5)   N32° 21.81'   W02° 57.75'
Arrive at a ruined village and possibly a nomad encampment near a broken bridge on the old route on the south side of the oued. Cross the Oued Safsaf easily here and rejoin Olaf following the original piste eastwards. There are some small plots and a well pump nearby.

56 (109)   N32° 21.48'   W02° 56.79'
After a cobbled ford take the left track by the tree. Right goes to a washout.

62 (103)   N32° 20.49'   W02° 53.54'
Go over a damaged ford. In 500m a minor

track splits right. We headed left into hills via a tricky oued crossing. The track from the right rejoins soon after.

63.5 (101.5)   N32° 20.44'   W02° 52.63'
Cross the wide Oued Safsaf to the south side over the remains of a broken ford. You're now heading into the Korima Pass gorge on a wide, red-earth track which rises above the oued below.

66 (99)   N32° 20.82'   W02° 51.29'
Korima Pass with thick oleanders in the Oued Safsaf and palm trees with ruins on the north bank. Another nice spot for a break or a camp.

69.5 (95.5)   N32° 20.29'   W02° 49.55'
Fork left.

70 (95)   N32° 20.21'   W02° 49.27'
Cross the Oued Safsaf, and head along the north-eastern bank to the SE.

71.5 (93.5)   N32° 19.73'   W02° 48.62'
Broken ford. Cross the ford and in 500m you get to a junction at N32° 19.67' W02° 48.39' where Route ME5 goes south to the N10 and Bouanane. For Bouarfa cross the oued on a ford and on the far side take the track to the right (SE). Left leads up into the hills and some old mines.

79 (86)   N32° 17.56'   W02° 44.79'
A piste joins from the right.

83.5 (81.5)   N32° 16.90'   W02° 42.17'
An old track joins from the right.

94 (71)   N32° 16.39'   W02° 34.78'
Well (20m) on the north side of the track.

109 (56)   N32° 15.57'   W02° 26.25'
Two kilometres before you reach the N10 highway the piste **becomes old tarmac** with buildings and cultivation nearby. At the highway turn left for Bouarfa.

165   N32° 31.89'   W01° 57.71'
AFRIQUIA fuel in **Bouarfa** town centre with a bigger fuel station on the northern out-skirts; to get there turn left (north) at the roundabout. Bouarfa has become a thriving town complete with local versions of Starbucks, promenading students and a couple of **hotels**.

ME5   KORIMA PASS – BOUANANE   53KM
March 2004 ~ Mercedes 190D

Description
This route was blundered through in 2004 while looking for a way to the **Korima Pass** and now adds up to just a way of getting off Route ME4 and 22km to the N10 highway to head back south and west. There are no markers but tracks are clear with little chance of straying into the jebels. You can be in Bouanane (fuel and basic hotel) in less than two hours. The **map** is on p98-9.

0km   N32° 19.70'   W02° 48.30'
At KM72 on Route ME4 before the big oued with a concrete ford, head south west, passing a few buildings until the track leads south.

3 (50)   N32° 18.10'   W02° 48.50'
Cross the oued with a broken concrete bridge. Half a kilometre later (N32° 17.6' W02° 48.5') the track splits. Take the right fork, an easy track across a flat valley of gravel with jebels on either side.

5 (48)
A distinctive cone hill 8km to the west as you continue along the valley.

11 (42)
On the horizon you can see a radio mast on top of Jebel Zelmou; the border with Algeria. A little while later, a track leads off to the right; you continue south.

13 (40)
Cross another oued and carry on south until you come across a track heading SE. Follow this track via N32° 11.8'   W02° 49.7' towards a mine.

16 (37)   N32° 11.70'   W02° 48.20'
Mine buildings. Take care not to end up in the crusher. Drive out south along the mine access road to the highway.

22 (31)   N32° 08.70'   W02° 46.60'
Rejoin the N10 highway. A sign here points back to 'Ksar Anbag', possibly the name of the mine.

53   N32° 02.20'   W03° 03.10'
Bouanane fuel station. You'll find a basic hotel, cafés and shops in the town square.
    Although I've not driven it, there is now a sealed road north and west to **Beni Tajite**.

ME6   FIGUIG – BOUARFA   110KM
April 2008 ~ Mazda pickup

Description
Figuig has a curious 'Land's End' appeal, stuck as it is in Morocco's south-easternmost corner and within sight of Beni Ounif in Algeria whose different-coloured street lighting highlight its separation at night. Up to 1994, for trans-Sahara travellers, this border was a convenient way of getting into Algeria. Then the border closed as Algeria entered a bloody decade of bomb-ings and massacres. Although there was talk of re-opening it in 2011 following the Arab revolutions, it's not likely to happen while Algeria gets its way.
    Some guidebooks suggest **Figuig** slipped into decline following the bor-der closure, but the town's wealth was always in its palmeries, not cross-border trade (which continues semi-officially with the smuggling of fuel and other commodities). In the early 1980s Figuig looked much as it does now if not poorer; it was never a medieval caravan port like other Moroccan oases.

Having made the effort of getting here, many travellers choose to spend a day or two relaxing and wandering around. A contributing factor in this is the *Hotel Figuig*, the town's only worthwhile hotel and **camping** spot. Situated on a bluff overlooking the palmeries below, the *Figuig* is no pimped-up faux-kasbah serving tour groups by the coachload. Nor is it a neglected roach palace, but seems to occupy a category all of its own.

Up in town there's fast internet, a garage for repairs as well as all the usual shops. **Petrol** (but not diesel) may be in short supply, probably connected with the smuggling activities. On a bike it's something to think about when you take the 110km ride out from Bouarfa (the tarmac and this route are about the same distance). And of course if you're set on knocking out every last mile of the Grand Moroccan Traverse stringing this book's off-road routes together, or are setting off to follow the **Desert Highway** (see p114), you don't get the badge unless you visit Figuig.

Scenically this track is merely a novel way of arriving in or leaving Figuig. It sets off right along the Algerian border where it's said trained mules of undefined nationality undertake smuggling sorties, but there's usually no problem with tourists driving this route. Entering a pass between the Jebel Maïz and the Jebel Amour a **dam** has been completed since this route was logged and will mean diversions to the description below. Beyond the reservoir you emerge into the broad, *raïma*-dotted plain and the sealed road running east to Iche or west to the N17 and Bouarfa.

If you want to string out the off-roading, once you rejoin the N17 at KM82, head back south for 28km to where a tarmac side road leads to a telecom tower. Here a piste sets off west along the Algerian frontier for some 65km, passing the remains of **Mengoub station** (about 52km from the tower) on the former French colonial railway to what was then Colomb-Bechar in present day Algeria. The nearby 'General Leclerc Monument' on the Michelin map is over the undefined border and commemorates a commander of the Free French forces who distinguished himself in Chad and Libya in WWII, but whose plane crashed here in 1947.

After the station, the track rejoins the N10 highway close to ME4 KM109.

Off road

In fair weather at least there are no problems, whatever your vehicle.

Route finding

All the paper maps and of course Olaf show the orientation of this piste before the dam. You'll see many side routes so keep an eye out for the key waypoints. Although many maps seem to show **Iche** as just over the border in Algeria, the small oasis is actually in Morocco and may be worth a visit. You won't see much traffic on this route; the **map** is over the page.

Fuel and water

Bouarfa and Figuig. Petrol may be in short supply in Figuig. Diesel seems OK. There are a couple of wells on the piste.

Suggested duration

Allow three hours to do the trip with a car or a motorbike.

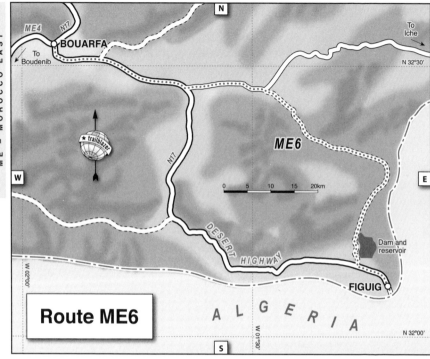

Route ME6

0km   **N32° 07.20' W01° 13.93'**
SHELL in **Figuig** town centre. Head north
out of town for Bouarfa.

8.2 (101.8)   N32° 09.15' W01° 18.19'
A couple of kilometres after a checkpoint
(where it's worth checking the status of
this route) by a post indicating 'Bouarfa
99' turn right **onto the piste** and head
north towards the jebel. In a kilometre
and a half cross a wide, shingle oued.

20 (90)   N32° 15.08' W01° 16.11'
Pass a small fort on the right and head
into the pass between the Jebel Maïz and
the Jebel Amour.

25 (85)   N32° 17.42' W01° 14.77'
Head past another bigger fort on the right.
About 2km later you pass a marabout
(shrine) on the right of the piste.

31.5 (78.5)
You'll notice buildings and a water tower
right of piste with a big fort and some
greenery a kilometre to the NE.

36.5 (73.5)   N32° 19.46' W01° 20.29'
Cross a wide oued with a broken ford
towards the **dam** which, if you can, you'll
pass on the hillside to the west.

40 (70)   N32° 20.36' W01° 21.15'
You pass some weathered granite boulders which have their uses.

42.5 (67.5)   N32° 20.81' W01° 22.46'
Fork left. In 600m a track joins from the
left at N32° 20.95' W01° 22.87'.

44.5 (65.5)   N32° 21.48' W01° 23.30'
Another track joins from the left. Then, as
you cross a ditch-oued where the track
splits again, keep right and then 300m on
cross a wide, stony oued.

50 (60)   N32° 24.15' W01° 24.76'
Cross the Oued Moulay El Harrane; the
left fork is better. Soon a rough track joins
from the right.

52 (58)   N32° 25.08' W01° 25.24'
Olaf rejoins from the left and soon another

track joins from the left just before a high-banked oued crossing.

57 (53)   N32° 26.97' W01° 27.17'
Fork right. Soon after there's a small oued crossing with a shady tree and 400m later a track joins from the left, having taken an easier way across the oued.

58 (52)   N32° 27.42' W01° 27.65'
Well and some buildings on the left just before another crossing of the Safsaf. Leave Olaf and strike out NW.

63 (47)   N32° 28.54' W01° 30.00'
Cross a ford. Various tracks go left and

right but the main route NW is obvious and the road is not far. There may be a few nomads' tents hereabouts.

68 (42)   N32° 29.45' W01° 32.87'
Join the tarmac running to Iche and turn left (west).

82 (28)   N32° 27.45' W01° 40.91'
Rejoin the N17 near a radio tower and turn right (NW) for Bouarfa.

110   N32° 31.91' W01° 57.70'
AFRIQUIA fuel in **Bouarfa** town centre. There is another fuel station on the Oujda road, north out of town.

ME7   BENI TAJITE – AOUFOUS   119KM
October 2008 ~ Yamaha Ténéré

Description
The off-road stage is a fun way of getting down to the N10 for Erg Chebbi. The **Col de Belkassem** is the off-roading crux and the view up there was nice enough, as were the crumbling ruins of **Tazouguerte's** old ksar. Back on the N10 'Desert Highway', turn south at the N13 Er Rachidia junction, passing the many oases lining the Ziz valley. As an extension to Route ME1, ME7 can be an undemanding taster for an off-road novice.

Off road
The only tricky bit is getting over the rocky Col de Belkassem. Between there and Tazouguerte there were several wash-outs where a **regular car** may struggle. If you've come down ME1 on a **bike**, this is a great way to reach the N10, though from there on at pedalling speeds things may get a bit dull and windy.
    Adventurers could spice things up on the way down south, by crossing the Guir bridge on the N10, turning left onto the sands and working their way cross-country towards KM75 on Route ME2. Then at KM124 pick up MS11 all the way to Erg Chebbi.

Route finding
The trickiest part can be getting out of Beni Tajite and on course for the Col. Once clear of town make KM26 a 'Go to' and follow the GPS; the tracks are there. After that expect detours around wash-outs. The route **map** is on p107.

Fuel and water
Either end for fuel, plus a station about 16km west of the N10-N13 junction on the way to Er Rachidia. Away from the towns and villages no wells were noted on the short off-road section but there's always the Oued Guir.

Suggested duration
The 30km off-road section to Tazouguerte can be done in an hour or so.

ME – MOROCCO EAST

0km **N32° 17.59' W03° 27.91'**
Ziz at the north end of **Beni Tajite**. Head south along the road on the east side of the Ziz for 250m and at the main road, turn right. Head up this road NW for 350m past the barracks on the left and at around N32° 17.60' W03° 28.15' turn SW down an avenue of trees and curve west out **on a piste** into the desert.

6 (113) **N32° 16.22' W03° 31.05'**
Junction marked by a concrete block where ME3 comes in from Gourrama. You continue SW towards the Col which sits across the Jebel Hajiba.

21 (98) **N32° 10.17' W03° 39.14'**
Crest a low pass with a cairn.

26 (93) **N32° 08.62' W03° 41.48'**
Col de Belkassem pass (1236m) with enough space to camp with a view. Getting down the far side can be rough.

34 (85) **N32° 04.79' W03° 47.13'**
Join the tarmac south of Tazouguerte and turn left to the ruins of old **Tazouguerte** and the palmerie down in the canyon.

43 (76) **N32° 00.81' W03° 46.35'**
Join the N10 at the Guir bridge. Sometimes a small café here. Turn west.

95 (24) **N31° 51.68' W04° 16.13'**
Junction with the N13 **Er Rachidia** road, turn left to follow the scenic Ziz valley past the so-called *Oases du Ziz*.

A kilometre west of the junction the long-established *Meski Source Bleu* **campsite** keeps going with good shade, a spring-fed swimming pool and a resto.

119 **N31° 41.90' W04°10.80'**
Afriquia in the palmerie at the south end of **Aoufous**. Erfoud is around another 20km further on but if you've got any sense you'll be heading for MS11 on p90.

ME8 THE TRACK TO BOU REDINE 80KM RETURN

May 2008 ~ Mazda pickup

Between Midelt and Rich some paper maps show a fairly prominent track leading east from Nzala via Aït Alla to Bou Redine where the track takes an intriguingly winding route through the ranges to Gourrama.

The unsigned track starts 40km south of Midelt by two radio masts at a snow gate (N32° 32.2' W04° 29.1') below the 1900m **Tizi-n-Tairhemt** to the north. It leads off north of the Jebel Aouja, passing south of **Aït Alla** some 10km from the asphalt.

Here at N32° 32.2' W04° 23.50' head for N32° 32.2' W04° 23.2' and at N32° 32.1' W04° 22.61' stay in the oued where the track squeezes past the bushes and over a broken culvert. The track continues in and out of the oued and over rolling hills, and after 27km slips north to a parallel valley and **Inml** village. Continue oued-skipping for 3km until N32° 33.7' W04° 11.6' on the outskirts of Bou Redine (or 'Boudin' as it was signed).

Here the main track leads north and on some maps leads 8km to Aït Alou Kchamene to pick up a piste which links with the ME1 scenic drive at N32° 39.5' W04° 04.5', some 22km all up. See map on the website. The track south from Bou Redine depicted on paper maps and copied by Google maps **does not exist**; a 2350-metre high jebel does.

Old French maps show a more plausible thin black line continuing east along the valley for 20km or more before turning south through a gap and cutting back west and south to Gourrama. We were told at Bou Redine that a piste did indeed continue to Gourrama but that it was 'up and down'. As one cannot be sure what locals categorise as difficult, we continued down the oued for another 4 or 5km up to N32° 34.13' W04° 09.23' near an abandoned mine on the north side of the valley set below a high ridge.

By now the track was barely visible. I walked on a kilometre or two towards a pass on terrain passable to a lithe 4WD or bike. Looking on Google maps the village of Ksar Almou Abtour (about 11km on) is accessed from the north via Tagentatcha (KM65 on ME1). So according to the old maps it was at least another 17km of 'walking-pace' terrain before the track turned south through the jebel to head back south-west for 25km to Tiouzaguine from where it drops another 15km through various villages leading to Gourrama.

Barging onward off-piste (as opposed to off-road) is not in the spirit of this book, but the canyon route north of Bou Redine must almost certainly lead by and by to ME1.

Routes ME1, ME3 & ME7

ME – MOROCCO EAST

To Guercif

MISSOUR

N15

To Midelt

ME1

N 33°00'

0   5   10   15   20km

Taoura

Azdad

ME1

To Anoual

Talsint

N 32°30'

W

E

GOURRAMA

To Rich

ME4

BENI TAJITE

ME3

To Bouanane

Atchana
(ruined fort)

ME7

Col de Belkassem
(1236m)

Tazouguerte

Guir
Bridge

DESERT HIGHWAY

N10

DESERT HIGHWAY

To Er Rachidia

N10

N 32°00'

Boudenib

ME2

To Bouanane

N10

ME7

ME2

★ trailblazer

AOUFOUS

To Erfoud

W 04°00'

W 03°30'

S

HIGH ATLAS

Outline of the High Atlas region

Stretching from Midelt south-west to Aoulouz, 'MH' is the biggest region in this book. It includes the geologically separate Jebel Sirwa and Jebel Sarhro massifs south of the High Atlas which are neither the Sahara or the Anti Atlas. Along with the 'MS' zone, this is the most visited area in this part of Morocco where the landscapes and Berber culture sum up the appeal of the south. Certainly you'd want to attempt either **Trans Atlas Routes** MH1 or -2, as well as a couple of tracks in the Sirwa and Sarhro massifs.

Visually the High Atlas itself is not so dramatic compared to the arid south and some villages can have a gloomy, sodden feel. The lower elevations of the Sirwa and noticeably more arid Sarhro massifs are more reliable destinations in mid-winter.

MH Routes

MH1	Midelt – Agoudal – Dades	317KM	p109
MH2	Tinerhir – Imilchil – El Kebab	241KM	p114
MH3	Dades – Todra 'Gorge to Gorge'	45KM	p118
MH4	Tinerhir – Iknioun – Nekob	112KM	p120
MH5	Alnif – Iknioun – Dades	116KM	p125
MH6	Aguim – Aoulouz	125KM	p127
MH7	Aoulouz – Askaoun – Tazenacht	166KM	p128
MH8	Taliouine – Askaoun – Aguim	133KM	p133
MH9	Tazenacht – Taliouine	94KM	p135
MH10	Dades – Iknioun – Alnif	113KM	p136
MH11	Two Rivers Loop	306KM	p138
MH12	Ouarzazate – Demnate	158KM	p139
MH13	Goulmina – Tagountsa Tunnel	187KM	p140
MH14	Nekob – Skoura	137KM	p141

TRANS ATLAS: MH1   MIDELT – AGOUDAL – DADES   317KM
May 2008 ~ Mazda pickup

Description
For those looking to string out the crossing of the High Atlas, this run won't leave you disappointed. It gets off to a great start following the popular **Cirque du Jaffar** out of Midelt, under the snow-bound slopes of the 3700-metre Jebel Ayachi. The 'cirque' refers to the amphitheatre-like valley head you drop into and climb out of and is just one highlight on this route. You rejoin the tarmac at KM37 which, barring the latest flood damage, continues all the way through mountain villages to the Imilchil–Rich road and onwards south to Agoudal.

Here starts the main crossing of the range, unsealed and likely to remain so now the parallel crossing to Ait Hani has been completed. Even in good conditions it'll be slow progress to the 2906m Tizi-n-Ouano, the highest route in this book. The descent commences alongside the gorge of the upper Dades to Msemrir and the resumption of tarmac down the Dades Gorge, bedecked with all the rich fruits of tour-bus tourism. If you've enjoyed the wilds, Boumalne du Dades is not such a propitious spot to end up. Ideally you'll have got here in time to head into the Jebel Sarhro massif directly ahead.

Off road
The descent into the Oued Jaffar can be the roughest section of the route but piste or asphalt, anywhere prone to flood damage will get gnarly and in winter over the top from Agoudal to Tilmi won't be a snow-clearance priority. Mud and snow make things exhausting on a heavy **motorcycle** without knobbly tyres and in such conditions it could be an epic for sure.

Setting off in a **regular car** at any time is bound to be an adventure too and on a **mountain bike** it will be a fair old trek. If you don't want to camp you'll have to plan your riding days quite closely.

Route finding
As is so often the case, getting out of Midelt can be tricky but once on the way tarmac leads all the way to Agoudal from where there's only one way over the top. Olaf no longer lines up with the sealed road in the middle of this route.

Traffic will amount to other off-road recreationists in the Cirque, and locals, including road crews. Over the Tizi you're back in the domain of adventure tourists again. The **map** is on pp116-17.

Fuel and water
Fuel only at each end and Imilchil for sure, though there may be some in the bigger villages at a price. There's plenty of water running in the creeks, in the village wells, from stores and maybe the heavens too.

Suggested duration
Of all the routes in this book MH1 can get quite a beating from the elements, so allow for an overnight or keep the wick turned up. In good conditions a mountain biker could cover this route in 3 or 4 tough days and end up with quite a sense of achievement.

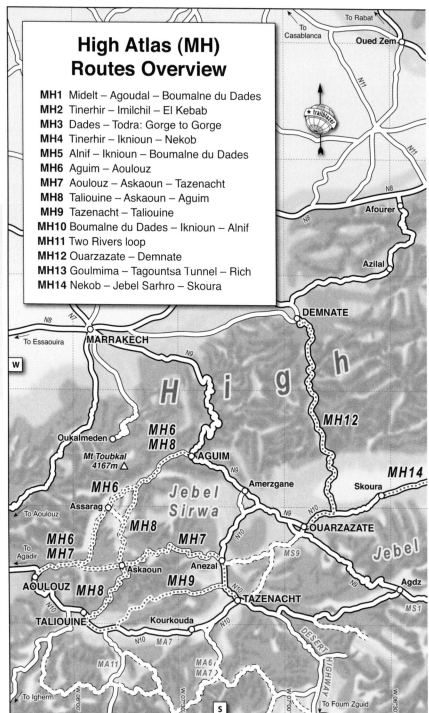

High Atlas (MH)
Routes Overview

MH1 Midelt – Agoudal – Boumalne du Dades
MH2 Tinerhir – Imilchil – El Kebab
MH3 Dades – Todra: Gorge to Gorge
MH4 Tinerhir – Iknioun – Nekob
MH5 Alnif – Iknioun – Boumalne du Dades
MH6 Aguim – Aoulouz
MH7 Aoulouz – Askaoun – Tazenacht
MH8 Taliouine – Askaoun – Aguim
MH9 Tazenacht – Taliouine
MH10 Boumalne du Dades – Iknioun – Alnif
MH11 Two Rivers loop
MH12 Ouarzazate – Demnate
MH13 Goulmima – Tagountsa Tunnel – Rich
MH14 Nekob – Jebel Sarhro – Skoura

N

To Azrou
To Azrou

Khenifra

To Missour

EL KEBAB

MIDELT

N 33°00'

Kasbah Tadla

N8

MH2

MH1

N 32°30'

A   t   l   a   s

To Gourrama

MH11   Tagountsa
                        Tunnel   Rich

Imilchil

MH11
MH13

Agoudal

MH13

N.32°00'

MH1

MH2

Amellago

MH11

Er Rachidia

MH3

To
Boudenib

Aït Hani

MH13

N10

GOULMIMA

MH1

MH2

E

TINERHIR

N 31°30'

N10   N10

BOUMALNE
DU DADES

MH4

N10

0   10   20   30   40   50km

To Erfoud

MH5
MH10

MH10

To Rissani

Sarhro   Iknioun

DESERT HIGHWAY

MS4

N12

MS12

MH4   MH5

ALNIF

Tazoualit

N 31°00'

MS4

NEKOB

DESERT   HIGHWAY

Fezzou

N12

To
Merzouga

MS1

Tazzarine

Engravings

Oum
Jrane

Tafraoute

MS3

MS1

MS3
MS6

N 30°30'

MS2

N9

MS4

MS6

A   L   G   E   R   I   A

To
Foum
Zguid   Zagora

MS5

MS4   To
Tagounite

To Tagounite

Tamegroute

N9

S

W 05°30'

W 05°00'

W 04°30'

0km   **N32° 41.07' W04° 44.60'**
Midelt town centre roundabout with SHELL and TOTAL fuel stations. One way of getting to the start is to head north past a red and white bollard in the road and over a bridge with red and white posts.

In 600m (N32° 41.31' W04° 44.80') turn left onto a minor road. If you're coming from the north you'll see a brown sign indicating 'Circuit Touristique Jaffar' pointing right.

1.3 (315.7)   **N32° 40.93' W04° 44.89'**
Turn right below some ruins. The general direction is SW.

6 (311)   **N32° 38.53' W04° 45.88'**
Tarmac ends. Carry on past junctions left and right. The way ahead is clear.

13 (304)   **N32° 36.25' W04° 49.07'**
Junction; continue SW. In 4km you'll find yourself turning south through the cedars towards the mountains. At KM21 you may pass between barbed wire fences.

25.5 (291.5)   **N32° 33.77' W04° 54.09'**
Fork with an arrow on a rock. Curve left, south, up into the pass where the track becomes rubbly. The other track to the right turns north then west.

26.5 (290.5)   **N32° 33.20' W04° 53.68'**
Come over the pass (2262m; flat space to camp) and enter the **Cirque**. Start a loose descent, in a car inching round a huge fallen boulder on the off-side. Down below are flat-roofed dwellings.

At KM29 turn sharp right as you cross a oued and begin climbing round a spur.

30 (287)   **N32° 32.47' W04° 53.74'**
Junction. Left may be rough so descend right to the valley floor and meet the kids who've heard you coming and may have prepared their traps!

30.5 (286.5)   **N32° 32.35' W04° 53.81'**
Cross a oued prior to climbing back out of the cirque. For us the kids half-heartedly blocked the way here with stones. There are no real options to go wrong but once you're ascending to the NW past fence posts through cedar woods to either side, you're on the right track.

34.5 (282.5)
The cirque is behind you now as the ground opens out onto a good earth road.

38 (279)
A nice camp spot as you cross a small oued.

44.5 (272.5)   **N32° 32.29' W04° 58.49'**
Pass a settlement in the meadows with a view to the northern plains and the snowy peaks to the south. A rutted, dried-mud section may follow.

48.5 (268.5)   **N32° 31.77' W04° 59.49'**
About two-and-a-half hours driving from Midelt you get to this key junction where a sign says: 'Tiz-n Zou 10; Tounfite 30; Imilchil 130'. Turn right here if you're just doing the loop back towards Midelt otherwise continue straight ahead on a good forestry track for a few kilometres.

52 (265)
Ait Ouchchen village, meadows, poppies, wheat. All very scenic – in spring at least.

60 (257)   **N32° 31.06' W05° 03.46'**
Go straight down towards the villages making up **Tizi-n-Zou**.

63 (254)   **N32° 31.04' W05° 05.07'**
Cross what may still be a narrow bridge with railed sides. Or dive through the river if you're feeling sporty or are too wide. All around are cypress and cedar trees dotting the barren, ashen slopes.

73 (244)   **N32° 29.91' W05° 10.53'**
Junction. If not already on it then **join the tarmac** and turn left for Imilchil.

91.5 (225.5)   **N32° 23.49' W05° 09.97'**
A *gîte* in Tagoudit village.

93 (224)
Turn left at a sign 'Imilchil 85km' on a road which bypasses **Agoudim** village.

97 (220)   **N32° 21.56' W05° 11.05'**
Oudadn Auberge by an apple orchard, a lovely place for a lunch break, overnight or simply just to get snowed in.

110 (207)   **N32° 19.46' W05° 16.09'**
Anemzi village.

132 (185)   N32° 17.40'   W05° 23.83'
Junction at the edge of **Anefgou** village to the left. 'Imilchil 47'.

136 (181)
Tighiste village. Willows, grass and a National Park Forestry centre.

147 (170)   N32° 12.45'   W05° 27.31'
The track tops out at 2649m. On the far side are pastures with horses; it looks a good spot for camping.

151 (166)
Tilhri or Tabanast village.

163 (154)   N32° 09.14'   W05° 34.46'
Reach the R317 road. Left is for Agoudal and Dades. Right is for **Imilchil** (9km, **fuel**) on Route MH2.

174 (143)   N32° 05.99'   W05° 30.62'
Turn right and pass through villages.

190 (127)   N32° 00.53'   W05° 29.39'
Agoudal centre at 2350m. The road follows MH2 SE over the oued to Todra. You turn right, join the main route out of town and head for the hills.

197 (120)   N31° 58.70'   W05° 32.72''
Go straight not left at a 'Grotte Akhiam' sign. Drive in the oued. In 1km pass buildings on the right with possible diversions. There are signs and blue arrows on the rocks to show the route.

After another 1.5km there's a **cistern** on the left and soon a narrow passage above a gully. In a kilometre or so the grassy pastures could make nice wild camps.

204 (113)   N31° 57.25'   W05° 36.09'
Short cut directly uphill, otherwise go left.

213 (104)   N31° 54.70'   W05° 39.73'
Tizi-n-Ouano highpoint at 2906m. Some buildings and a bit of rubbish. Good views to the south over the upper Dades.

219 (98)
Tilmi village lies far below with the deep gorge below left. In about 3km the big descent begins with occasional steep short cuts and washed-out bends.

229 (88)   N31° 50.93'   W05° 44.05'
Junction with a valley to the west. You carry on straight and in 500m cross a oued back on the valley floor with the orange *Gîte d'étape Ighounta* on the far bank. Crops and cultivation resume with flowery meadows all around in spring.

235 (82)   N31° 50.02'   W05° 45.70'
Cross a bridge in Aït Ali Ouikkou.

237 (80)
Izmaguene village.

240 (77)   N31° 48.03'   W05° 46.59'
Take the left track and in 500m cross a bridge over a oued. Soon there's a sign: '**Tilmi Centre**', a track joins from the left and you pass an old kasbah. All this is within one kilometre.

247 (70)   N31° 47.73'   W05° 46.65'
Sign: right to Asaka restaurant and Aït Mohamed. An Olaf loop rejoins from right (a split from around KM240). In a kilometre maybe a café.

251 (66)   N31° 43.11'   W05° 48.17'
Reach the upper turn-off for MH3 just before Msemrir.

255 (62)   N31° 41.77'   W05° 49.05'
Msemrir town centre (about three hours driving in good conditions from Agoudal) with a pharmacy, shops and auberges.

285 (32)   N31° 31.74'   W05° 55.49'
From around KM280 the hotels begin and at this point, by a cliff-edge hotel, is the much-photographed '**Dades Gorge hairpins'** viewpoint.

The gorge-side hotels and restos multiply and in about 5km on the left is the posh *Chez Pierre* restaurant and auberge. Here you can have as good a meal as you'll eat in Morocco and it won't have to be a tajine, cous-cous or an omelette.

315 (2)   N31° 22.49'   W05° 59.55'
Dades central roundabout on the N10 highway. Turn left for fuel and Tinerhir or right for Ouarzazate.

317   N31° 22.07'   W05° 58.87'
SHELL fuel station on south side of Dades.

MH – HIGH ATLAS

TRANS ATLAS: MH2 TINERHIR – IMILCHIL – EL KEBAB 241km
May 2008 ~ Mazda pickup

You may learn that the High Atlas are not exactly the Torres del Paine at drivable elevations, and that the southern massifs of Sirwa and Sarhro have more colour. This transit also lacks the greater variety of Route MH1 which intersects it, but chances are it'll be passable when MH1 is not.

It kicks off from Tinerhir with a run through the **'Costa Todra'**, a rampant development bearing little relation to the impressive but not mind-blowing spectacle of the gorge itself, 15km up the road. Once there, you may pay a few dirhams to pass through (it's official; old guy with a hat and a satchel). The tall, narrow chasm is especially dramatic when the overhead sun lights up the walls. There may be climbers and almost certainly an all-day tourist souk selling brightly-coloured head scarves, boxed sets of trilobites and magic slippers.

With Todra behind you, pass through Tamtatoucht with auberges galore and the gnarly Gorge to Gorge track (MH3). Onward leads to the junction at Aït Hani (KM52, also MH11) where you set off into the barren ranges of the High Atlas, peaking right on time at the 2650m **Tizi-n-Tiherhouzine** (KM63).

Agoudal (KM85; 2350m) and **Imilchil** (KM121; fuel) have several places to stay. From here it's an unchallenging and increasingly pastoral descent down to the lowlands, or at least as low as they get before the land rises again to become the Middle Atlas. At KM231 having passed Sidi Yakia Oussad down to the left you get to the junction with the R503 by a couple of roadhouses. Right is for Midelt, left is for Khenifra. Turn left and if you're seeing it through all the way to El Kebab, fork right in 200 metres up an unsigned minor road (the actual road sign is back a bit). Follow this winding road over the hill and drop down the other side into the valley of the Oued Srou and El Kebab, just one place to end the crossing though there's fuel in Aghbala at KM196.

MS10 FIGUIG TO ATLANTIC: THE DESERT HIGHWAY 1500km
2008 and 2012 – Mazda pickup, Yamaha Ténéré, BMW F650GS

The 1500km network of sealed roads connecting Figuig to the Atlantic makes a classic and easy overland journey for those in a rental car, motorhome, riding a touring motorcycle or for cyclists looking to get stuck into a long, mostly level road tour. The tarmac is in good shape and **fuel stops** are never more than 200km apart, even if you won't necessarily find European-style roadside services.

In either direction and on a daily basis it'll offer as much desert scenery as your windscreen or visor can accommodate and pushbikes excepted, it's possible to spend every night in some sort of hotel, or at worst a municipal campsite. In places it's even possible to get off the highway without damaging all but the lowest vehicle. Places listed below in bold are on, or close to the MS10 and have **fuel** and **hotels** too. Map p114-15.

> ... in either direction and on a daily basis it'll offer as much stark desert scenery as your windscreen or visor can accommodate...

From **Figuig** (where petrol may be limited, see p103) overlooking the Algerian border it's a striking run though the jebels along the N17 to **Bouarfa** from where you scoot back south towards the frontier following the N10 and passing **Bouanane** (basic hotel). At Bounane a road branches up to **Beni Tajite** and Gourrama, or soon after Boudenib you may choose to leave the relatively dull stretch of the N10 for **Gourrama**. Here you can work your way back down through the Ziz Gorge and through the sprawling modern university town of **Er Rachidia** and rejoin the N10 for Merzouga. It's a detour worth taking.

The N13 leads down the oasis-filled Ziz valley via **Aoufous** to **Erfoud** and **Rissani** where most will make the 90km round trip to admire the dunes of Erg Chebbi alongside **Merzouga** – fairly small by Saharan standards but unique to Morocco. Many of the auberges alongside the dunes north of Merzouga will be accessible along tracks not needing huge clearance if taken slowly.

West of Rissani the N12 'Route of Fossils' is one of the best stretches of the Desert Highway, even if many of the trilobites you'll be offered are cast from plaster. You pass nameless ranges to the south, villages with long-ruined hilltop ksars and after **Alnif**, the volcanic spikes of Jebel Sarhro. Tazzarine and **Nekob** have hotels too, as does **Agdz** soon after the bridge over the Draa river. Here the 'Valley of the Casbahs' runs down to **Zagora** (parallel to Rissani), home of the famous *'Timbuktu, 52 jours'* sign. Note that some maps indicate a sealed road linking Zagora to just north of Foum Zguid. Although such a connection would make sense, it's not complete yet. Not to worry, you're about to take a much more enjoyable drive from Agdz west along the R108, passing more striking jebels, picturesque villages with tiny mosques, rustling palmeries and crumbling kasbahs as well as the occasional café and very little traffic.

At the junction with the R111, **Tazenacht**, just up the road, is worth the detour both for the spectacle on the drive back, and if you're after buying textiles in a relaxed, non-city souk setting. On the way back south you pass though the narrow walls of the **Tizi Taguergoust** pass which peels back dramatically to reveal the desert beyond. Otherwise, turn south from Agdz down the R111 and pass through the gap or 'foum' in the ranges into friendly **Foum Zguid**, a far cry from places further east on the tourist axis.

Leaving town on the N12 you really feel you're heading out into the Sahara; a thousand miles to the south, Timbuktu is the next town of any consequence. At Tissint you pass back through the ranges of the Jebel Bani and west of town can take a right turn and reverse Route MA11 up to **Taliouine**, a great drive into the Anti Atlas. Back on the Desert Highway, **Tata** has good hotels, restaurants, ATMs and camping right in town. If you've a day to spare you can take a great mountain drive north up to **Igherm** (the end of Route MA11) and loop back down the R109 to Tata.

Beyond Tata, there's fuel at **Akka** if you know where to look (see Route MA3) and room to camp out in the desert if you so wish. The N12 carries on west here via **Aït Herbil** to **Bou Izkarn** on the coast road. Much nicer is the road down to **Assa**. Out of town, if the sun is low a great stage beckons as the R103 climbs up over the **Targoumite Pass** with views back to the desert before dropping down towards **Fask**. Once through **Guelmim** you may find the faded charms of oceanside **Sidi Ifni** a more ambient end to your tour than inland **Tan-Tan** which is merely faded, albeit with the lure of the Western Sahara beyond.

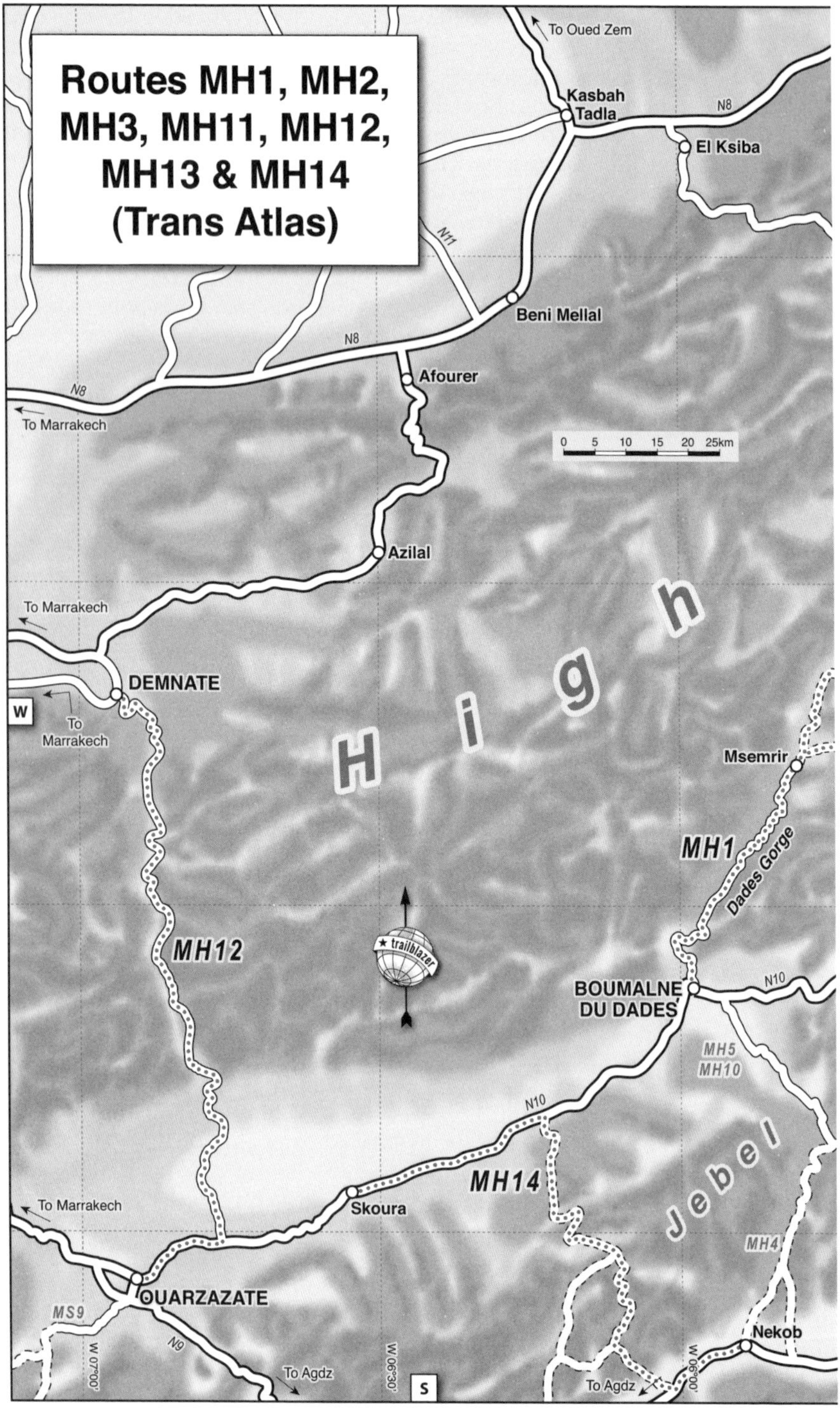

MH – HIGH ATLAS

Routes MH1, MH2,
MH3, MH11, MH12,
MH13 & MH14
(Trans Atlas)

To Oued Zem

Kasbah
Tadla

N8

El Ksiba

N11

Beni Mellal

N8

Afourer

To Marrakech

0 5 10 15 20 25km

Azilal

To Marrakech

DEMNATE

W

To
Marrakech

H i g h

Msemrir

MH1

Dades Gorge

MH12

trailblazer

BOUMALNE
DU DADES

N10

MH5
MH10

N10

J e b e l

MH14

To Marrakech

Skoura

MH4

OUARZAZATE

MS9

Nekob

N9

W 07°00'

To Agdz

W 06°30'

S

To Agdz

W 06°00'

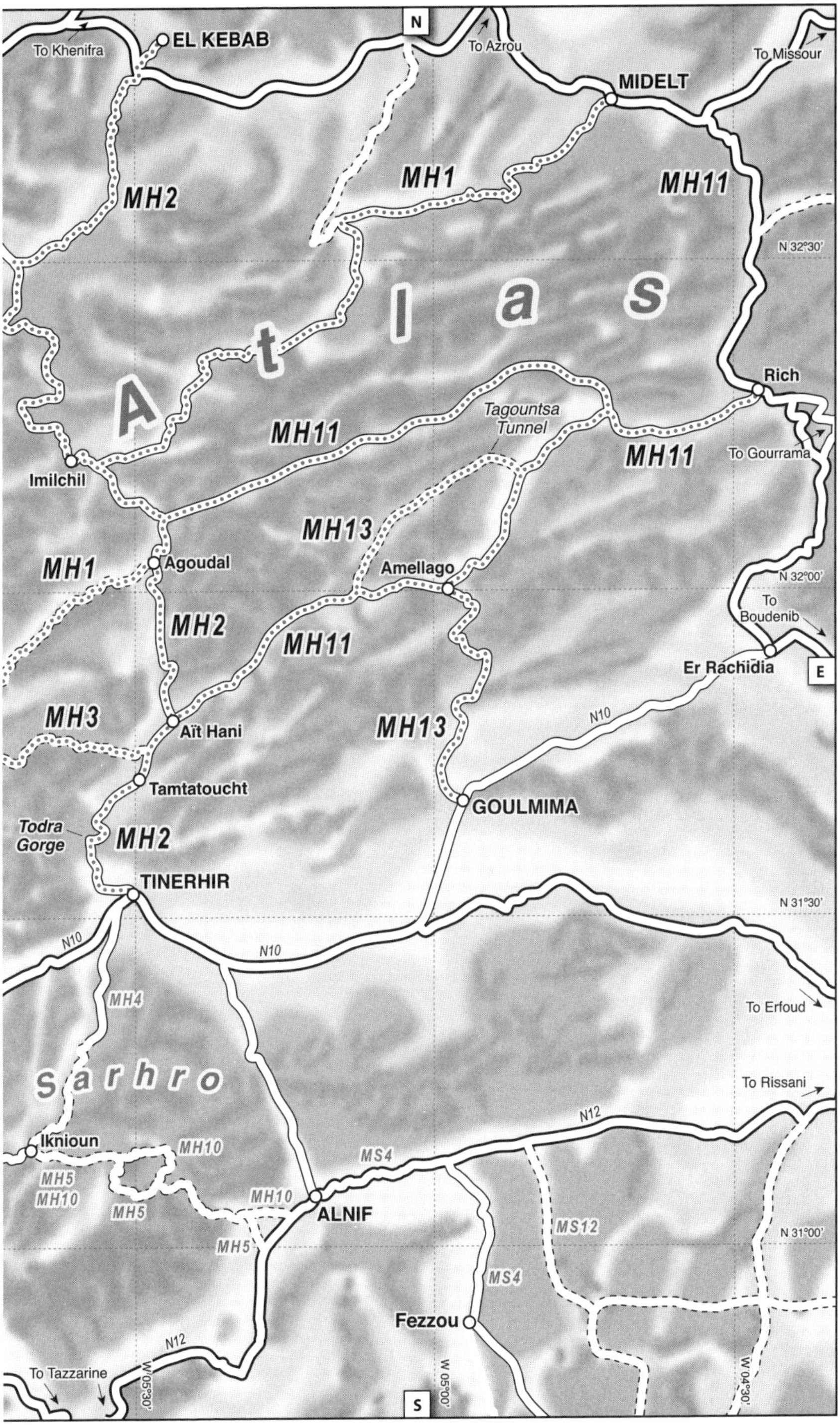
N
To Khenifra
EL KEBAB
To Azrou
To Missour
MIDELT
MH1
MH2
MH11
N 32°30'
A t l a s
Rich
Tagountsa Tunnel
MH11
MH11
To Gourrama
Imilchil
MH13
MH1
Agoudal
Amellago
N 32°00'
MH2
MH11
To Boudenib
Er Rachidia
E
MH3
Aït Hani
N10
MH13
Tamtatoucht
GOULMIMA
Todra Gorge
MH2
TINERHIR
N 31°30'
N10
N10
MH4
To Erfoud
Sarhro
To Rissani
N12
Iknioun
MH10
MS4
MH5
MH10
MH10
MH5
ALNIF
MS12
MH5
N 31°00'
MS4
Fezzou
N12
To Tazzarine
W 05°30'
W 05°00'
W 04°30'
S

MH3 DADES – TODRA 'GORGE TO GORGE' 45KM
May 2008 ~ Mazda pickup

Description
Situated astride the two well-touristed gorges, for a while this was a popular high-clearance, off-road challenge between the two villages of Msemrir and Tamtatoucht. Even the two main guidebooks attempted brief accounts, although only the Lonely Planet guide read like the writer had actually done it.

This route description takes the option to end at the tarmac 7km north of Tamtatoucht, a village once notorious for misguiding travellers attempting to access the route from that end. I tried it myself in the late '90s, before the tarmac reached Tamtatoucht, but gave up trying to outwit the hostile *faux guides*. Msemrir by comparison is close enough to the start of the clear route to make effective misguiding all the more difficult, but they may try anyway.

These hassles only exist at either end; once on the route you're unlikely to encounter any confusion or tricks; only Berber shepherds inhabit this bleak valley begging or selling trinkets.

We did this route on an overcast day so the scrubby hills were not exactly a blaze of glory but even then, it's comparatively dull once you've a chance to relax out of the limestone gorge at the start. The scenery gets better at the eastern end as you emerge high above the Aït Hani plains, but MH3 has neither the barren purity of the desert or the lushness of the best oasis routes.

Off road
You'll hear many yarns about the horrors of this route and one guidebook claimed the crossing was easier east to west. If anything the opposite is true.

Nevertheless, after MH5, this is technically the second **toughest route** in this book (though way easier and more popular than MH5) and following rains can become briefly impassable. The tough sections are at either end, though inching your way into the narrow limestone gorge right at the start may alarm you as to what lies ahead.

This gnarly section ends at KM10 and in good weather, no matter what you're told, what lies ahead is straightforward both technically and especially navigationally. Of course all this does not account for mud, running water, ripped out riverbanks and even snow. The crossing tops out at a not-insubstantial 2639m which may well be snowbound in mid-winter.

Although I've made hasty assumptions before, MH5 is strictly for **4WDs**, **trail bikes** and **MTBs** and even they must turn back in bad conditions. I've heard of big GSs doing this route, something not so unexpected in the conditions we had in May.

There is **frequent traffic** in the main season. We saw at least 15 Toyotas either carrying groups or self-drive rentals piloted by somewhat bemused occupants a little out of their comfort zone, plus a bunch of mountain bikers supported by a Land Rover and a few motorbikers. Up to that point it was more tourists than I'd seen after three weeks in Morocco. Our thought was that they could have picked so many more interesting routes in Morocco but what do I know! Gorge to Gorge remains a classic, convenient, short and intense mini-adventure.

Route finding

Can be tricky with locals out to mislead you but thanks to Olaf, GPS, the inter-net and books like this you're one step ahead of them. They like to spin the yarn that like the shifting dunes of the Sahara, the route changes from year to year and all your space-age gadgetry and route descriptions are to no avail.

The route might shift by a few metres here and there, but basically it goes up one valley to the **Tizi-n-Uguent Zegsaoun** pass at KM17.8 and more or less down the next, using the original track where it still exists, or the riverbeds where the track has gone. There is no ambiguity here, but as you look down over the Aït Hani plains many routes lead back into the gorge link route which is one reason why it's easier to find the start from Msemrir. If ascending from Tamtatoucht, the key point if heading to Msemrir is KM38.5; from here west-wards all is clear – in a route-finding sense at least. The **map**'s on pp116-17.

Fuel and water

Boumalne du Dades is 62km from the start at Msemrir and Tinerhir is 45km from where this route joins the tarmac so that adds up to a **152km fuel range**. The next fuel north is at Imilchil. No wells were seen but the creeks flowed at the far end (in May).

Suggested duration

We took three hours plodding steadily in a 4WD and let a few other cars past. A sprightly moto could do it in less than two hours. On a mountain bike it can be done in a short day but would require overnighting in Msemrir, a fairly stiff haul up from Dades. It would of course be more fun without full luggage.

0km   N31° 41.77'   W05° 49.05'
Msemrir. Wind your way north through town with several auberges and cafés.

2.3 (42.7)   N31° 42.74'   W05° 48.23'
Junction at a blue sign and a spring with a **well** nearby and maybe a chancer or two. Three tracks diverge; the clear track uphill right seems the obvious one but isn't for you. Straight ahead is one of the Olaf tracks but in spring it may be overgrown, ploughed over or unclear. That is the orig-inal way into the limestone gorge, passing along the right side of a cultivated patch. It meets the route below around KM4.

3.1 (41.9)   N31° 43.12'   W05° 48.18'
With the above route from the blue sign unclear, we carried on round to the NW on the main track for a kilometre and with the help of Olaf turned right off the piste at this point and down into the field. Very soon another track joined from right.

3.5 (41.5)   N31° 43.15'   W05° 48.01'
Head east on a track across the field.

3.9 (41.1)   N31° 43.10'   W05° 47.75'
Cross the field and head for a red earth track heading east. Both Olaf routes have converged.

4.4 (40.6)   N31° 43.16'   W05° 47.45'
A track joins from the left. Head into the narrow limestone gorge where the track goes in and out of the stony oued. There's no single clear way, just follow the path of least resistance. In a car it can be tortuous, low range stuff for a while. You can imag-ine that after heavy rain this gorge would get quite a rinse.

10.2 (34.8)   N31° 43.59'   W05° 44.50'
Emerge with some relief from the gorge. The track eases right up and either fol-lows the original piste or dips in and out of the oued.

18 (27)   N31° 44.58'   W05° 41.30'
You're at 2639m on the **Tizi-n-Uguent Zegsaoun** watershed. Depending on the condition of the track you can take the direct route steeply down to the left.

MH – HIGH ATLAS

21.5 (23.5)
After several switchbacks on the way down from the pass you drop into a oued, but are still at 2450m.

23.6 (21.4)   N31° 45.28'   W05° 39.21'
Still in the oued you pass through a red rock defile.

26 (19)   N31° 44.98'   W05° 38.09'
Leave the oued.

26.5 (18.5)   N31° 45.06'   W05° 37.76'
At this junction cross a oued and go steeply uphill, or take the alternative track which goes to the left for an easier crossing and which joins this route 200m later.

32.2 (12.8)
Pass a cave on the left and enter a stream. In 500m you drive out on the north side of a oued. A low range ascent follows.

33.8 (11.2)
Pass caves occupied by shepherds on the left high above the valley floor.

35.2 (9.8)   N31° 44.35'   W05° 33.61'
A couple of kilometres of low range slabs begins. In a couple of hundred metres at N31° 44.26' W05° 33.56' head left steeply downhill on slabs.

In 500m head round the north side of a rounded hill. A short cut steeply down to the left looked a bit washed-out to us but was probably fine.

37.3 (7.7)   N31° 44.10'   W05° 33.03'
The steep short cut above rejoins your track from the left above *Auberge Taghrot* at N31° 44.15' W05° 33.02'. Another track here leads steeply uphill and links up somewhere above.

38.5 (6.5)   N31° 43.91'   W05° 32.74'
Key junction. Turn south for Tamtatoucht about 8km away (making a total crossing distance of around 47km). We went left towards the tarmac road. In 500m take the left track at N31° 43.84' W05° 32.64' and continue winding your way westwards. Around here there may be deviations to get round muddy sections.

41 (4)   N31° 43.71'   W05° 31.47'
Fork left; a more direct if rougher route to the tarmac.

43 (2)
Pylons visible ahead by the road.

44 (1)   N31° 44.08'   W05° 30.06'
Cross a small oued.

45   N31° 44.22'   W05° 29.71'
Join the tarmac at a nondescript point about 7 or 8km north of **Tamtatoucht** and about the same distance south of **Aït Hani**. There are several auberges in Tamtatoucht, and that's even before you've got to the **Todra Gorge** and Tinerhir.

MH4   TINERHIR – IKNIOUN – NEKOB   112KM
March 2012 ~ BMW 1200GS

Description
Situated between the desert and the High Atlas, the distinctive **Jebel Sarhro** massif is considered separate from the Atlas. However it's similarly mountainous and may experience the same weather over 2000m and so, like the Jebel Sirwa, gets grouped in the MH zone.

Crossing the basalt massif of the Jebel Sarhro, this is a popular piste for the right reasons, making a direct and spectacular link between the ever-popular locales of the Todra Gorge and Zagora in the south. It rises gradually over the high plains north of Iknioun and then turns west and south up to the 2316m Tizi-n-Tazazert pass.

From here the vegetation as well as the scenery take a dramatic turn as a series of basalt ridges, flat-topped mesas and ravines of twisted black rock unrolls before you. It's a fabulous descent and you'll want to stop again and again to marvel at and photograph your surroundings.

It's best done heading southwards as described below, allowing the drama of the Sarhro ranges to unfold before you in the afternoon light.

Off road

The track gets rough once over the top but despite this fact, old Mercedes vans still manage it and anyway, coming down is less of a strain on a **2WD**; you just have to ease gently over the bigger rock steps. Being bare rock as opposed to loose stones and earth there's nothing for any heavy rain to wash out, though there may be some puddles and creek crossings further down as you pass the cultivated area after the *Auberge Tazlout* at KM84. Apart from these possibly muddy patches and of course allowing for the weather, **motorcycles** as large as they come running road tyres manage this route fine, and I even saw a pair of loaded up MTB-ers nearing Nekob one time.

With an easy asphalt link coming up from Dades to Iknioun, the northern half of this route gets less traffic than it used to, but it all meets up on the impressive south side of Sarhro.

Route finding

Assuming nothing has changed too radically it's all straightforward: up one side, down the other. The **map** is over the page.

Fuel and water

Tinerhir and Nekob for fuel. There can be snow on the pass, run-off on the north side and water at the auberges and villages plus the odd well.

Suggested duration

It's a slow descent in a car so allow a short day to cover the 112km.

0km   N31° 31.24' W05° 32.00'
TOTAL fuel station in **Tinerhir**. Leave to the west through the town but after around 220m, close to a *Banque Populaire*, turn south at the lights at the sign for the *Hotel Timbuktu*. Go down this road, past shops and then houses to the very end of this road past new housing.

3.5 (107.5)   N31° 29.60' W05° 32.04'
At the corner and follow the gravel track heading SSW past a low walled enclosure on your left with a hill with a turret on top visible to the right. Some reports say the first 20km have been **sealed**.

8 (104)
Enter a village with a palmerie. Continue SSW passing a pink mosque on the right as you leave.

10 (102)
Pass an access track to the radio mast on the right. Keep left. The track becomes stony. In 2km cross a oued after which the track turns towards the SSW.

14 (98)
The track follows a river bed for 500m and soon you start climbing into the hills. Then, after a kilometre or so, the track flattens out and snakes along a valley.

22 (90)
Cross a oued and continue along its western bank. The heading is generally SW as you drive along the creek bed.

24 (88)
Leave the oued and start climbing sharply into the hills above. Within a kilometre

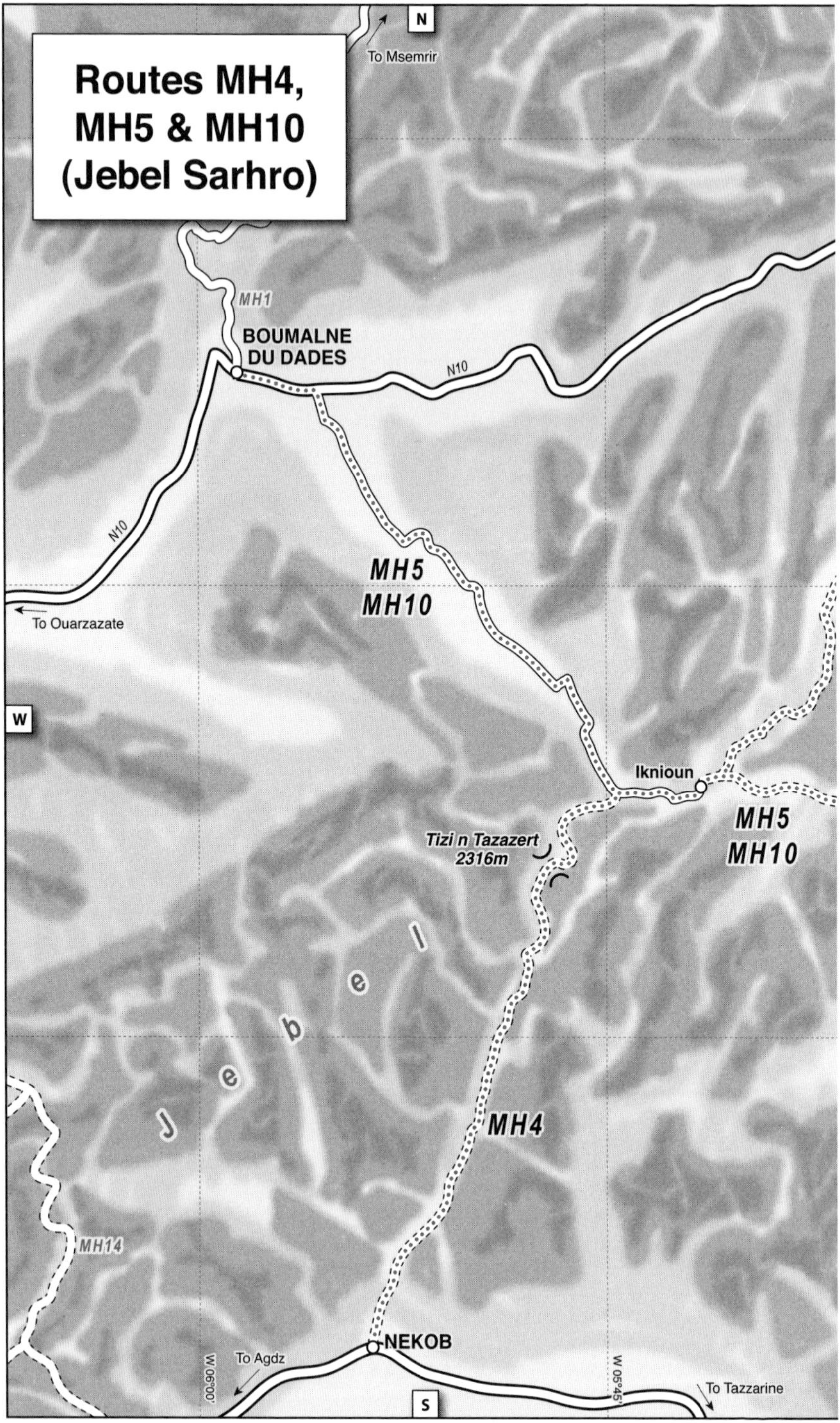

Routes MH4, MH5 & MH10 (Jebel Sarhro)

N

To Msemrir

MH1

BOUMALNE DU DADES

N10

N10

To Ouarzazate

MH-HIGH ATLAS

W

MH5
MH10

Iknioun

MH5
MH10

Tizi n Tazazert
2316m

J e b e l

MH4

MH14

NEKOB

To Agdz

W 06°00'

W 05°45'

To Tazzarine

S

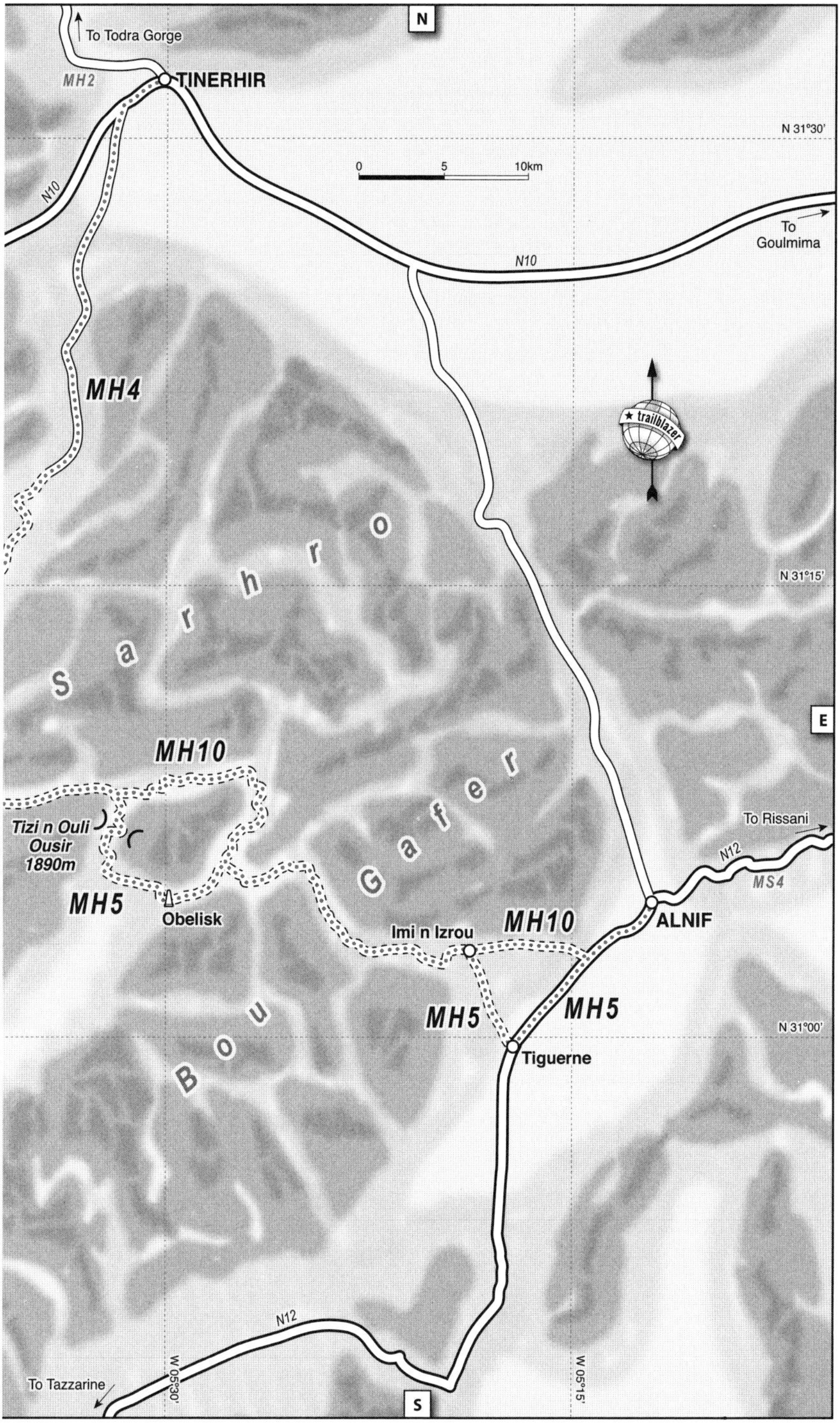

N

To Todra Gorge

MH2

TINERHIR

0   5   10km

N 31°30'

N10

N10

To Goulmima

MH4

MH – HIGH ATLAS

N 31°15'

S a r h r o

MH10

E

Tizi n Ouli Ousir 1890m

G a f e r

To Rissani

MH5

Obelisk

N12

MS4

Imi n Izrou   *MH10*   ALNIF

MH5

B o u

MH5   *MH5*

N 31°00'

Tiguerne

N12

To Tazzarine

W 05°30'

W 05°15'

S

you get to a distinctive extruded fin of black rock after which the track twists upwards again.

28 (84)   N31° 19.60' W05° 35.40'
A track joins from the right, with buildings visible below.

30 (82)
Elevation 1850m. The track flattens out to give a view of the possibly snow-topped mountains to the east. About 500m later you descend, with a village below.

32 (80)
A track goes off to the right. Go left. In a few hundred metres pass some buildings. The track resumes its ascent.

34 (78)   N31° 17.80' W05° 35.60'
Take the right fork, bearing SSW. A kilometre later pass a **well** and 2km later (KM37.6) a thin flat sandy oued, resembling a track, crosses the piste.

40 (72)
After some buildings and stone ruins, a couple of tracks join from the right.

43 (69)
Track joins from the left.

44 (68)   N31° 13.10' W05° 37.30'
Junction with the Agoultine mine track to the east. Head SW past a village.

49 (63)
A large **well** on the right.

53 (59)   N31° 10.56' W05° 40.06'
Junction. Turn right for Iknioun. Left is Route MH5 coming from Alnif and the less gnarly MH10 going to Alnif.

54 (58)   N31° 10.24' W05° 40.46'
Iknioun. A busy little town with a couple of cafés and an auberge right in the centre. Follow **tarmac** out of town along the valley to the west, past a copse with the 2712m Sarhro high point of Amaloun-n-Mansour to your left.

59 (53)   N31° 10.22' W05° 43.58'
The tarmac to Dades runs off to the NW; you leave it here to the west **along a piste**.

60 (52)
Aït Moraid. Your chance to buy cedar wood cups. They sure smell nice.

63 (49)   N31° 09.56' W05° 45.75'
Junction, keep left and south, descending for a few hundred metres then climb again. A number of false passes follow.

66 (46)   N31° 08.34' W05° 46.11'
Tizi-n-Tazazert Pass (2316m). Over the next 6km or so you pass the *Café Tizi* and the exposed and even more basic *Hotel Café Tiza*. From here the rock-step descent sets in with great views.

84 (28)   N31° 03.24' W05° 47.27'
With the major part of the descent over, the *Auberge Tazlout Bab n Ali* is a nice spot to end up if you don't want to push on to Nekob. There's another auberge down the road.

Cultivation resumes as the track passes dry stone walls. Soon you cross a oued and continue along its western bank.

95 (17)   N30° 58.55' W05° 48.99'
Fork: left is down to village of Tirhremt-n-Oudrar, you curve right and uphill. Soon after, around some sharp bends you may find your route briefly splits from Olaf.

100 (12)   N30° 56.62' W05° 49.67'
A track branches off to the left and joins the highway 5km east of Nekob. Keep right for the regular way to Nekob.

107.5 (4.5)   N30° 53.86' W05° 52.09'
A track and pylons join from the right which lead to a village. In less than a kilometre another track joins from the right at N30° 53.38' W05° 52.03'.

109 (3)   N30° 52.99' W05° 52.24'
Arrive at the oued and cross it, coming out by a blue sign near some radio masts (N30° 52.99' W05° 52.23'; a handy point to aim for if doing this route in reverse and taking the track NW from the side of the *Ziz*). From here follow tracks to the SE and enter Nekob.

112   N30° 52.16' W05° 52.68'
Zizmo fuel station on the SW edge of **Nekob**. Several auberges around.

MH5 ALNIF – IKNIOUN – DADES 116KM

April and November 2008 ~ Mazda pickup, Yamaha Ténéré

Description

For a few kilometres this route is a lot harder than anything else in this book, following an abandoned track that's destined to be ever less used by vehicles between KM42 and KM55 following the completion of the MH11 bypass. Depending on who's been through since the last rains, the route may be impassable. The only people to travel it seem to be bike riders and 4WD drivers looking for a challenge. On this route they'll surely get it.

As on many pistes of this type in Morocco, it's interesting to observe the change in the villagers as the altitude and remoteness increase. Up high the peasants are poorer and behave conservatively. Just 20km away and 1000m lower down in sat dish country, the kids are riding bikes and whoop hyperactively as you pass by.

While it might be comparable with the Jebel Sirwa massif, geologically-distinctive Jebel Sarhro's south side is a lot drier. Where Sirwa feels alpine in places, fed by Toubkal's run off, Sarhro has a Mediterranean, or, given the gradients, maybe even a Corsican feel in its foliage, colouring, scents and wildlife. Once I saw a pair of lizards whose back halves were as blue as the sky.

Off road

In the right hands a Jeep or a Defender 90 would crawl over this route with little more than a shrug. A locking rear diff won't do any harm but unless your axles can flex like Olga Korbut following an olive oil sauna, at the cost of some axle clearance, consider **reducing tyre pressures** to improve rock traction.

I managed to ride and push my laden **motorbike** up to the pass from the north but this small victory was soured by the oil dripping from a cracked crankcase, collapsed forks, a dented rim, flat tyre and a sore head! Either way I'm sure glad I wasn't on a 1200GSA. On a moto or an MTB, this is a route worth doing as a loop with the clobber left at a hotel.

Route finding

This route is fully Olaffed. It's hard to get lost driving up the valley but at the sharp end it can get hard to follow the actual track in some washed-out creeks. Here it pays to get out and walk so you don't end up having to back up. The only local traffic to be found on the high ground will be donkeys; beyond the villages you're on your own for the meaty part of the route. Finally I can say with some confidence that you will not encounter any Transit or Merc vans traversing the full length of MH5. At KM55 the difficulties dissolve as you join the improved Iknioun–Alnif track. The **map**'s on pp122-3.

Fuel and water

Alnif and Dades for fuel. Several wells as indicated.

Suggested duration

In a 4WD give yourself a full day, possibly including some time to recce and for road building. Motorbikes will have fewer delays but need some skill to keep upright, while MTBers will want to make two fun days of it.

0km   **N31° 06.75'   W05° 10.34'**
Alnif *Ziz* on the east side of town with a resto and internet over the road. For **hotels** here see the end of Route MS4.

Drive west through town, past the other *Ziz* at the west end of town and take the Olaffed turn-off (N31° 05.3'   W05° 12.6) about 5km after the *Ziz*.

17 (99)   **N31° 05.56'   W05° 17.27'**
A track joins from the left by the Oued Tazlaft below **Imi-n Izrou**.

Within a kilometre you cross the oued (with a **well** on the right) and drive steeply up through town, passing a building on the left with coloured balcony balustrades. There's no need to follow the Olaf detour around to the left unless you're very shy.

19 (97)   **N31° 05.22'   W05° 17.97'**
Leave town to the west and pass through the gap in the range along the south side of the Oued Tazlaft. Tazlaft village is ahead. Go up the valley, passing some finely made dry stone buildings.

31 (85)   **N31° 07.10'   W05° 23.20'**
The track turns west towards the peaks.

38 (78)   **N31° 08.01'   W05° 26.43'**
This junction is where MH11 (KM81.5) comes in from the north, the easier way to Iknioun, avoiding the Tizi-n-Ouli Ousir.

39 (77)   **N31° 07.44'   W05° 27.06'**
Pass a **well** (25m) on the left of the piste.

42 (74)
Crest a rise and you see what lies ahead...

44 (72)
Cross a oued, a steep climb commences.

47 (69)   **N31° 07.68'   W05° 30.51'**
You reach an ominous obelisk indicating '1710m'. It commemorates one of the last battles for colonial dominance in 1933 over the Aït Atta Berbers. The truly gnarly section now begins.

48 (68)   **N31° 08.32'   W05° 30.71'**
Cross a stream in a small gorge. Depending on your ground clearance and presence of recent tracks, the best way ahead may require a short walk.

51 (65)   **N31° 08.94'   W05° 30.91'**
A saddle west of a cone hill where the track drops into a bowl and climbs up to Tizi-n-Ouli Ousir about 2km away.

54 (62)   **N31° 09.65'   W05° 30.59'**
Tizi-n-Ouli Ousir pass, 1890m. From here a very stony few hundred metres leads down to the Iknioun–Alnif track. On a bike or in a car you'll have to inch down to avoid possible damage to your undercarriage.

55 (61)   **N31° 10.17'   W05° 30.58'**
Join the better track and turn left or west for Iknioun and Dades. Turning right here follows MH11 back to Alnif, something you might wish you'd known about if getting this far has cost you.

59 (57)   **N31° 10.20'   W05° 32.35'**
A **well** on the right and cultivation all around. Soon there's another **well** on the left.

64 (52)   **N31° 09.94'   W05° 34.94'**
Crest a 1957m pass with a view of the Iknioun valley ahead. As you continue down, tracks join from left and right, with several **wells** in the next few kilometres.

72 (44)   **N31° 10.56'   W05° 40.06'**
The track from Tinerhir (Route MH4) joins from right with a red and white radio tower on the left.

73 (43)   **N31° 10.27'   W05° 40.44'**
Iknioun centre with an auberge, lots of Yamaha 50s and a couple of cafés. **Start of the tarmac**. A kilometre out of town there's a shady copse on the right.

78 (48)   **N31° 10.22'   W05° 43.58'**
Route MH4 over the Tizi-n-Tazazert pass leaves the tarmac to the left and heads west as your road turns NW.

111 (5)   **N31° 21.84'   W05° 54.85'**
Join the N10 highway. Turn left for Dades or right for Tinerhir.

116   **N31° 22.01'   W05° 58.05'**
Inov fuel station on the eastern edge of **Boumalne du Dades**.

MH6   AGUIM – AOULOUZ   125KM
April 2008 ~ Mazda pickup

Description
If you've just come from Marrakech over the Tizi-n-Tichka and are looking to get yourself west, this route will take you there over the southern side of the High Atlas. After you turn off the N9 the tarmac ends beneath the slopes of **Jebel Toubkal** where a rough track drops down past cascades and through a string of villages to the valley floor, bringing to mind the Hunza valley of northern Pakistan, although Moroccan towns are actually more picturesque. You re-emerge at Aoulouz, midway between Taroudant and Talioune.

Off road
The road out of Aguim is sealed but twisting and narrow and once the asphalt ends at KM37 it's initially a rough and possibly muddy descent into the upper Souss valley. But, incredibly, **Transit vans** possibly older than you and with a full load manage it daily; at times you may need to back up for them. In rain this would become a messy run but at least you'll be slithering downhill.

Route finding
Nothing to tax the brain here; ride up the hill and down the other side. If you get in a muddle there are plenty of people to ask. Not all the branches and forks appearing on Olaf were evident, possibly due to roadworks and the fact that it got dark around me.

There are plenty of **other routes** criss-crossing this region; broadly speaking the **Jebel Sirwa** massif. You could make a great couple of days of it by linking parts of Routes MH7 and MH8. If coming over from Ouarzazate you could start this route by taking the mostly sealed road to Bou Tazoult about 40km before Aguim, joining this route at KM17 near Sour. The **map** for this route is on pp130-1.

Fuel and water
Fuel at Aguim and Aoulouz and plenty of water all around.

Suggested duration
This can be done in a day out of Marrakech or Ouarzazate. The off-road stage is fairly congested or steep, with comparatively few opportunities for a secluded overnight stop. Neither Aguim nor Aoulouz look great places to stay, but at the far end Talioune or Taroudant will have plenty of what you want.

0km   N31° 09.50'   W07° 27.78'
TOTAL fuel station at the south end of **Aguim**. Head north for 500m and turn NW. Pass through several villages.

17 (108)   N31° 07.83'   W07° 35.65'
There's no clear sign of the way SE to Bou Tazoult, but it crosses the oued just after a hairpin before Sour and joins the N9 at N31° 05.42' W07° 17.84'.

22 (103)   N31° 05.67'   W07° 37.19'
Village of **Sour**.

37 (88)   N31° 02.16'   W07° 42.36'
At a wide saddle below Toubkal and with a red radio mast 500m to the NE, Route MH8 leaves the tar to the south for Askaoun. **The tarmac ends** a couple of hundred metres further west at N31° 02.17' W07° 42.55'.

From here allow up to 3 hours to Aoulouz as you drop down from the pass past possibly running water, red rock shelves, grassy green meadows and several villages.

53 (72)   N30° 59.60' W07° 48.89'
After a long and at times tortuous descent you pass a hotel-café, near the village of **Assarag** which appears on some maps.
A right turn here leads up a tortuous route about 12km to a viewpoint over **Lac Ifni** right below the summit of Toubkal.

60 (65)   N30° 57.34' W07° 49.58'
Turn down some sharp hairpins and the worst of the descent is behind you. Around here a track possibly leads out SE to points on Route MH8.

64 (61)   N30° 56.11' W07° 51.43'
Cross a river and the track improves.

79 (46)   N30° 50.58' W07° 54.00'
Junction with a track that leads east to Timgdal, or to KM30 on Route MH7.

101 (24)   N30° 44.35' W07° 58.91'
If it hasn't happened already, **join the tarmac** near a reservoir on the south side of the road. Within a kilometre you pass the turn-off left which passes below the dam wall and leads back up east to Askaoun; Route MH7 to Tazenacht.

119 (6)   N30° 42.44' W08° 08.48'
A tarmac road joins from the left and the road becomes wider.

121 (4)   N30° 42.04' W08° 09.17'
Roundabout on the main N10 Taroudant –Taliouine road. Turn left or south.

125   N30° 40.41' W08° 10.54'
Aoulouz town centre MOBIL, with a SHELL serving a few hundred metres further on.

MH7   AOULOUZ – ASKAOUN – TAZENACHT   166KM
April and November 2008 ~ Mazda pickup and Yamaha Ténéré.

Description
A thrilling traversal up and over the highest drivable point of the **Jebel Sirwa** massif where the sub-alpine meadows produce grass green enough to induce travel sickness. Out of Aoulouz you follow a tar road as far as the reservoir and then branch off around KM24 for the valley drive up to the heights of Askaoun, the crossroads of the Sirwa, and where route MH8 comes up from Taliouine on the way up to Aguim. Your route lies east where you rattle your way over two 2500m-plus passes surrounded by patches of either snow or dazzling emerald pastures. You round the north side of 3304m-high Jebel Sirwa, just a few kilometres away and from where the track improves with more spectacular views across the valleys and plains as you wind down to Tachakoucht, with a particularly good-looking old town, having met the ever-encroaching tarmac.

At Anezal on the N10 highway, Tazenacht is only 26km to the south over an impressive pass and viewpoint, but alphaphiles can take the road north to Amerzgane and Aguim to pick up Route MH6 back to Aoulouz via Assarag and Aouzioua, so completing one of the few tours in Morocco composed of towns and villages only beginning with 'A'.

In April at least, while Taliouine and points south were cooking, up in the Sirwa streams trickled off the passes, purple and yellow flowers shimmered in the cool breeze and birds twittered about their business. The greenery and views were a real tonic for the eyes and anywhere up near the two passes it's worth stopping to listen to the sounds of nature.

Off road

On a bike Aoulouz to Askaoun can take just over an hour from the reservoir turn-off to the top. This is still 'Transit country' though and the road is only a little wider than those vans; something to bear in mind on the hairpin section after KM37.

The last few kilometres before Askaoun can get gnarly, as it can do over the two high passes east of Askaoun. But that didn't dissuade an old Golf creeping slowly down the Tizi-n-Tleta. As I was reminded elsewhere, tracks in Morocco exist primarily for local people to get around in normal cars.

On a heavy GS and the like, it would still be a great ride as the very rough sections are quite short and the rewards worthwhile. With its copious water points and sheltered spots, this route, or versions of it, would also make a great mountain bike ride.

Route finding

Straightforward, it's fully Olaffed and for once reasonably accurate on the maps, although there's little traffic on the piste. For the **map** see pp130-1.

Fuel and water

Aoulouz and Tazenacht, as well as a Zɪz the eastern point of the N10/N9 triangle of roads near Aït Benhaddou. There's plenty of water trickling down off the mountain as fresh as a daisy. You pass a well as you approach Askaoun.

Suggested duration

A full day as described but it would be a shame not to spend a night out, ideally over 8000ft.

0km   N30° 40.27' W08° 10.71'
Aoulouz main street *SHELL*. Head NE out of town on the road to Taroudant.

5 (161)   N30° 42.03' W08° 09.20'
Cross the bridge over the Oued Souss and at the roundabout turn right for Aouzioua.

6.5 (159.5)
A road leads off to the right; you carry on straight, NE.

18 (148)
Aouzioua town with a few stores.

23.5 (142.5) N30° 44.18' W07° 59.34'
Leave the tarmac and turn right to pass through gardens right below the dam wall and head up the other side.

25 (141)   N30° 44.01' W07° 59.10'
Turn sharp left here and continue uphill to follow the south bank of the reservoir eastwards.

30 (136)   N30° 42.47' W07° 57.10'
Cross a big bridge and turn right. Turning left here may lead to KM79 on MH6.

33 (133)   N30° 42.09' W07° 55.75'
After a brief downhill stretch turn left off the track and soon cross a concrete bridge to the north side of the river.

35 (131)
Tizzouguine village.

37 (129)   N30° 42.12' W07° 53.53'
Around here you leave the river and get stuck into the steep climb up to Askaoun.

64 (102)   N30° 44.27' W07° 46.65'
Cross MH8 south of **Askaoun**, just after a **well**. At this point if you can get to KM65 without crushing someone's prize marrows then give it a go. Otherwise turn north along the pine avenue for 300m to the flag stand in front of an official-looking building. Now turn back SE through the trees for 350m toward the minibus

MH – HIGH ATLAS

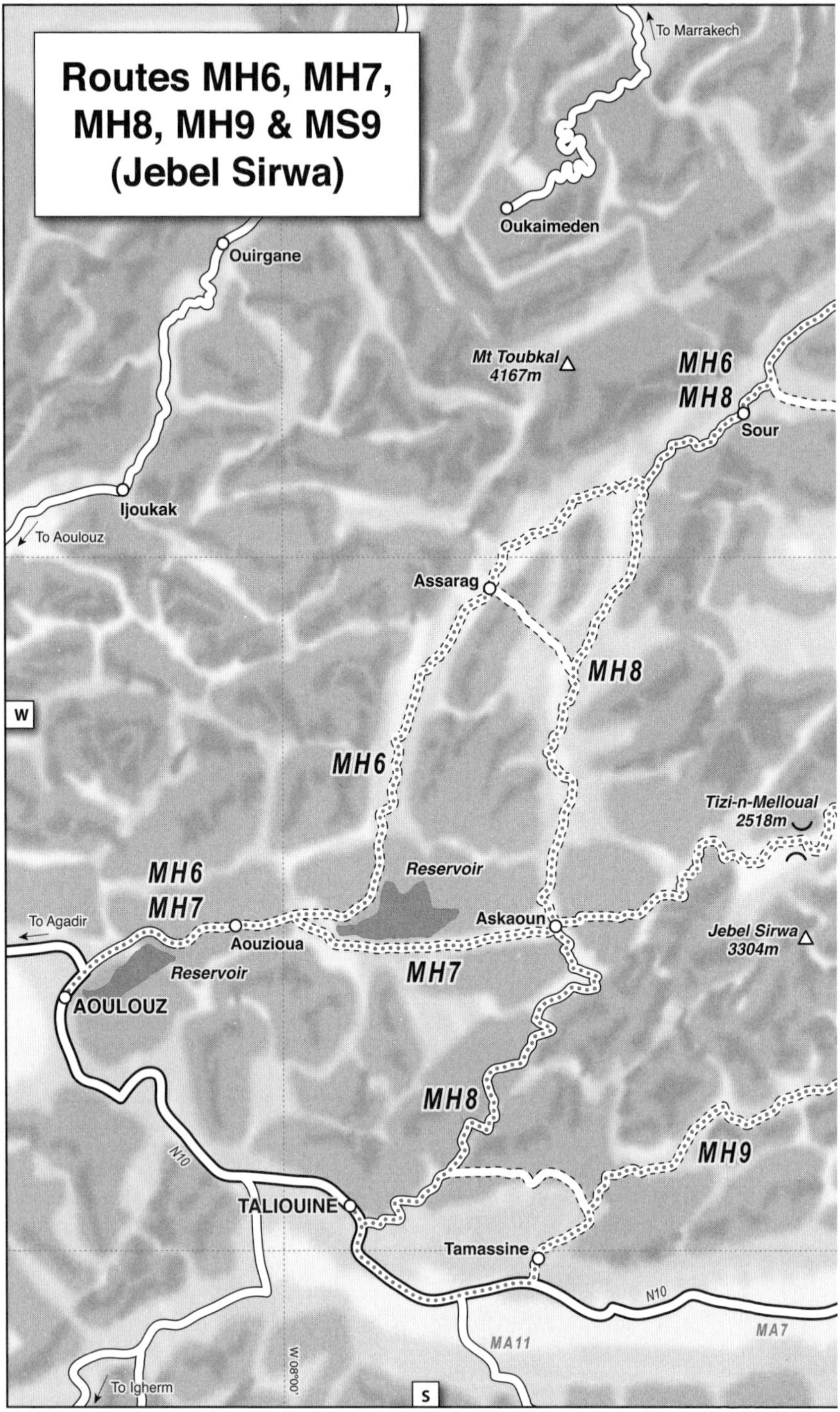

Routes MH6, MH7, MH8, MH9 & MS9 (Jebel Sirwa)

To Marrakech

Oukaimeden

Ouirgane

Ijoukak

To Aoulouz →

Mt Toubkal △
4167m

MH6
MH8
Sour

Assarag

MH8

MH6

Tizi-n-Mellloual
2518m

MH6
MH7

To Agadir ←

Reservoir

Askaoun

Jebel Sirwa △
3304m

Aouzioua

Reservoir

MH7

AOULOUZ

MH8

MH9

N10

TALIOUINE

Tamassine

N10

W 08°00'

MA11

MA7

To Igherm →

W

S

N

To Marrakech

N9

*Tizi-n-Tichka
2260m*

○ Telouet

N9

0   5   10   15   20km

★ trailblazer

AGUIM

N9

Amerzgane

○ Aït Benhaddou

N 31°00'

To Boumalne
du Dades

N10

MH12

N9

N10

OUARZAZATE

E

MS9

To Agdz

N9

Tachakoucht

MH7

Anezal

MS9

MH9

TAZENACHT

*MH7, MH8
MH9*

N10

DESERT HIGHWAY

To Agdz

N 30°30'

DESERT HIGHWAY

To
Foum Zguid

MA6, MA7

W 07°30'

W 07°00'

S

MH – HIGH ATLAS

park (N30° 44.30′ W07° 46.50′) by the arches. Drive on east into the market place and turn right, south, out of the square and then turn left (N30° 44.29′ W07° 46.46′). Then, after 200m (KM65), fork left at N30° 44.22′ W07° 46.39′.

66 (100)   N30° 44.27′ W07° 45.80′
Fork right and follow a rocky washed-out track with cairns by the track side.

71 (95)   N30° 44.46′ W07° 43.35′
Start of a rough ascent. Soon you enter a narrow pass, cross a concrete bridge and reach some ruins and grassy meadows suitable for camping.

76 (90)   N30° 45.26′ W07° 40.63′
Inch over rocks, turn a hairpin over a stream and head uphill. There are flat grassy camp spots around and according to the old maps a track leads 8km towards Jebel Sirwa summit. Note that getting on the actual summit of Jebel Sirwa involves some exposed scrambling; many trekkers don't take the risk.

79 (87)
At 2437m the track is better now.

81 (85)   N30° 46.54′ W07° 39.95′
This could be the **Tizi-n-Tleta** (2448m), a flat pass by some outcrops with stone sheep folds and goat holders. It's clearly used as a camping spot.

83 (83)
The track rises still further to 2514m as a valley opens out to the east with a transhumance hamlet visible below.

85 (81)   N30° 47.40′ W07° 38.77′
Junction with a track leading down to the hamlet and on to other villages to the north. In a kilometre there's a sharp bend over a stream, another idyllic camping spot and base for a trek towards Jebel Sirwa summit; just 9km away at 166°.

88 (78)   N30° 46.97′ W07° 37.76′
Tizi-n-Melloul at 2518m; high point on this route which is now a good track.

90 (76)   N30° 46.89′ W07° 36.82′
The descent begins and after a couple of hairpins another track leads down to a

hamlet as you come to a vista of the parched Ouarzazate plain to the east. Tachakoucht is also visible 15km away.

104 (62)   N30° 48.83′ W07° 33.09′
Junction at a sign; **tarmac** resumes.

110 (56)   N30° 47.95′ W07° 31.54′
Tachakoucht, still at just under 2000m.

126 (40)
Tamazight village to the SW as the road swings sharply east.

140 (26)   N30° 45.46′ W07° 17.37′
Join the N10 highway at **Anezal**: a few cafés, shops and an auberge. Tazenacht is a particularly great drive over the **Tizi-n-Bachkoum** to another nice town with mellow people.

Otherwise north leads past the seemingly abandoned **Gas Haven** 'roadhouse' – a mirage of South-west Americana but actually a film set from a 2006 remake of Wes Craven's 1977 desert mutant-psycho slasher *The Hills Have Eyes*.

A short distance later, after the Oued Iriri, the road forks: left or north for **Amerzgane** (fuel, 41km from Anezal), a nice small town with cafés and a couple of roadside **B&Bs** a few kilometres to the north on the Marrakech road. Forking right leads to Ouarzazate which is 62km from Anezal with a ZIZ at the point of the triangle of roads where the N10 meets the N9.

Note that the N10 between Tazenacht and the ZIZ at the triangle is barely two cars wide and full of bends and climbs so whichever way you go, keep your wits about you **after dark**, especially on a bike.

166   N30° 34.69′ W07° 12.34′
Tazenacht SHELL on the north side of town with an AFRIQUIA on the west exit to Taliouine, a ZIZ on the south exit to Foum Zguid and a no-name fuel station in town just in case the other three all run out. Right opposite this town centre fuel station is a string of cafés, restaurants and a couple of cheap hotels.

For a better impression of the roads south of Tazenacht which go east to Agdz and south to Foum Zguid see The Desert Highway: MS10. For more on Tazenacht see Route MA6.

MH – HIGH ATLAS

MH8   TALIOUINE – ASKAOUN – AGUIM   133KM
April 2008 ~ Mazda pickup

Description
A great route up from Taliouine onto the sub-alpine ranges of Jebel Sirwa and the High Atlas itself. You pass from the domain of goat and palm to that of sheep, golfing-calibre grass and even cattle and horses. You rejoin the tarmac close to Jebel Toubkal's summit whose northern slopes you'll have been watching all day, most clearly on cloud-free mornings.

The scenery is wonderfully refreshing if you've come up from the baking desert. You'll see why in Islam green is the colour of paradise, and alpine scenes on thick laminated posters adorn café and roadhouse walls.

As you cross through the pass at KM71.5 the land changes from wild Mediterranean to pastoral. Here shepherds tend their flocks and herds with dogs, trickling streams feed bright green grass and crossing a limestone basin you can't help being reminded of England's majestic Yorkshire Dales.

Off road
This route takes a sporty direct route from KM58 to 68 after which the track hugs the very edge of the flower-speckled mountainside up to the pass. Beyond here the water which gives this route such a verdant feel could also turn it into a mud bath, so be ready for anything, especially in mid-winter.

In good, dry conditions a **regular car** could manage this (though not from KM58 – an Olaf diversion may exist to the west) and **big bikes** too will have a great ride. On a **mountain bike** most of the height is gained along the tarmac stage to Askaoun. Here you might want to spend the night to give yourself a full day to get back to the tarmac and maybe even Aguim.

Route finding
It can get a bit complicated so pay close attention as the route isn't all Olaffed. Minibuses trundle up to Askaoun, but you won't see many beyond that. At the top end, the narrow tarmac road is relatively busy with Transits, Bedfords and mules running between Aoulouz and Aguim and is not something to leave for the dark with weary reflexes. Where's the **map**? On pp130-1.

Fuel and water
Taliouine and Aguim for fuel with plenty of water in the villages and streams.

Suggested duration
This route can easily be done in a day as long as conditions are good, but Aguim is no Shangri La, so either plan to head on over to Marrakech, back down to Ouarzazate (see KM133) or camp out from around KM61.5.

0km   **N30° 31.91'   W07° 55.31'**
Taliouine town centre fuel. Head east on the road to Tazenacht past a couple of auberges. There's an old ksar to the south of the road which may well be worth a wander.

1.5 (131.5)
Turn north for Askaoun, a twisty but asphalted scenic drive. At around KM40 you pass a nice mountain village with a rounded, castle-like ksar of dark stone beneath which might lie a thick shaggy

MH – HIGH ATLAS

carpet of ripening corn. In the spring it could be the Alps.

48 (85)   N30° 43.71' W07° 46.53'
A piste heads off left by a well, signed for 'Houzioua' (MH7 coming from Aoulouz).

49.5 (83.5)   N30° 44.43' W07° 46.65'
Askaoun. A line of trees leads to a square with a flag ahead of a building with a radio mast. (The market square is to the SE.) **Tarmac ends**. Head left of this building, NW. Soon you cross over a pass towards the pylons at N30° 46.52' W07° 46.82'.

55 (78)   N30° 46.92' W07° 46.59'
Arabic sign for somewhere to the right.

56.5 (76.5)
Taouyaot ahead and a place in Arabic signed to the right. In 500m or so you cross a concrete bridge over a stream.

58 (75)   N30° 48.11' W07° 46.10'
The gardens of **Anrouz** village. Soon after this point fork right to the north: N30° 48.41' W07° 46.05'. You're leaving Olaf and carry on north.

60 (73)   N30° 48.91' W07° 45.97'
Junction; keep right and head to a village. Within 500m pass a red-walled compound on the right with glass on the wall tops. Half a kilometre later a promising sign proclaims 'Aguim' in English.

61.5 (71.5)   N30° 49.89' W07° 45.85'
Here a track leads down right to a village. Keep left. Although the way ahead gets a bit thin, work your way around to N30° 49.88' W07° 46.03', about 500m further on, then take lesser tracks up the hill to reach N30° 49.97' W07° 46.26', another half a kilometre on (KM62.5). Struggle along a washed-out track for a bit; don't worry, it's the right way – or one of them. There are quiet camping spots from here up to the pass, 10km away.

68 (65)   N30° 51.15' W07° 46.86'
Just after some weathered boulders and an axle-flexing section is a **junction** with a fork leading downhill (west) to what looks like a more promising-looking track but down at this point a sign indicates

'Aguim' is back up hill to where you are now. So you've just taken a less-used direct route.

There now begins a precipitous section to a pass – not a good place to be texting at the wheel or 'bars although there are enough flat spots for scenic camps. The sunny southern aspect is popular with Mediterranean-looking plants.

71.5 (61.5)
Head through the pass (2342m) and past some old buildings. The scenery and vegetation suddenly mutates into a duller upland plain. In 500m another sign indicates Aguim.

73 (60)   N30° 53.07' W07° 46.18'
A sign left for Assarag, only around 10km away. Right is for Aguim. The landscape here is bleaker, with fewer flowers but with grass pasture and a smoother track.

79 (54)
With a view of **Jebel Toubkal** to the NW, you top out at **2521m**.

82 (51)   N30° 56.81' W07° 44.30'
You drop down into a grassy limestone basin with horses, sheep and dogs, and streams and karst outcrops.

90 (43)   N31° 00.54' W07° 42.79'
Limestone pass. Drop down and soon spot the radio tower behind the road.

92 (41)   N31° 01.39' W07° 42.52'
The seemingly little-used short cut you passed earlier joins from the left.

96 (37)   N31° 02.17' W07° 42.36'
Join the asphalt with the red radio mast nearby. Turn right for Aguim, about an hour away.

111 (22)
Sour is the name of this village.

132 (1)   N31° 09.76' W07° 27.95'
Junction with the N9 Marrakech–Ouarzazate road in **Aguim**. Turn right, south, for the fuel station.

133   N31° 09.50' W07° 27.78'
TOTAL fuel in Aguim.

MH9   TAZENACHT – TALIOUINE   94KM
November 2008 ~ Yamaha Ténéré

Description
This route, now possibly largely sealed, links a string of villages south of Jebel Sirwa to the north. You follow a road rising towards the route's 1804m high point soon after which you bounce off southwards. Despite the muddy finale I experienced, it's a fun and undemanding route if you feel you've been up and down the N10 to the south one time too many.

Off road
Only the few poorly-drained miles of mud around KM67 might give even a 4WD something to think about, but this was following very heavy rains. Other than that, the route should be easy, even in a **2WD**.

Route finding
The route is Olaffed and maybe even sealed up to KM48. I saw only one or two cars and vans serving the villages. Note that the villages named on most maps and those names found locally rarely match. The map is on pp130-1.

Fuel and water
Fuel in Tazenacht and also Tinfat, a few kilometres after you rejoin the N10. There are plenty of villages and streams for water.

Suggested duration
Half a day will get you through, or a good day out can be had out of Ouarzazate by doing this after Route MS9 and a lunch in Tazenacht. Coming through on MS9 you get a good view of the Jebel Sirwa summit turret which at KM42 is just 12km to the north.

0km   **N30° 34.70'   W07° 12.34'**
Tazenacht SHELL on the north side of town. Take the road north towards Ouarzazate and Marrakech.

8 (86)
Pass sign for Taghdoute to the west.

9 (85)   **N30° 37.91'   W07° 15.92'**
Turn off to the west by a yellow sign onto a new tarmac road. How far it goes, you're about to find out.

23.5 (70.5)   **N30° 36.10'   W07° 23.64'**
Cross a oued and go straight, not NW for Mouidat village. A few kilometres on pass through **Nekob** village from where, despite the paper maps, a goat track leads south to the N10.

30.5 (63.5)
Tamejecht village.

35 (59)   **N30° 36.22'   W07° 30.12'**
Drive through what could be **Tafrent** village and in 500m keep left, not right for Taouzoute. This was a bit washed-out but joined up with the track coming north from town in a kilometre or two.

38 (56)
Aflan Oussir to the north. Continue west, passing the 1804m high point on this route.

41 (53)   **N30° 35.08'   W07° 33.11'**
Aït ou Almane (or some such) followed by another village in 1500m. A couple of hundred metres on, keep left in case it isn't obvious. Olaf is your friend.

46 (48)   **N30° 35.34'   W07° 35.39'**
Reach a main junction and a sign, still only just below 1800m, and turn SW. Right or NE leads to Aït Amrane, Tizgui

and trekking access to the summit of Jebel Sirwa 12km to the north.

48.5 (45.5)
Pass round Assaïs village to the south after which follow a few more villages.

55.5 (38.5)   N30° 32.84'   W07° 39.21'
The top of a 1536m pass with a view to **Azgour** village ahead.

57 (37)
Drop down to cross a river, rise out steeply on the far side and head right and then west.

59 (35)   N30° 32.77'   W07° 40.74'
T–junction. Leave Olaf here and turn south and west for Tinfat and the highway. On the way you pass a couple of **wells**. Right leads 20km to **Zagmouzere** (archway where the track meets the road: N30° 34.13' W07° 51.34') on MH8, a few kilometres north of Taliouine.

67 (27)
Around here, just a short distance from Tamassine, it got very muddy and instead

of Transits, tractors shouldering piles of passengers were serving the villages – but this was a week after exceptional storms in the region. If it looks bad for you too, turn back and take Olaf to Zagmouzere.

69 (25)   N30° 29.37'   W07° 44.12'
Pass by **Tamassine**'s custard and olive mosque.

71 (23)   N30° 28.44'   W07° 44.45'
Arrive at **Tinfat** on the N10 highway by the basic *Café de Siroura* and turn west for Taliouine.

75 (19)   N30° 28.14'   W07° 46.54'
A basic *SHELL* fuel station with not much around to make a worthy end to this route. Carry on west towards Taliouine, crossing a dramatic pass after which the scenery changes noticeably.

94   N30° 31.49'   W07° 53.22'
ZIZMO **Taliouine** westside, a few kilometres before the town centre where there are several auberges. See the website under Updates for a link to accommodation information.

MH10 DADES – IKNIOUN – ALNIF   113KM
November 2008 ~ Yamaha Ténéré

Description
Stuffed in between the Alnif and Boumalne du Dades (or just 'Dades') roads, the **Jebel Sarhro** massif is a geologically distinctive area and I'd not be surprised to learn it possessed its own unique biosphere too. At their heights the ranges claw at the sky in jagged ranks unique to Morocco, evoking southern Algeria's Hoggar at Assekrem. The rock may not all be volcanic but it sure looks igneous.

As you inch away from Iknioun this route takes you as deep into those ranges as you can get on anything with wheels. The track rises up to look out over the gnarliest peaks looming over valleys from which there seems no exit; in moody light calling it all Wagnerian wouldn't be a stretch. And best of all it's a lot easier on your vehicle than its ugly sister MH5, and no less dramatic.

Off road
Unlike adjacent MH5, you won't have to do so much as a foot recce on this route unless it's to work out a good angle for an action shot. **Four-wheel drives**, although maybe not plain old cars, will take it all in their stride and even a big **motorbike** will manage it with a bit of ungainly paddling here and there. Some climbs and hairpins were awkward, but my bike felt particularly over-

loaded when I wobbled through. I predict **mountain bikers** will have a great ride; a gradual tarmac ascent from Dades up to Iknioun, then mostly level or downhill dirt with good camping around KM71, close to a well.

Route finding
The only mistake you might make if you don't have Olaf is possibly taking a wrong turning to a village or farmstead between Iknioun and KM62, but this error soon becomes evident when you're entangled in someone's washing line and fluttering chickens. Beyond KM62 the crutch that has been Olaf is kicked away until you rejoin MH5 at KM81.5, but there are only a couple of alternative turn-offs until you get to the Oued Tazlaft and the regular piste back to Izrou and the highway. The only traffic I saw after Iknioun was a couple of Transits as I neared Izrou. For the **map** see pp122-3.

Fuel and water
Alnif and Dades for fuel. Several wells as indicated.

Suggested duration
I took three and a half hours on a bike going slowly and stopping frequently so a car could manage it in about the same time. Cyclists would have more fun making two days of it.

MH – HIGH ATLAS

0km   N31° 22.06'   W05° 58.88'
SHELL fuel east of **Boumalne du Dades**.

6.5 (106.5)
Turn off south to Iknioun.

44 (69)   N31° 10.29'   W05° 40.43'
Iknioun; tarmac ends. Pass through town. After 1km MH4 comes up from Tinerhir. Fork right on a narrow track past hamlets below the 2712m mass of Amaloun-n-Mansour mountain, the **highest point** in the Jebel Sarhro massif.

56 (57)   N31° 09.86'   W05° 34.81'
At this hairpin go left, back off the pass.

62.5 (50.5)   N31° 10.17'   W05° 30.58'
Just by some rounded rocks Route MH5 comes in from the SE via the **Tizi-n-Ouli Ousir**; you don't want to go there.

68.5 (44.5)   N31° 10.59'   W05° 27.65'
Well (4m) on the right.

71 (42)   N31° 10.67'   W05° 26.34'
Viewpoint to the north after a loose climb to a flat area with space to camp at 1700m.

73.5 (39.5)
Another great viewpoint to the SW this

time over successive jagged ranges. In about 500m fork right.

76 (37)   N31° 09.65'   W05° 25.15'
Cross a oued with a lone palm by a stone farmstead. After the climb ignore the two tracks leading left to a distant building.

80 (33)   N31° 08.36'   W05° 26.25'
Gardens and buildings. You now cross the upper Oued Tazlaft which you'll parallel nearly all the way back to the highway.

81.5 (31.5)   N31° 08.01'   W05° 26.43'
Join Route MH5 at around KM38 and turn left or east for Alnif.

101 (12)   N31° 05.56'   W05° 17.23'
Track forks just after the oued on the east side of **Imi-n-Izrou**: left is the direct route east to the highway just west of Alnif.

108 (5)   N31° 05.35'   W05° 12.63'
Reach the tarmac and turn left for Alnif.

113   N31° 06.75'   W05° 10.34'
ZIZ fuel, **Alnif** west side about a kilometre from town.

TRANS ATLAS: MH11   TWO RIVERS LOOP   306KM
March 2012 ~ BMW F650GS

This 300km scenic drive takes you out along a pair of parallel valleys which are linked at the west end by cresting the 2650m **Tizi-n-Tiherhouzine** which separates them. The lack of traffic makes it an enjoyable way of enjoying the High Atlas with a campervan, bike, whatever.

You're actually following the course of **two major rivers**, the Ziz in the northern valley and the Rheris along the southern stage. They both rise within a few kilometres of each other just east of Agoudal. A couple of hundred kilometres later, once they've each carved impressive **gorges** south of Rich and a narrower canyon north of Goulmima, near Rissani, they almost meet again as they feed the gardens there before diverging once more. Then, just south of Remilia (KM156 MS6), close to the Algerian border and over 400km from their sources, the two rivers finally become one, only to spill uselessly into the northern Sahara where the simoon disperses their combined outwash over the sands of the Grand Erg Occidental.

Besides the starting point, if you spring a leak there's more **fuel** at KM4 just over the bridge at the west edge of Rich, as well as Imilchil, 30km north of the KM116 junction. Agoudal at KM132 will be your best bet for a **feed**, though there are over a dozen smaller villages along the way. The map is on pp116-17.

Description

Start at the *AFRIQUIA* on the N13 and drive the couple of clicks into Rich. At the end of the boulevard or 'town square' turn left, then first right, to the end then left and first right again where the road curves down to the river and the bridge (there's a map on the website). Over the bridge you pass the Ziz and at KM26 get to a junction where you must chose to go up the Ziz or down to meet the Rheris. Up the Ziz river it is then, over to the north side and up into the valley where villages cultivate the slender river banks until the trees thin out as the barren hillsides encroach. At 2160m Outerbate (KM99) is the last village before the Ziz becomes a large stream and you reach the junction at KM116.

Turn left here where a string of villages leads to Agoudal at KM132 and from where you set off towards the 2626m (8618') **Tizi-n-Tiherhouzine** pass to cross the two rivers' watershed and to the south side of the High Atlas. During the time you spend up here it's not impossible to get a twinge of the 'altitudes'. Switchbacks lead down to Aït Hani and the junction (KM168) south to Todra and Tinerhir. You carry on north-east for Assoul to pass through the impressive **gorge** around Imiter; the first real manifestation of the Rheris where stone-lined allotments and pink almond trees border the river hemmed in by the ochre gorge walls under which lie Mesa Verde-like dwellings. With the sun dropping behind you it could all be a treat for the eye.

Amellago junction is KM236 where you can drop down through another amazing canyon to Goulmima (52km), or take the high road 44km across the Amane plain to the KM26 junction for Rich and the *AFRIQUIA* back at KM306. (Note the parallel yellow road via 'Ait B. Akki 'on the RKH map doesn't exist).

TRANS ATLAS: MH12   OUARZAZATE – DEMNATE   158KM
November 2008 ~ Yamaha Ténéré

The main Trans-Atlas crossing is the N9 over the 2260m Tizi-n-Tichka, linking Marrakech with Ouarzazate. Just to the west the less-used R203 climbs over the 2092m Tizi-n-Test, also running from Marrakech.

Chances are you'll use these passes but MH12 makes an obscure alternative. The R307 is a narrow backroad and initially you might count the traffic on the fingers of one hand and wonder why they bothered to seal it all. Perhaps a tarmac capping resists the erosion better. There are few sweeping vistas here; the nature of MH12 is climbing and dropping over two near 2200m crests separated midway by a trough.

Up here **landslides** are frequent, closures not uncommon and road repairs near continuous. You can see why. The road is a platform cut into steep scree slopes that drop straight to the valley floor. Any rain or snowmelt loosens this debris which smothers the carriageway while bigger rocks mash the asphalt. The rubble is never fully cleared and with no Armco or parapet, it's not always the bend swinging jaunt you'll get into on the Tizi-n-Tichka or Test.

Allow about four hours on a bike; any road vehicle including a campervan could manage as long as the rockfalls aren't too bad. The only **accommodation** spotted was a sign for a *gîte* in Tourfine and possibly a café or two, although the villages from here onwards have small shops. On a loaded bicycle it would be quite a two-day work-out, much quieter than the Tichka but not as elevated as MH1 or MH2. The map is on pp116-17.

Description
Start at the top-of-the-hill SHELL in **Ouarzazate's** town centre. Head east on the N10 to Dades passing the huge reservoir now the head of the **Oued Draa** which once flowed right to the Atlantic. At KM18 turn north onto the R307 and head for the hills. Traverse the arid peneplain at the foot of the Atlas then at KM45 just after a village the road turns west and gets stuck in. Soon you're swinging left and right as the road claws up the hillside. Although there's no sign for the 2190m **Tizi-n-Fedrhate** at KM73, this the high point looking down on the sun-blighted village of Tamzerit below.

From here you drop down just as steeply, possibly fording a shallow river where the more temperate vegetation emerges. By the time you reach *Toufrine* village (KM101 at 1625m, *gîte*) across the upper Tessout valley, you're at the bottom of the 'trough'. Traffic becomes marginally more frequent and the road's in better shape.

Soon after **Aït Tamlil** you'll have a view east to the brick-red slopes of Jebel Rhat, while directly to the south the north slope of the Jebel Anghomar (3610m) could be covered in thick snow. The 2059m **Tizi-n-Outfi** crops up at KM119. Now things become a bit lusher and busier; cypress and other pine trees appear, along with more taxi vans. The road drops away steeply and by and by you pass the flashy **hotel** situated by the natural limestone arch of **Imi-n-Ifri**, a local tourist attraction. **Demnate** at KM158 has hotels and ATMs, Marrakech is two hours away.

MH – HIGH ATLAS

MH13 GOULMIMA – TAGOUNTSA TUNNEL (LOOP)   187KM

March 2012 ~ BMW F650GS

Description

A scenic roundtrip on road and dirt from Goulmima that passes through two fabulous gorges carved over the eons by the Oued Rheris which you may meet later on MS6 or MS12. Soon after breaking out of **Goulmima's** enveloping palmerie you find yourself crossing and re-crossing the Rheris before entering an easterly equivalent of the Todra Gorge but without roadside *checheries*. Instead it's the real thing, nomads padding silently along the road, leading their flocks or mule caravans to the markets in town. Then, out of the second gorge past Imiter, you turn into the hills and climb past Tana village and a thin track up the valley to the Tizi Tagountsa pass with an impressive view south-east over the Plaine d'Amane.

The ensuing novelty involves the piste curling under itself through a **tunnel** as it drops steeply from the escarpment. The story goes that the Aït Morrhad were forever ambushing the French columns at the Imiter gorge and so, having practised on the nearby N13 Gorges du Ziz 'Tunnel du Legionnaire' six years earlier, in 1934 they outdid themselves by building a road high over the valley side above the gorge, including the short tunnel where a regular hairpin bend wouldn't fit. Once back down on the plain, a return to Goulmima is optional as there's a great auberge in Aït Youb (KM55).

Off road

The track stage is well drained, stony and slow up to the pass, but a regular car with clearance will manage, as will a big bike with low gearing. The piste stage would not be much fun on a mountain bike.

Route finding

At the start of the piste new tracks supercede Olaf and took some unravelling but no local vehicles venture beyond Tana village up to the pass so from there all is clear. There was no evidence of 'Assel' village depicted on the maps. The route map is on p116-17.

Fuel and water

Goulmima is your only fuel on this route with water from the village wells.

Suggested duration

An easy day's ride or drive.

0km   N31° 40.40'   W04° 57.99'
ZIZ fuel at the SW end of Goulmima. Head NE through town passing shops, cafés and a hotel or two.

2.5 (184.5)
Pass under the arch and reach a round-about. The sign here for 'Amellago 53' is easy to miss from your direction, but turn sharp left here by going nearly round the roundabout and then split right, NW up a

backstreet. Continue along this road until you suddenly burst out of the rustling shade into the dazzling desert and soon cross a branch of the Rheris.

20 (167)
Village of Tadirhoust. If it's already past your bedtime there's a *gîte* here, while at the north end is a fine ruined ksar. Beyond the village is the first of many fords you cross as the gorge walls rise around you

from KM36. You then climb out of the gorge back into the open, but now the desert has given way to a scrubby upland plateau, the Plaine d'Amane.

52 (135)
The tiny hamlet of **Amellago** where the road forks right for Rich and from where you'll return in a few hours. You go left for Aït Youb and the Imiter gorge.

55 (132)   N32° 00.19'   W05° 02.22'
Aït Youb village and *Chez Moha* south of the track (waypoint above). A great place to overnight on this route.

72 (115)   N32° 00.49'   W05° 09.34'
After the Imiter gorge, turn off right just before a bridge. In 100m turn right over a ditch and follow the track NE past buildings. About 800m from the road turn right at a junction (N32° 00.77' W05° 09.18') down to the river and pylons.

74.5 (112.5)   N32° 01.43'   W05° 08.86'
At this junction by a telecom tower I turned right with Olaf to cross the oued and follow trackside pylons.
Straight also leads to the Tana over the same distance and is the newer track.

83 (104)   N32° 04.81'   W05° 06.36'
Whichever track you took, they join up by the fields here close to **Tana** village. Ask directions: "Tagountsa, tunnel?" or head for N32° 05.09' W05° 06.02' by the oued south of the village and follow the track past goal posts and around a low gorge bend at N32° 05.27' W05° 05.78'. The track gets rougher but is now clear.

102 (85)   N32° 09.59'   W04° 56.81'
Having come up the valley passing the odd gnarled juniper tree and sheep corrals you reach the **Tizi Tagountsa** high point (2251m) below a radio mast.
Walk southwards to grab a great view off the cliff edge across the Amane plain 500m below and where your track leads.
That done descend steeply and curl through the short **tunnel** marked 'Route du Tagountsa, Les Troups du Maroc'.

113 (74)
Reach the Rich–Amellago road at **Agoudim** village by a pylon and burned out kasbah. Head SW to Amellago (KM135) and back to Goulmima.

187
Zizmo, Goulmima after a great day out.

MH – HIGH ATLAS

MH14 NEKOB – SKOURA (SARHRO WEST)   137KM
March 2012 ~ BMW F650GS, Yamaha TTR250

Description
Route MH4 may be known as the classic traverse of the Jebel Sarhro massif, but even on the dull, rainy day we had, this version a little to the west is no less impressive and could be a great way of combining a double crossing of this unique range with, as you'll read, some additional branches. Following this route, you rise up, drop right down, rise up again to over 2000 metres and then commence a 40km glide down to the Oued Dades valley.

Off road
It's a well-formed track most of the way, though some steep climbs will warm the clutches of high geared vehicles. A big GS will manage fine in dry conditions and there's nothing to stop an MTB-er either, other than something really good on telly.

Route finding
On the first stage, without St Olaf to guide us, we made a couple of non-terminal errors but from the high point back down it's all clear apart from actually reaching the N10 highway.

There's an alternative, Olaffed start to this route near the N9 junction just before you cross the Oued Draa at N30° 41.72' W06° 10.40' (climb the ridge ahead then turn north) and which meets this route up near the high point at KM46. It's doubtless another great route or could be a fun way of turning back down south from KM46 because as on MH4, the south side of the Sarhro massif is the more dramatic. From KM31 you may choose to follow another alternative route north-west to join Olaf early by following another SD-card filling variation in this fabulous mountain area. For the map see pp116-17.

Fuel and water

Nekob and Skoura for fuel, although at KM100 there's fuel at the east end of El Kelaa some 12km north-east. There's water from the villages and streams.

Suggested duration

We rode it in about six hours so a fairly easy day's ride or drive.

0km   N30° 51.64' W05° 53.31'
AFRIQUIA fuel a couple of clicks west of Nekob centre. Fill her up and head SW down the road.

10.5 (126.5)   N30° 48.77' W05° 58.90'
By a pair of stone blocks, turn right off the N12 and cross 3km towards the hills and the mouth of a oued. Follow the track into the narrow valley, passing villages and their surrounding gardens.

20 (117)   N30° 51.72' W06° 04.59'
Cross the oued by some gardens and climb steeply. In about 8km you top out at over 1600 metres and commence a steep descent back into an adjacent valley.

31 (106)   N30° 53.55' W06° 05.67'
Down in the valley we followed the oued to the NE, although an alternative heads WNW to rise 500m in 9km and pick up Olaf early at N30° 55.31' W06° 08.59'.

38 (99)   N30° 56.25' W06° 04.05'
Leave the oued steeply to the left up a hairpin and begin climbing again. Within a kilometre turn right.

46 (91)   N30° 57.81' W06° 05.26'
Now on a high plateau at nearly 2000m, Olaf joins up from the SW.

48 (89)
Keep left – right is a dead end down to a shepherd's enclosure.

56 (81)
A 2040m high point with cairns though you may have reached this height already. From here it's a less dramatic 40km descent back into the cultivation zone with occasional villages and easy route finding until you near the outskirts of 'Aït Hamoudene'.

95 (42)
Approach a cluster of separate villages close to the N10 road indicated as 'Aït Hamoudene' on old maps and all wrapped around the Oued Dades. It flows between you and the road; your task is to find your way to one of the few bridges across it.

96 (41)   N31° 10.56' W06° 11.79'
At this crossroads turn left, west, and follow the broad track all the way down past buildings, a ruined ksar and over a causeway through some gardens.

97.5 (39.5)
Just after the gardens a narrow red and white bridge crosses the Oued Dades.

100 (37)   N31° 11.49' W06° 12.95'
Arrive at the N10 with a signboard pointing back to where you've come from indicating 'Ikdaren' and 'Aït Gmat'. El Kelaa fuel is 12km east or turn west for Skoura.

137
INOV roadhouse on the east end of Skoura. From here Ouarzazate is about 40km.

SAHARA

Outline of the Sahara region

Though occupying barely a slither of the world's largest desert, the Moroccan Sahara has a strong appeal; the chance to explore an iconic wilderness. And in mid-July, you won't be quibbling over geographical nuances as to whether it's the 'real Sahara' or not.

But we're in Morocco so distances are short. Only a few routes demand an overnight stop, but a night out in the desert is why you're here; if you don't know that yet, you will the morning after.

Another attraction here is that routes are **less rocky** than elsewhere, with small dunes in between the two main sand seas of Chebbi and Chegaga. At its best such terrain is more exhilarating than following a stone-bound track through the hills, although real dunes are another thing altogether: see p162-3.

In the high season outside of summer you won't be alone. Land Rovers shuffle tour groups daily between Zagora and Merzouga so it's worth remembering the Anti Atlas is also largely arid, as of course is the Moroccan West.

MS Routes

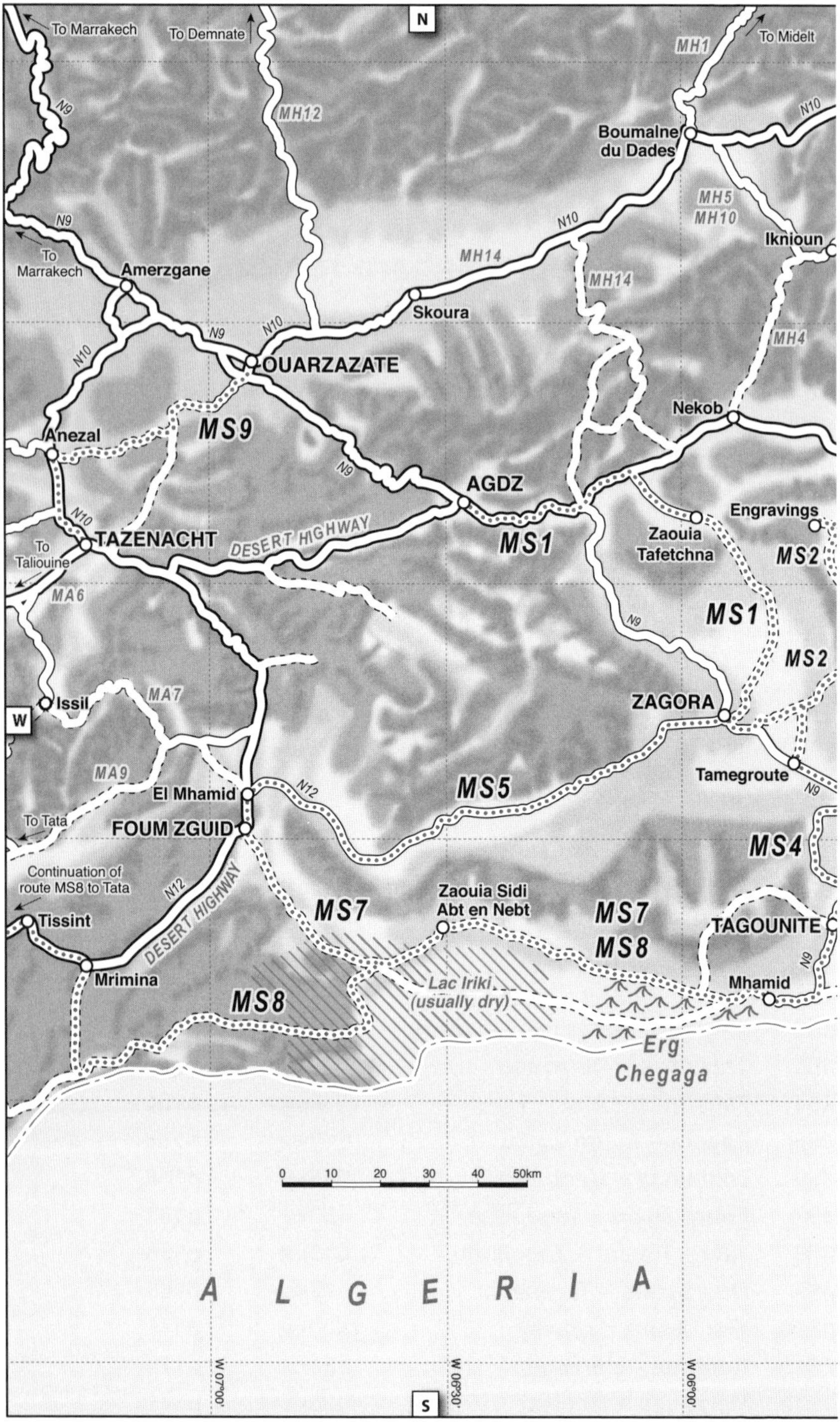
N
To Marrakech
To Demnate
To Midelt
MH1
MH12
N9
N10
Boumalne du Dades
MH5
MH10
Iknioun
N10
MH14
MH14
To Marrakech
Amerzgane
Skoura
MH4
N9
N10
N10
OUARZAZATE
Nekob
Anezal
MS9
N9
AGDZ
N10
DESERT HIGHWAY
Engravings
TAZENACHT
MS1
Zaouia Tafetchna
MS2
To Talïouine
MA6
MS1
N9
MS2
Issil
MA7
ZAGORA
W
MA9
Tamegroute
El Mhamid
N12
MS5
N9
To Tata
FOUM ZGUID
MS4
Continuation of route MS8 to Tata
N12
DESERT HIGHWAY
MS7
Zaouia Sidi Abt en Nebt
MS7
MS8
Tissint
TAGOUNITE
N9
Mrimina
Mhamid
MS8
Lac Iriki (usually dry)
Erg Chegaga
0
10
20
30
40
50km
A L G E R I A
W 07°00'
W 06°30'
W 06°00'
S

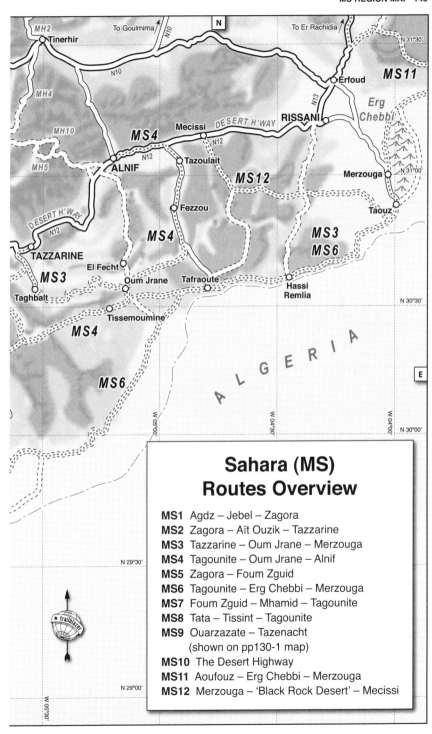

MS1   AGDZ – ZAGORA   121KM
April 2008 ~ Mazda pickup

Description
Passing palm-shrouded villages with their own crumbling ruins and backed by dramatic jebels, the 'Vallée des Kasbahs' N9 road to Zagora is no eyesore, MS1 is an barren desert alternative, following a piste which uses the **Jebel Rhart** as a berm to swing you into Zagora.

Off road
A couple of rocky oued crossings may give a 2WD's exhaust a fright, but other than that it's plain sailing. Bikes have nothing much to fear from MS1. A mountain biker will find this route easy, but at **cycling** speeds it's well worth the scoot down the scenic N9 road sooner or later.

Route finding
Straightforward; there aren't too many wrong directions you can wander off in, but you won't see that much traffic. The route **map** is below.

Fuel and water
Agdz and Zagora for fuel; water from the villages. No wells were noted.

Suggested duration
A couple of hours with an engine; cycling will take at least a full day.

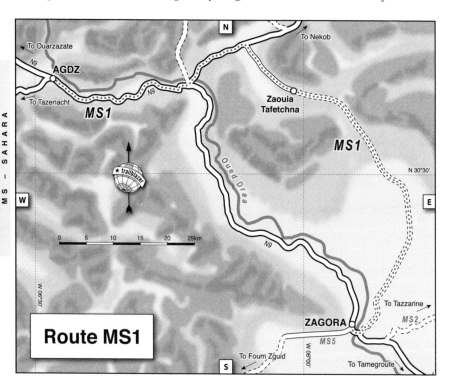

0km   N30° 41.52'   W06° 26.83'
Z1Z south side of **Agdz**. Head south.

28.5 (92.5)
Turn left over the Draa and take the N12
near the alternative start to MH14.

45 (76)   N30° 45.43'   W06° 03.59'
Turn right onto a tar road for Zaouia
Tafetchna crossing a 1178m pass.

59 (62)   N30° 41.08'   W05° 57.18'
The **tarmac ends** by a red tower in **Zaouia
Tafetchna**. Follow a track through town.

60 (61)   N30° 40.77'   W05° 56.61'
Drive in and out of the oued on the edge
of town and then at N30° 40.69'   W05°
56.54' leave the oued to follow a graded
track passing dry stone walls and heading
for a pass.

66 (55)   N30° 40.65'   W05° 53.42'
Crest a 1041m pass. A kilometre later a
track leads off to Tazzarine.

73 (48)   N30° 38.43'   W05° 50.45'
Junction, turn left and cross a stony oued
with a water tower and village ahead
which you pass to your right.

76 (45)   N30° 37.35'   W05° 49.31'
Fork, keep right (straight). The long
escarpment of the **Jebel Rhart** is ahead.

80 (41)   N30° 35.64'   W05° 47.77'
Top of a 924m pass with a rocky descent
and a village far ahead.

85 (36)   N30° 33.67'   W05° 46.29'
Sandy oued with the old kasbah nearby.

85.5 (35.5)
Pass the kasbah of Anoui on the right but
keep heading directly south.

93.5 (27.5)   N30° 30.40'   W05° 43.59'
Gardens and a palmerie on the left.

96 (25)
Various tracks come and go as you
approach a village; keep heading south.

97 (24)   N30° 28.56'   W05° 43.23'
Fork left to avoid the kids or head through
the village if you have no fear.

98 (23)   N30° 28.02'   W05° 43.17'
Rejoin the other track by the water tower.

101 (20)   N30° 26.82'   W05° 43.81'
Fork left here with buildings on the right
and a palmerie soon after; continue WSW.

102 (19)
A track joins from the right; continue SW.
If you happen to be driving in the dark
the lights of Zagora are visible ahead. The
piste gets fast and dusty.

110 (11)   N30° 22.59'   W05° 46.96'
Pass a water tower on the right.

111 (10)   N30° 22.23'   W05° 47.26'
Cross an irrigation canal.

112 (9)   N30° 21.96'   W05° 47.37'
Pass under some pylons and then cross
three fords. At N30° 21.21'   W05° 47.31'
pass gardens and more pylons, cross a
sanded-in canal and pass between walls
and palmeries. At N30° 20.93'   W05°
47.32' continue straight.

115 (6)   N30° 20.31'   W05° 47.88'
Recross the canal and follow the track
past the garden walls.

116 (5)   N30° 20.03'   W05° 48.45'
Cross tracks and pass a sign for a kasbah
hotel, then recross the canal and keep
going straight. At this waypoint you **join
the tarmac**. Turn right and head into
Zagora. At the junction with the Mhamid
road turn right, passing the many
pimped-out kasbah hotels popular with
tour groups.
    By now you'll probably have attracted
a moped posse of touts eager to provide
you with a range of Zagora's many services and products.

119 (2)
Cross the oued and go up the hill towards
the town centre. You level off by some sort
of palace on your left and drive up the
main road.

121   N30° 19.70'   W05° 50.30'
Zagora town centre; C*MH* fuel station on
the main road.

MS2   ZAGORA – AÏT OUAZIK – TAZZARINE   100KM
May 2008 ~ Mazda pickup

Description
This is a great way of getting to the Tazzarine area and is about half the distance of the road though probably no quicker. It starts with a rubbly approach to the pass at KM32 from where the rubble continues until you turn north along the back side of the Jebel Rhart.

All being well you continue up the Ouazik valley to the village of that name. This route then takes you on an excursion to view some prehistoric **rock engravings** a couple of kilometres west of the village, but be warned, unless we missed something, they're not of the calibre you can see in Fezzan, Tassili N'Ajjer or the Gilf Kebir and are about as basic as genuine prehistoric engravings get, no matter what the guidebooks tell you.

With those ticked off, you head back and up a valley east of Aït Ouazik and pick up the sealed Tarhbalt road in time for lunch in Tazzarine.

Off road
Nothing difficult here apart from the shaking you get from the rubble track up to the pass and turn-off north, as well as some oued stages further up. High clearance **2WDs** and **big bikes** won't have kittens.

Route finding
All the current paper maps copy each others' mistake depicting an old French road cutting directly north-north-west up to Tazzarine avoiding Aït Ouazik (where it's even marked). This isn't the route you follow and is so old now it's hard to see any trace of where it once headed over the escarpment at around N30° 34.30' (according to old French maps) or possibly at N30° 33.00' (on Google Earth). Despite all that, there are no navigational issues. MS2 can be an alternative start to Routes MS3/MS5 and MS4 from Zagora.

Plenty of tourist 4WDs shoot through this way, linking Erg Chebbi with Zagora, but on the northern stage up to Aït Ouazik traffic is less common. The **map** is on pp152-3.

Fuel and water
Fuel at each end only and water in a couple of wells and villages along the way.

Suggested duration
Allow yourself a morning's drive or ride if you go via the engravings.

0km   **N30° 19.71'   W05° 50.29'**
Zagora CMH fuel station. Head south down the main road and after 700m turn downhill to the left. Cross the oued and pass through the flashy kasbah resorts and Amerzrou suburb.

2.5 (97.5)   N30° 19.09'   W05° 49.71'
Pass the junction left for Route MS1 up to Agdz and carry on through Amerzrou.

8 (92)   N30° 18.26'   W05° 46.99'
At a sign indicating 'Tazzarine 90km' turn left onto a stony track.

11 (89)
The piste descends to the desert floor as it turns SE.

12 (88)   N30° 19.26'   W05° 45.50'
Cross a small oued and turn east.

22.5 (77.5)   N30° 21.95'   W05° 39.90'
Route MS4 comes up on the right from
Tagounite. There's a **well** 200m away.

24 (76)
Another track joins from the right as your
track turns NE.

31.5 (68.5)   N30° 25.25'   W05° 36.21'
Tracks join from the left as you approach
the **Taflalet pass**. Low vehicles will want
to pick their way carefully up the pass.

33.5 (66.5)   N30° 25.50'   W05° 34.98'
A piste splits to the right – a parallel, possibly less rough route. Soon there's another but in a car it's best to soldier on.

41 (59)   N30° 27.96'   W05° 31.39'
Turn north and cross a bouldery oued
soon.

43 (57)   N30° 28.92'   W05° 31.81'
Parallel track joins from the left with a
sandy creek on the right for a break.

44.5 (55.5)
You pass a graveyard on the left. The track
is hard sand and smooth.

47.5 (52.5)   N30° 31.11'   W05° 32.44'
Pass a **well** about 200m to the left.

52 (48)   N30° 32.99'   W05° 33.80'
Another **well** to the left of the piste and
maybe some nomad tents.

63 (37)
Some palms on left and pink oleanders in
the oued. Track improves shortly.

68 (32)   N30° 39.74'   W05° 37.38'
Nice spot on the right for a camp.

69 (31)   N30° 40.38'   W05° 37.37'
Junction. Turn right for a direct route to
Tazzarine. Straight on for rock art. You
soon pass a football field on the left.

70.5 (29.5)   N30° 41.01'   W05° 37.79'
Join a track by a wall near a 'Stop' sign in
Arabic. Turn left.

71.5 (28.5)   N30° 41.06'   W05° 38.26'
Junction. Go right (although left possibly
leads directly to engravings).

73.5 (26.5)   N30° 41.66'   W05° 39.28'
Turn south towards the next waypoint.
We parked at N30° 41.59' W05° 39.32' and
took a 2km round-trip to the **engravings**
at N30° 41.19' W05° 39.49'.

79 (21)   N30° 40.00'   W05° 37.59'
Heading back past the 'Stop' sign, you
meet the piste coming up from KM69.
Continue through village past an old ksar.

80 (20)   N30° 41.28'   W05° 37.25'
Cross a oued, leave the village and head
into the valley.

84 (16)   N30° 40.65'   W05° 35.14'
Turn NE on a corrugated track with a **well**
on right and pylons nearby.

91.5 (8.5)   N30° 43.42'   W05° 32.13'
Fork right towards a building.

92 (8)   N30° 43.77   W05° 31.73'
Join the tarmac. Turn left for Tazzarine.
Right leads to Taghbalt: Route MS3.

100   N30° 46.92'   W05° 33.80'
It's the ZIZ in **Tazzarine** town centre with
an omelette café opposite. Next?

MS3   TAZZARINE – OUM JRANE – MERZOUGA   228KM
May 2008 ~ Mazda pickup

Description
Taking a low run eastwards to Erg Chebbi, at what was the tarmac's end in
Taghbalt you follow the banks of the large **Oued Taghbalt**, fringed by many
gardens and palmeries until you cross it at KM48 and head out into the barren, stony desert. This track eventually brings you back to the oued and
presently round to the fabled settlement of Oum Jrane from where you drop

down to the white sign at KM76.5 and head directly east to pick up Route MS6 coming up from Tagounite. Here both routes follow the same path through chotts (salt pans) as well as a string of auberges through to Taouz and fuel in Merzouga. You'll see it all along this route, the customary oueds and jebels are joined by wide open and sandy stages culminating with the well-earned spectacle of Erg Chebbi.

Off road
The nastiest section is the notorious couple of kilometres before Remlia at KM139 where you cross the path of **Oued Rheris** just as it prepares to join Oued Ziz. If it's not actually flowing it leaves piles of silt and sand.

Beyond Remlia the track is merely washed-out and hardened mud ruts, crossing chotts by turns smooth and bumpy. At Taouz you rejoin the tarmac to the lone fuel station just north of Merzouga.

Route finding
It took a bit of trial and error to get from Taghbalt to the Oued Taghbalt crossing at KM48 but now we're all the wiser. From there onwards, out in the desert untrammelled by confusing tracks, it's less confusing.

This is one of several satisfyingly long Saharan routes in this area which can be mixed and matched with each other to make your own itinerary, starting or ending at places like Tagounite, Tamegroute, Zagora to the south, or Agdz and Mecissi to the north. The route **map** is on pp152-3.

Fuel and water
Fuel at each end plus whatever they can get away with at Oum Jrane. Water from wells and villages along the route as marked.

Suggested duration
This route is do-able in one long day but why wear yourself out?

0km   **N30° 46.92' W05° 33.82'**
Z*IZ* in **Tazzarine** centre. Head SE out of town for Taghbalt, not right for Nekob and Ouarzazate. Follow the **tarmac to its end** at Taghbalt.

36 (192)
Cross the oued and enter **Taghbalt**.

37 (191)   **N30° 37.75' W05° 21.08'**
At the water tower follow the track around to the left.

37.5 (190.5)   N30° 37.76' W05° 20.93'
Fork, head SE by a sandy oued.

38 (190)   N30° 37.55' W05° 20.66'
Turn left steeply down into the palm-filled oued and cross it.

39 (189)   N30° 37.47' W05° 20.20'
Cross the oued again. On the far side turn left at N30° 37.40' W05° 19.96' below the cliff with a mosque on top.

40 (188)   N30° 37.56' W05° 19.71'
The track climbs out of the oued to a T-junction. Turn left here and follow the banks of the major Oued Taghbalt.

48.5 (179.5)   N30° 38.33' W05° 15.21'
Having followed the oued past fields and gardens, just after a school drop down and cross the wide oued to the north.

49 (179)   N30° 38.53' W05° 15.15'
Drive steeply out of the oued and at this junction go straight not right, though this may be a direct route to KM62.5.

52.5 (175.5) N30° 39.86' W05° 15.47'
T-junction, turn right. A nice descent into
a oued soon follows.

57 (171) N30° 40.78' W05° 13.60'
Fork right.

61 (167) N30° 39.50' W05° 11.77'
A track joins from the left. Soon you arrive
at a village and palmerie.

62.5 (165.5) N30° 39.40' W05° 11.02'
This is possibly a junction heading south
to Oued Taghbalt from KM49. Continue
east over a oued towards telegraph poles.

63 (165) N30° 39.35' W05° 10.56'
Drive through the village of **Taksha**.

64 (164) N30° 39.06' W05° 10.33'
Pass a school on the right with a blue and
yellow map of Morocco on the wall. Soon
you come to a junction. Turn left for Oum
Jrane. The piste runs just above the wide
Oued Taghbalt which you follow more or
less all the way to Oum Jrane.

66.5 (161.5) N30° 38.70' W05° 09.25'
The western outskirts of Oum Jrane.

68 (160) N30° 39.13' W05° 08.39'
Leave the oued via slabs. In 500m a track
joins from the left.

69.5 (158.5) N30° 39.08' W05° 07.85'
A track heads off south. Take it and head
for KM76.5 if you don't want to experience Oum Jrane. Otherwise continue SE
towards some buildings.

71.5 (156.5) N30° 38.39' W05° 06.75'
Oum Jrane west end. From here you have
a chance again to head south to KM76.5 to
avoid the town, or even freestyle SE
towards KM83.

72 (156) N30° 38.53' W05° 06.41'
Oum Jrane town centre; Morocco's
'Timbuktu' and site of a lost Templar
hoard. There are a couple of shops and
offers of **fuel** and **water**. To pick up MS4
to Alnif go to the school at the east end of
town and turn north over the oued.
Otherwise this route heads SE out of
town, following any track towards
KM76.5, below.

76.5 (151.5) N30° 36.40' W05° 05.62'
Crossroads. White sign indicating
'Auberge 5km' pointing back to Oum
Jrane. A route cuts south from here to pick
up MS6 on its way up from Tagounite.

You turn east and follow any east-
bound track. Fast, smooth going; not
something you often get in Morocco.

83 (145) N30° 36.92' W05° 01.92'
A track joins from the left and from here
on it occasionally gets sandy.

97 (131) N30° 37.79' W04° 52.58'
Another track comes in from the left.
There are low hills to east and the track
gets a bit rough following the fast stage.
North of a hillock you cross a sandy oued.

100 (128) N30° 37.92' W04° 51.97'
Another sandy oued beside a hill with
trees to north. Any track east is good here.

104 (124) N30° 38.15' W04° 49.37'
Route MS6 joins from the SW by a three-
stone cairn. There is a long, low sand
dune ahead.

105 (123) N30° 38.23' W04° 48.71'
Cross this dune easily. *Auberge Dinosaur
Kem Kem* lies just to the south. Kem Kem
is the local name for this vicinity.

110 (118) N30° 38.58' W04° 45.45'
A **marabout** (shrine) is just to the north of
the piste and *Auberge Marabout* to the
south beside the sand dune.

112 (116) N30° 38.48' W04° 43.91'
Pass another auberge and blue-grey hills
to the SE: Jebel Zireg with a radio mast on
top. On the far side is Algeria. Start crossing the chott of Lake Maider.

117 (111) N30° 39.98' W04° 41.48'
Signs point to **Tafraoute** auberges nearby;
the piste goes straight ahead over a pass.

119 (109) N30° 40.16' W04° 40.18'
You're over the pass and entering a valley
with a crenellated ridge to the north and
dunes to the south.

130 (98) N30° 40.58' W04° 33.43'
A sandy section starts around here.

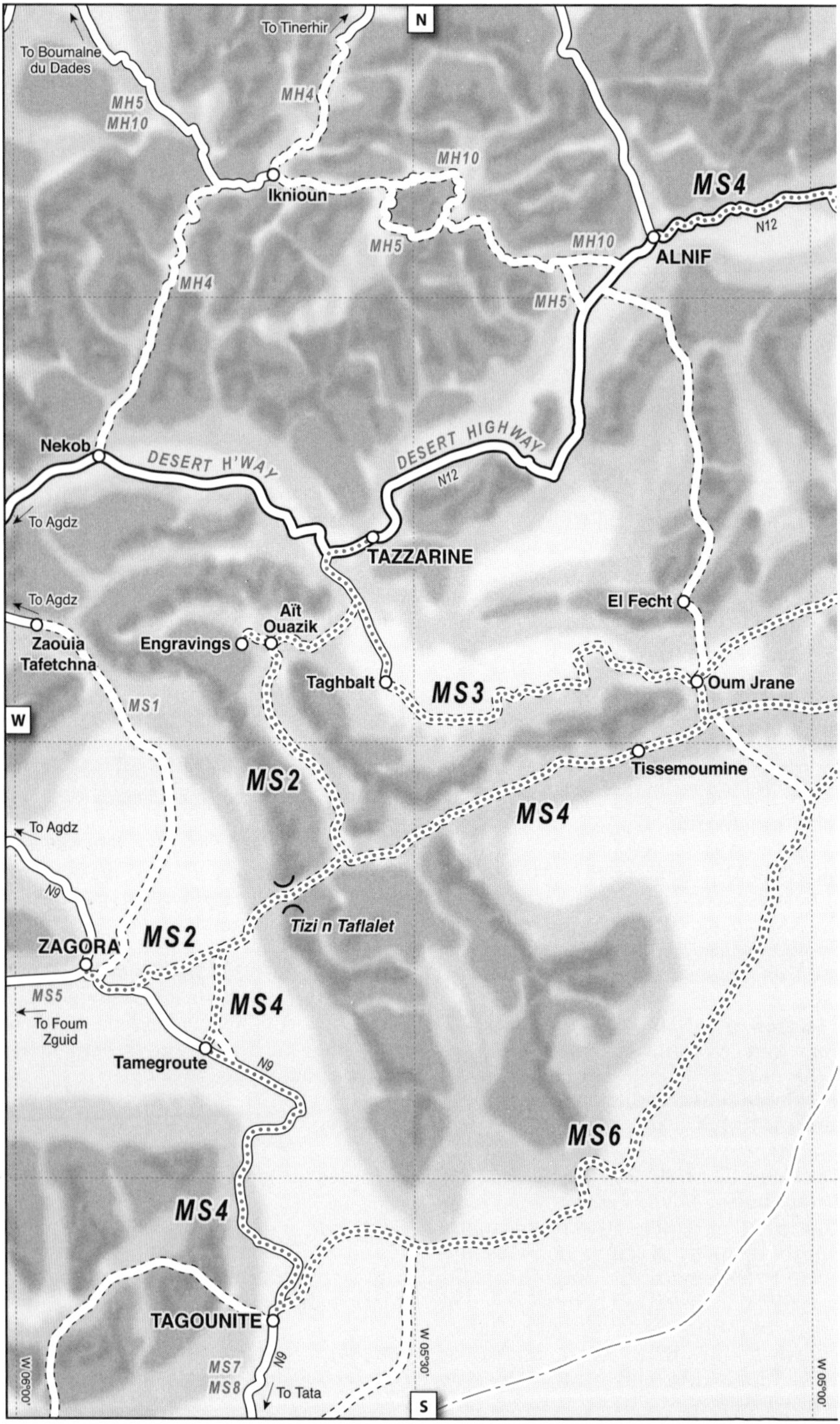
N
To Tinerhir
To Boumalne du Dades
MH5
MH10
MH4
Iknioun
MH10
MS4
MH5
MH10
ALNIF
N12
MH4
MH5
Nekob
DESERT H'WAY
DESERT HIGHWAY
N12
To Agdz
TAZZARINE
To Agdz
Aït Ouazik
Zaouia Tafetchna
Engravings
El Fecht
Taghbalt
MS3
Oum Jrane
MS1
W
Tissemoumine
MS2
MS4
To Agdz
N9
Tizi n Taflalet
ZAGORA
MS2
MS5
To Foum Zguid
MS4
Tamegroute
N9
MS6
MS4
TAGOUNITE
W 06°00'
W 05°30'
W 05°00'
MS7
MS8
N9
To Tata
S

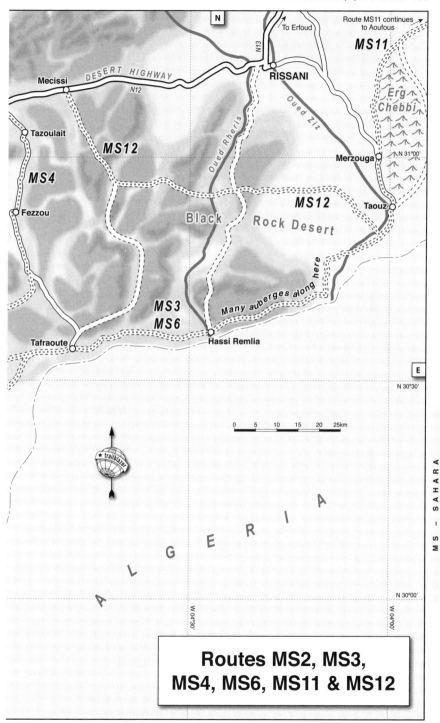

Routes MS2, MS3,
MS4, MS6, MS11 & MS12

134 (94)   N30° 40.18'   W04° 30.89'
A track and a sign point north to connect
with MS12 somewhere. Continue east.

139 (89)   N30° 40.51'   W04° 28.36'
Sign: 'Auberge Oasis Ramlia 7km'. Low
dunes appear ahead. Brace yourself for
many winding tracks around small dunes
and bushes and nastier **feche-feche** powder. Consider lowering your tyre pressures and stay north where the oued is
narrower. Head up to N30° 41.5' or so,
bypassing **Remlia** altogether.

145 (83)   N30° 41.14'   W04° 25.00'
Auberge Ramlia where a piste runs north
40km to MS12. Continue NE on a stony
track. In about 2km there is a junction of
pistes.

149 (79)   N30° 42.39'   W04° 22.98'
Another auberge to the left with its name
in stones on the hill behind. Soon there's a
sandy descent towards a chott. Cross it
following occasional cairns on either side.
From this point you're following the
course of **Oued Ziz** upstream.

162 (66)   N30° 43.05'   W04° 19.10'
Cross various salt pans between stretches
of black stone *hamada* (plain).

166 (62)   N30° 44.68'   W04° 12.74'
Auberges aplenty hereabouts.

173 (55)   N30° 47.7'   W04° 09.6'
At KM171 white-painted cairns lead

down across the Oued Ziz via a village,
but it's simpler to cross the oued here.

176 (52)   N30° 46.70'   W04° 08.65'
A sign indicates 'Auberge Hassi Ouzima
2km' and the 'white-cairn/village' route
joins from the right. Head north occasionally passing twin cairn markers.

184 (44)   N30° 50.62'   W04° 08.16'
Signs for more auberges. A track joins
from the left. Head along the edge of a
dried-mud oued to a junction. Turn left
down into the oued among gravel
hillocks.

194 (34)   N30° 52.42'   W04° 02.58'
Pass along a sunken section of track. Black
hamada follows.

198 (30)   N30° 54.22'   W03° 59.69'
Crest a rise near Taouz with a radio tower
on the left. Tarmac just ahead.

199 (29)   N30° 54.53'   W03° 59.58'
Join the tarmac just north of Taouz. Turn
right for Merzouga.

223 (5)   N31° 06.02'   W04° 01.08'
Merzouga junction. Turn sharp right for
the village (post office, shops and a grubby souk). The auberges are spread out all
to the north.

228   N31° 08.13'   W04° 03.11'
Afriquia fuel station in the desert.

MS4   TAGOUNITE – OUM JRANE – ALNIF   233KM
March 2008 ~ Mazda pickup

Description
One of the better routes in this region, taking a less-used axis towards the
north-east. Once the road section is knocked out, in a car it's a rough, rubbly
start until you're well past the Tizi-n-Taflalet Pass. Here the terrain opens out
as you turn for the north at KM128 towards Oum Jrane, situated along the
south banks of the Oued Taghbalt.

At this point you strike off to the north-east following increasingly thin
tracks which rise over a pass, cross a sandy oued and then the Jebel Atchana
before picking up a more-used piste to Fezzou. Here tarmac leads to the N12
Alnif highway.

Off road

No great hardships lie in store for **big bikes** and only the sandy oued crossing at KM152 will take some gumption in a **2WD**. If you can get past that, then the rest of the piste is do-able, but there are many other alternative ways north.

Route finding

This route crosses a popular zone for tour group convoys shuttling between Zagora and Erg Chebbi, but once you leave Oum Jrane it all gets much quieter. Compared to what's normal in Morocco, the track then gets a bit 'thin' until you rejoin it on the north-north-west-bound stretch to Fezzou village. The map is on pp152-3.

Fuel and water

Fuel at each end or in Oum Jrane at a price. Reaching the N12 at KM214, there's fuel but not much else at Mecissi, 12km east; it's twice that distance to Alnif. There's water from only a couple of wells and of course the villages.

Suggested duration

Even with the highway start and end, it could be a long day to Alnif so consider a desert camp after Oum Jrane if you have the means.

0km   N30° 00.29'   W05° 34.55'
Tagounite ZIZ at the north end of town. Go north over a pass in the Jebel Bani and head into Tamegroute.

46 (187)   N30° 15.25'   W05° 40.09'
A couple of kilometres before **Tamegroute** split right onto a dirt road heading NW to...

47.5 (185.5)   N30° 15.83'   W05° 40.81'
… this point where a wide stony track runs NE near the marketplace arch. Continue NE. When you pass…

48.5 (184.5)   N30° 15.94'   W05° 40.75'
…a blue door on the corner you know you're on the right track out of town.

60 (173)   N30° 21.63'   W05° 40.07'
A junction with Route MS2 coming over from Zagora. Soon you get to a **well** (25m). Another Zagora junction is just ahead (KM22.5 of MS2) before you cross a oued and head for the Taflalet Pass.

64 (169)   N30° 22.54'   W05° 38.52'
Junction with a track from the south.

68 (165)
You're now turning into the pass.

70 (163)   N30° 25.24'   W05° 36.21'
Join another track from Zagora as you head into the **Tizi-n-Taflalet**.

72 (161)   N30° 25.49'   W05° 34.99'
Junction to the south with red painted rocks to probably a better track which meets up at KM81. There is another junction 750m later doing the same thing; your last chance. Great ranges all around.

76 (157)
You start wishing you'd taken that parallel track. In 500m at N30° 27.05' W05° 32.67' a track goes off to the south.

79 (154)   N30° 27.91'   W05° 31.49'
Junction where MS2 goes up to Tazzarine. There's another crossroads in 500m.

80 (153)   N30° 28.04'   W05° 31.19'
Muddy **well** (15m) near some blue-grey rock slabs. You turn SE soon after.

81 (152)   N30° 27.75'   W05° 30.78'
Basic tourist camp with a **well** and tank where you meet the alternative track you wish you'd taken at KM72. Turn left to the east and within 500m (N30° 27.77' W05° 30.49') at a red-marked rock, fork right.

85 (148)   N30° 28.22'   W05° 28.37'
Tracks join from the right.

86.5 (146.5)   N30° 28.37'   W05° 27.48'
Village on the right as the track curves NE through a low pass and joins tracks you may have split from earlier. The trees have been stripped to stumps around here for firewood.

92 (141)   N30° 30.16'   W05° 24.59'
Sanded-up mud-block garden wall of Imi-n-Ou Assit. A kilometre after the village fork left at N30° 30.51'   W05° 23.81' (though the tracks may well join up later).

94 (139)   N30° 30.85'   W05° 23.43'
Fork right; left heads for the hills and, according to the paper maps, may reach KM38 on Route MS3. Google Earth shows the piste as an interesting-looking track following a canyon winding through the jebel about 18km to **Taghbalt**.

96 (137)   N30° 31.26'   W05° 22.40'
Oued by a couple of buildings and a palmerie. At around KM98 the track speeds up for a bit before the valley narrows through a grassy oued – possibly a good lunch spot. Then the valley opens out again and you can speed up. This route continues directly ENE to the way-point below.

110 (123)   N30° 34.56'   W05° 14.90'
Sign for Oum Jrane auberge, 15km. Continue ENE. If you're following Olaf, in about 3km it heads NE for Oum Jrane, probably via a more direct route. If you go this way, aim for KM129.5, the school on the east side of Oum Jrane. Back on this route, you'll notice a lone water tower on the hill to the south. You continue ENE, enjoying a fast smooth track.

119 (114)   N30° 35.42'   W05° 09.56'
The white mosque of **Tissemoumine** is visible directly to the north as you zip along a smooth sand sheet.

126 (107)   N30° 36.40'   W05° 05.62'
White sign for 'Auberge Restaurant Camping Aumjrane, 5km' pointing north. Turn north here. Straight ahead are Routes MS3 and soon MS6 for Merzouga.

129 (104)   N30° 38.33'   W05° 06.18'
The southern outskirts of **Oum Jrane**. For the centre of town head 500m to the NW where you'll find a few stores offering water, maybe fuel and an auberge somewhere.

Despite the kids stampeding towards you, Oum Jrane could be worth a wander. Just to the NW of the town centre the old town sits on a cliff, overlooking the broad **Oued Taghbalt** you're about to cross.

Otherwise head 500m north (KM132.5, N30° 38.62' W05° 06.25') for the pink and yellow school at the east end of town. Pass the school and turn north to cross the oued. Look back left and you can see the old town above the oued.

131 (102)   N30° 38.96'   W05° 06.35
A thin track leads off to the NE. Directly north goes to the more used route to **Rzou** or **El Fecht** and **Aït Sadane**, close to the N12 highway between Alnif and Tazzarine.

Carry on NE. In a kilometre and just before a grassy oued crossing, you'll see the symbol used to define Berber or Amazigh identity marked out on the hill alongside an Arabic word. Continue NE for 2km to pass over a low saddle between two sand-swept hills.

137 (96)   N30° 41.48'   W05° 03.91'
Keep heading NE even though tracks head off to the ENE.

144 (89)   N30° 43.31'   W05° 00.65'
Pass a few sanded-over ruins with several broken drilling cores lying around.

The landscape improves and soon you get to a junction with a track near 5°W that runs between **El Fecht** (about 11km to the west) and **Tafraoute**, KM134 on Route MS6 and about 32km to the east.

147 (84)
Head NE on thin tracks.

149 (86)   N30° 44.55'   W04° 57.97'
Pass a cairn and head ENE towards a ridge.

150 (83)   N30° 44.89'   W04° 56.96'
Tracks converge on a white pile of rocks to mark the crossing point over a sandy oued. 2WDs will struggle here. Carry on

ENE for the pass, passing blue grey marble outcrops.

152 (81)   N30° 45.37'   W04° 55.50'
Sandy pass.

155 (78)   N30° 45.55'   W04° 54.37'
A junction just after a dune, take the left fork to the NE. Right heads about 23km down to Tafraoute, KM134 on MS6. Fork left in 1km with another fork soon.

162 (71)   N30° 48.00'   W04° 50.71'
Join a northbound track on dark grey hamada. In 3km you'll see dunes to the east with trees and greenery. It could be a good camping spot.

171 (62)
Join a well-formed corrugated track.

172 (61)   N30° 52.99'   W04° 52.61'
A track leads off to the NW to follow the Oued Dahmane to a not very obvious

passage through the Jebel Tiberguent at N30° 55.2' W05° 04.7' towards **Ait Sadane**, among other places. You continue north.

175 (58)   N30° 54.21'   W04° 52.98'
Pass the ruins of Tamgannt kasbah and an old graveyard. Radio tower of Fezzou ahead.

179 (54)   N30° 55.85'   W04° 53.90'
Join what's probably a road that continues as a truck route 30km to Tafraoute.

180 (53)   N30° 56.49'   W04° 54.14'
Fezzou village centre.

210 (23)   N31° 11.20'   W04° 57.20'
Join the N12 highway near **Timerzit**, just off the highway to the NW.

233   N31° 06.97'   W05° 09.72'
AFRIQUIA fuel on the east side of **Alnif** with a couple of hotels at the other end.

MS5   ZAGORA – FOUM ZGUID   130KM
March 2004 ~ Mercedes 190D

Description
This valley-bound alternative to Route MS7 follows the north slopes of Jebel Bani and gets easier by the year as the long predicted sealing draws closer. Initially it passes through allotments and gardens supplying Zagora's hotels, and then becomes more remote with a few nomadic encampments.

Off road
Reports of asphalting are premature even if Google Maps confidently displays this route as the 'N12' and in real life the road has been prepared. The latest news is that the road has been almost entirely graded with only around 30 kilometres of stony piste remaining in the middle section.

Route finding
As things stand there will be little confusion with the new prepared road. The **map** is on p165.

Fuel and water
Each end for fuel with a well at KM31 and several gardens in the western half.

Suggested duration
Less than half a day will do you on this one.

0km   **N30° 19.70'   W05° 50.30'**
Zagora *CMH* fuel. Head south down the
main road and passing the ***Hotel de la
Palmerie*** on the right (N30° 19.4' W05°
50.4') turn right by the latest version of the
famed *'Timbuktu 52 jours'* sign) onto a
wide **track**.

8 (122)
Pass the aerodrome and continue west.

25 (105)   **N30° 12.20'   W06° 01.20'**
Pass a small oasis garden to the south
with a few buildings. There is another
oasis 5km further on with ruins.

31 (99)   **N30° 11.40'   W06° 04.80'**
More ruins and gardens and a **well** (8m).
Leave the abandoned village with a well
on your left.

37 (93)
A large pink house north of the track by a
fenced-off field, with a walled palmerie
and orchards a kilometre later.

50 (80)   **N30° 07.00'   W06° 14.20'**
More buildings with fields. The track now
heads NW, away from the Jebel.

56 (74)
Around this point the graded track may
become a stony piste. It heads towards a
oued line and the pink town of Bou Rbia.

60 (70)   **N30° 08.40'   W06° 20.50'**
The stony piste may split. Take the left
fork to the west towards Bou Rbia.

79 (51)   **N30° 03.70'   W06° 30.00'**
Cross the 6° 30' line right by a concrete
ford. From this point a fast, wide track
leads to El Mhamid.

116 (14)   **N30° 08.90'   W06° 47.70'**
You arrive at Smira village. From here in
2004 we drove alongside pylons through a
oued alongside an unfinished road.

124 (6)   **N30° 07.50'   W06° 52.40'**
Arrive at the eastern outskirts of El
Mhamid.

127 (3)   **N30° 07.50'   W06° 52.80'**
Reach the tarmac road in **El Mhamid**. If
reversing this route, the piste begins
opposite a pink building with a white sign
on the oued side in three languages asking you to keep the desert clean.

130   **N30° 05.40'   W06° 52.66'**
Foum Zguid fuel with unleaded at the
north end of town. For more on Foum
Zguid see the end of Route MA9.

MS6   TAGOUNITE – MERZOUGA   245KM
October 2003 ~ MTB (Raf Verbeelen). Part updated 2008 ~ Mazda pickup

Description
Along with seldom-undertaken Route MW6, this route, which also runs close
to the Algeria border, gives a taste of the true Sahara further south. It's also
remarkably smooth under wheel compared to other Moroccan pistes. Along
with an absorbing selection of landscapes, these features make this one of the
most popular desert itineraries in Morocco.

Starting from the Draa Valley you head north around the Jebel Bou
Debgane and then cross a large basin-like formation with Hassi Taffeta well in
its centre. Descending the eastern rim you then cross the Oued Mird to the fort
at Hassi Zguilma and begin the long north-north-east run up to Tafraoute
which is linked by a mine truck route from the north. From here things get a
bit tougher as the track follows a valley to the tricky Oued Rheris crossing then
continues over bumpy chotts to Taouz. After Taouz it's a sealed road run up to
Merzouga by the amazing dunes of Erg Chebbi-i-yay.

This route could be done in a long day, but it would be a shame not to spend at least one night out in the desert. Any number of spots between Tafenna and Taouz would make great overnight stops. Auberges have mushroomed alongside this popular piste, while Merzouga itself has a score of auberges facing Erg Chebbi.

Off road
Rough hairpin tracks lead steeply down into the basin of Tafenna, after which it's remarkably smooth until you get to the small dunes before Tafraoute. The toughest stage is winding in and out of the nasty hummock scrub, dunelettes and *feche-feche* of the **Oued Rheris** just before Hassi Remlia (KM156); **big bikes** may struggle here and even locals in 2WDs avoid it. Beyond Remlia rough chotts lead to Taouz. **Mountain bikers** have this route nailed in a week.

Route finding
It's all Olaffed, otherwise between Tagounite and KM18 you might find yourself blundering around the villages and adjacent irrigation canals, but from this point it's a clear run over Tafenna to Oued Mird where the lower loop that goes south of Jebel Bou Debgane joins this piste.

The long smooth run from Hassi Zguilma fort (KM56) up to the eastward turn of the piste has a few turn-offs, so keep an eye on your bearing. 'Agoult' on the paper maps doesn't appear to exist, but near here twin tyre markers lead you north-east over a featureless gravel plain, a few low dunes and a chott (the 'Lac') to Tafraoute.

From Tafraoute (missing from paper maps) to Hassi Remlia and the auberges around Ouzina is straightforward. From Ouzina tracks follow the course of the Oued Ziz to Taouz. The **map** is on pp152-3.

Fuel and water
Fuel each end and possibly Tafraoute and Remlia, from drums. Water from villages and wells along the route. The longest waterless stretch is from the fort at KM56 to Tamassint, KM109.

Suggested duration
Do-able in a long day but a night out in the desert or at one of the many auberges in the latter half is the way to go.

0km   N29° 59.38' W05° 35.08'
Tagounite ZIZ fuel on the north side of town. Drive south into the town centre for 1.5km and turn left at N29° 58.6' W05° 35.0' opposite the military barracks. You may see a very faint sign for 'Blida' (a village marked on the Michelin map) on the east side of the main street. This **track** leads along canals to a palmerie.

3.5 (241.5)
Walled village on both sides of the track. Heading ESE. When you emerge from the

village you may pass a sign for 'central Tagounite' as you continue through the palmerie.

7 (238)
A scrubby plain and 500m later the track turns almost north with the mass of **Jebel Bou Debgane** to the east. The track soon passes two concrete blocks and runs alongside a palmerie to the right.

9 (236)   N29° 59.00' W05° 30.80'
Blida. Having crossed a canal with sluice

gates where the track turns ENE and then a major ditch, you arrive at a junction with a small sign on a lamppost indicating 'Blida'. Turn left towards the red and white mast. Pass the mast on the left and a school on the right and continue through town towards the Jebel.

In a kilometre you reach a junction. Turn left and continue north with the Jebel to your right passing white cairns.

12 (233)
Fork right. After 1500m you pass the village of Aissfou on the left with its long palmerie. Continue NNE.

19 (226)   N30° 03.40'   W05° 29.00'
Junction. Turn right and continue NE. The track gets sandy and bumpy, veering ENE.

23 (222)   N30° 04.50'   W05° 26.70'
A track joins from the WNW coming from Zagora – our track now turns ESE.

28 (217)
The wide, smooth track starts to rise up the hamada and onto the Tafenna ridge.

31 (214)
Crest the ridge at 856m. The descent is rough. Soon you see the track cutting across the smooth flat centre of the 'basin' to the opposite ridge. At KM34 is Hassi Tafenna **well** (N30° 04.5' W05° 20.2').

38 (207)
Climb up the less rough eastern rim.

41 (204)
Hut on the right near the crest of the ridge (951m) which appears after 300m. From here a view stretches east over distant plateaux. Begin a gradual descent over the next 3km.

45 (200)   N30° 06.60'   W05° 15.10'
Junction with a cairn on the hamada between the ridge and Oued Mird. Right leads south of Jebel Bou Debgane back to the Draa valley.

Take the left fork NE across the hamada with a line of acacias running parallel to your left.

50 (195)   N30° 07.70'   W05° 12.40'
Cross a thicker band of trees as a track joins from the right. In less than a kilometre you get to some buildings and a small palmerie on the left of the track, with a pole marker on the right. The track becomes sandy for a few hundred metres.

53 (192)
Veer NE towards an escarpment.

56 (189)   N30° 09.40'   W05° 09.90'
Hassi Zguilma; a pink fort and checkpoint on a hill. Track leaves to the NNE.

60 (185)
Track joins from the left. Smooth going.

66 (179)   N30° 13.90'   W05° 06.80'
Tracks diverge. Take the left fork NE with cone-shaped hill to your right.

70 (175)   N30° 15.70'   W05° 05.40'
Track splits, keep left heading towards an Ayers Rock-like monolith. Soon more monoliths become visible ahead and to the NNE. Some corrugations.

75 (170)
A track joins from the right; having passed the red plateaux to the east, another track joins from the right 4km later (N30° 18.6' W05° 03.3').

81 (164)
Distinctive slab cairn with a hole, on the right of the piste. In a kilometre the track cuts across the piste with two white-painted cairns on the left. Both could mark the junction of a direct route north to Oum Jrane.

84 (161)   N30° 21.80'   W05° 00.90'
Could be a well on the right. The track becomes stonier with scrub and trees to the right.

90 (155)   N30° 25.50'   W04° 59.50'
After climbing a track joins from the right.

95 (150)   N30° 27.40'   W04° 59.20'
Reach a pair of tyres on either side of the now corrugated track. You see more tyre markers as the track heads NNE across a featureless gravel plain.

98 (147)   N30° 29.10'   W04° 58.40'
Two more tyre markers, another single
tyre at KM100 and another pair on a slight
rise to the left at KM102. Continue NE
across the gravel plain, aiming for tyre
markers ahead.

112 (133)   N30° 34.70'   W04° 53.00'
Two tyre markers on the right. with more
ahead and cairns from KM118.

121 (124)   N30° 38.15'   W04° 49.37'
Join MS3 and head east towards dunes.
The going now gets soft as you cross a low
dune (plenty of tracks) and continue over
the soft undulating sand.

122 (123)   N30° 38.23'   W04° 48.71'
Cross this dune easily on an improved
surface. *Auberge Dinosaur Kem Kem* lies
just to the south.

127 (118)   N30° 38.58'   W04° 45.45'
A marabout (shrine) is just to the north of
the piste and *Auberge Marabout* to the
south, beside the sand dune.

129 (116)   N30° 38.48'   W04° 43.91'
Pass another auberge and blue-grey rubble hills to the SE: Jebel Zireg with a radio
mast on top. Algeria lies beyond. Soon
you start across the seasonal chott known
as Lake Maider.

134 (111)   N30° 39.98'   W04° 41.48'
Signs for **Tafraoute** auberges. A mine
track leads north to the N12 via Fezzou
and there's a way through to MS12 too.

136 (109)   N30° 40.16'   W04° 40.18'
You're over the pass and in a valley with a
crenellated ridge to the north and dunes
to the south.

147 (98)   N30° 40.58'   W04° 33.43'
A sandy section starts around here.

151 (94)   N30° 40.18'   W04° 30.89'
A track and a sign point north for the Col
Mharech. Continue east on a bumpy piste.

156 (89)   N30° 40.51'   W04° 28.36'
Sign: 'Auberge Oasis Ramlia 7km'. Low
dunes appear as tracks wind around
small dunes, bushes and nastier powder.
    On big, heavy bikes it could be hard

work. Consider lowering tyre pressures
and stay well north towards the gap in the
range where the oued is narrower.

162 (83)   N30° 41.14'   W04° 25.00
Auberge Ramlia. A piste goes north 40km
to eventually cross MS12 at around KM71.
You head NE on a stony track.

166 (79)   N30° 42.39'   W04° 22.98'
An auberge to the left. Soon there's a
sandy descent towards a dry lake bed or
'chott'. Cross it following occasional
cairns on either side.

179 (66)   N30° 43.05'   W04° 19.10'
Cross various chotts between stretches of
stony hamada. Soon there are several
auberges by the trackside.

188 (57)   N30° 45.87'   W04° 10.39'
It's another auberge. You can cross over to
the south side of the Oued Ziz, but it's
simpler to continue ahead about 2km, and
cross at N30° 46.7' W04° 09.6'.

197 (48)   N30° 48.66'   W04° 08.23'
Occasional twin cairns hereabouts.

200 (45)   N30° 50.15'   W04° 08.44'
Soon the track forks but either fork will
do. More signs for various auberges.
Another track joins from the left. Head
along the edge of the oued.

202 (43)   N30° 50.69'   W04° 07.35'
Junction. Turn left into the oued.

211 (34)   N30° 52.42'   W04° 02.58'
Sunken track. Black hamada follows.

215 (30)   N30° 54.22'   W03° 59.69'
Crest a rise by Taouz with a radio tower
on the left. The tarmac is just ahead.

217 (28)   N30° 54.53'   W03° 59.58'
Join the tarmac at Taouz and go north.

240 (5)   N31° 06.02'   W04° 01.08'
Merzouga junction. Turn right for the village with shops and a grubby souk. The
auberges are all to the north.

245   N31° 08.13'   W04° 03.11'
An *AFRIQUIA* fuel station in the desert.

ERG CHEBBI

The good thing about the dunes of Erg Chebbi near Merzouga is that they look like something right out of the movies; the problem with this pint-sized sand sea is there's nowhere else like it in Morocco so it's been well and truly discovered. It is the grand terminus of Morocco's Axis of Tourism.

For many people Chebbi exemplifies the magical Sahara and they come here in their droves to walk, camel, ride and drive the sands. Moroccans have a saying 'See Ouarzazate and die' but many tourists would settle for seeing the dunes of Chebbi before giving up the ghost. The only other option, Erg Chegaga south of Zagora, lacks Chebbi's rosy hue and supine forms which see it glow so evocatively at sunset.

Erg Chebbi is actually one of the tiniest 'ergs' or sand seas in the Sahara, just seven kilometres wide by 30-odd long from north to south. Just over the border the Grand Erg Occidental in north-west Algeria runs for hundreds of kilometres in all directions – check out the comparative scale on online mapping satellite imagery. Despite the estimates and gross exaggerations you'll read or hear about, the highest dune here is just 150 metres above the desert floor. At Chegaga it's 100 metres.

On the Erg

Arriving at the Erg and never having driven or ridden in desert dunes before, for many off-roaders and particularly bikers, riding to the top of the tallest dune is their goal. On a light, unloaded bike it's do-able and easiest coming up from the east side. Many try blasting up any old way before getting bogged down, exhausted from falls or hurting themselves.

The nature of Erg Chebbi with its **small dune formations** actually makes it extremely challenging to drive on. Like the northern Grand Erg Oriental in north-eastern Algeria and Tunisia (Route A1 in *Sahara Overland*), these small dunes have no pattern and are like trying to jet-ski up and down over a stormy swell. Huge dunes develop a pattern of corridors which readily form between them and are much easier to negotiate.

Erg Chebbi may be small but in my experience it's not the type of terrain any normal Saharan piste would cross unless there was no choice, so be warned. To take a rental 4x4 into the dunes with no sand mats or means of re-inflating the tyres is asking for a recovery which may cost you dearly; the canny Merzougans know all about that.

MS7   FOUM ZGUID – MHAMID – TAGOUNITE   163KM

April 2008 ~ Mazda pickup

Description

Many people see this route as a handy link between the sealed roads at Mhamid and Foum Zguid; the road via Agdz is twice as far but actually a great drive. For the first half this route follows the Jebel Bani to the north, passing the usually dry chott of Lac Iriki. This is predominantly a rough, rocky trail that, depending on your suspension and how you slept last night, can make you wonder why they don't just seal it.

The nearby **dunes of Chegaga** are the main attraction. Your transit will be much more fun if you **get off the main track to the south**, bomb across Iriki and head into the small dunes as far as you like for a bit of exploration and experimentation.

With package tourists overnighting in the bivouacs of Erg Chegaga, this route is very popular and as a result nomad kids may desperately wave you down with empty water jugs from around KM75 onwards, but rest assured there are wells out here.

Driving or riding over virgin sand dunes is an invigorating and amazing experience, rather like skiing, but is also risky. While the sand may look soft to fall on, it's not. A bike cartwheeling behind you or the insides of your rolling car aren't either. Take your time and think about what you're doing and the consequences of getting stuck, particularly in a bowl or 'vortex'. Once a car has dropped into even the shallowest bowl, even with plates, there's no room to get enough momentum to drive yourself out.

As many know, the key to improving traction on soft sand is **reducing tyre pressures** to 1 bar (14.5psi). It's quite amazing to see where a car can go at these pressures – the tread pattern is comparatively immaterial. A light bike can manage with 0.7 bar or 10psi. As with a car, pressures this low transform a bike's handling and make dune riding **safer and more predictable** because you're able to go slower without getting bogged and so have more time to make decisions.

On dunes **momentum** is required to stop yourself sinking but caution is also essential so as not to shoot off a crest. Then there are challenges with perspective in the featureless glare of high sun angles or with the sun behind you. In these conditions it's quite

No one in their right mind would drive over dunes like these, but many try. © P. Hartleb

easy to ride off the crest without even seeing it. There's also the unpredictable hazard of other users: quads, bikes and 4x4s bombing around on a busy day. Some lose their heads here and end up rolling or mashing their vehicles. And with all these users comes the rubbish left by the irresponsible.

And finally there's also the conflict of tearing about while others attempt to commune less conspicuously with the sands. Give them some space and confine your dune-bashing further south to the lower dunes or go round the east side.

Off road

In a car you have to crawl along at walking pace at times. Coming through the dunes lining the Oued Mhamid at the end of the piste section you'll probably need **four-wheel drive**, while **bikers** will need to stand up and get pro-active. Lac Iriki might be considered an inland delta of the Oued Draa and although it rarely fills up, it frequently gets soggy. In a 4WD it's something to consider. On an **MTB** this route would be hard work away from the lake bed sections.

Route finding

Side tracks come and go but route-finding is all too clear with the Jebel always to the north and either stone cairns or a rubbly track that you can't miss. At KM104 maps show a piste following the curve of the Jebel Bani all the way to Tagounite; see KM263 of MS8. The **map** for this route is over the page.

Fuel and water

Still Tagounite for fuel, with water at wells and encampments along the route.

Suggested duration

Easily done in a day. Overnight camps may attract a nomad or two.

0km　　　　**N30° 05.40'　W06° 52.66'**
Foum Zguid fuel at the north end of town
For more see the end of MA9. Head south.

3 (160)　　　**N30° 04.00'　W06° 52.00'**
Head out of town and after a kilometre
turn left, SSE **onto the piste** heading for a
pink fort.

4 (159)
Fort with possibly a passport check. Continue SSE on corrugations. Saw-tooth
ranges to the south.

13 (150)　　　**N29° 57.90'　W06° 49.80'**
Fork left, SE at a wide oued. In 700m exit
the oued as a piste joins right.

21 (142)
Fork. The main corrugated track curves
right heading towards Jebel Hamsailikh.

29 (134)
Pass north of the mesa and in 500m cross
a sandy oued with grassy tussocks.

30 (133)
Back on a stony hamada heading SSE
towards Oued Mdaouer.

35 (128)　　　**N29° 50.70'　W06° 40.30'**
Fork left ENE. Dunes ahead.

37 (126)
Smooth going then cross a bumpy clay-
pan and oued (KM39.6). Cairns.

41 (122)
Sandy oued crossing. Continue NE.

47 (116)　　　**N29° 52.75'　W06° 34.60'**
Pink fort checkpoint from where a smooth
track crosses the lake to Zaouia Sidi Abt.

65 (98)　　　**N29° 58.20'　W06° 26.00'**
Zaouia Sidi Abt en Nebt. A few buildings
and the mausoleum. In a kilometre leave
the village ESE on a stony track. A bone-
shaking 30km stage begins.

72 (91)　　　**N29° 58.57'　W06° 21.98'**
Pass a village and in a kilometre fork left.

77 (86)　　　**N29° 57.89'　W06° 19.17'**
Checkpoint on a hill, a **well** 30m south.

80 (83)　　　**N29° 56.91'　W06° 17.84'**
Junction; go straight, not right.

97 (66)　　　**N29° 54.29'　W06° 08.48'**
Forking right here might be better.

99 (64)　　　**N29° 53.07'　W06° 07.23'**
Junction; a piste goes south into the dunes
and a fort. Soon you pass an auberge. The
stony section is over.

104 (59)
A junction for the track to Tagounite.
Right for Mhamid.

106 (57)　　　**N29° 52.55'　W06° 03.54'**
Cross the deep channel of Oued el Rharg.

111 (52)　　　**N29° 52.19'　W06° 00.54'**
Junction. A track goes NE to Tagounite
(52km) via a gap in Jebel Bani. For
Mhamid continue SSE. It may help to
stick KM138 in the GPS and press 'Go to'
following the best track.

124 (39)　　　**N29° 50.22'　W05° 53.02'**
Metre-high dunes appear near Mhamid.

127 (36)　　　**N29° 49.80'　W05° 51.39'**
Work your way along generally heading
east towards KM138.

138 (25)　　　**N29° 50.25'　W05° 45.24'**
After a very sandy 100m the dunes end.
Carry on SE towards a water tower.

139 (24)　　　**N29° 49.91'　W05° 44.75'**
Join the main piste from Mhamid.
Buildings ahead. The northern arc you've
taken may have missed the worst of the
sand.

142 (21)　　　**N29° 49.68'　W05° 43.72'**
Join the tarmac on the edge of Mhamid,
passing a few cafés and shops.

143 (20)　　　**N29° 49.49'　W05° 43.21'**
Mhamid roundabout. The village is a
staging point for bivouacs in Erg Chegaga
with wall-to-wall nomad crafts and touts.

163　　　　**N29° 59.38'　W05° 35.08'**
Tagounite ZIZ. With no 'things to see and
do' as in Tamegroute up the road, you can
walk around Tagounite without disguise.

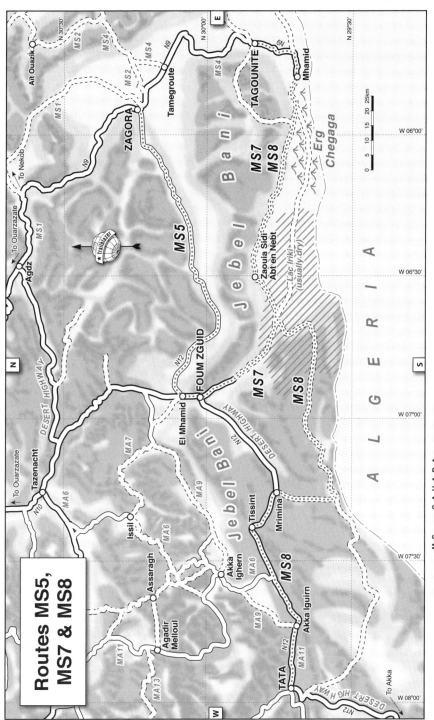

Routes MS5, MS7 & MS8

MS8   TATA – TISSINT – TAGOUNITE   315KM
April 2008 ~ Mazda pickup

Description
West of Tata as far as Zag on the closed road to Smara, the borderlands are a
restricted area. (Routes MW1 and MW6 skirt round this region.) Venture south
of the Desert Highway here (and maybe even a little *east* of Tata) and you'll be
spotted and escorted back to the road. However, lately tourists have managed
to follow pistes *south* then *east* of Tata to pick up MS8 at around KM109 while
covering about the same distance. (It's all Olaffed or assemble your own key
waypoints from Google sat imagery). It starts 8km south of the fuel at KM0
below. Turn left or south-south-east – the tar ends in 7km at N29° 37.63' W07°
56.78'). Taking this start plus the detour north-east at KM263 will add up to a
substantial 300km piste.

Otherwise, this route picks up a former **Dakar Rally** track which, like
Route MW2, is as well marked as any piste in Morocco. It works its way north
of the fringes of the **Oued Draa** which marks the border hereabouts and then
moves north towards the mud flats of **Lac Iriki**. At a pink fort you then join
Route MS7 for the run into Mhamid or the direct route to Tagounite.

Off road
Big bikes will manage fine but whatever your vehicle it's better not alone.
Though not on this route, the **dunes of Chegaga** are not far away and a worthwhile deviation. This route, or versions of it across Lac Iriki, is popular and
although I saw no other tourist cars until well past Zaouia Sidi, chances are
you will.

Route finding
It's a seemingly complex meander along the piste but is initially very well
marked with Dakar cairns up to the pink fort at KM199 and largely Olaffed
too. The **map** is on p165.

Fuel and water
Fuel only at each end or possibly Mhamid if you ask around. Once on the piste
the only well spotted was around KM228.

Suggested duration
Just about do-able in a day but much better to camp out in the desert.

0km   N29° 44.31'   W07° 58.42'
Tata fuel on the south side of town. Head
into town and turn right to follow the
wide boulevard heading east for Foum
Zguid. For hotels here see end of MA6.

49 (266)   N29° 50.33'   W07° 29.99'
Pass the turn off north for Route MA6 and
MA11 coming down from Akka Ighern
and Tazenacht.

70 (245)   N29° 54.42'   W07° 19.12'
Frequent checkpoint in **Tissint** as the road
bends sharply right. A café on the bend
and stores down the road.

87 (228)   N29° 49.53'   W07° 12.24'
Just before Oued Mellah and a warning
roadsign, **turn south onto a track** which
soon becomes corrugated. There are
Dakar Rally balises every 10m or so. Olaf
runs to the west and soon joins up.

104 (211)   N29° 40.69'   W07° 13.80'
An observation post is visible on the hill
to the SE and an army base on the other
side of a oued. What you're about to do is
loop south around the base, turn east and
north again to KM113.

108 (207)   N29° 38.93'   W07° 13.62'
Having crossed a side oued near the base,
you pass beneath the scrutiny of another
observation post on a hill to the east.

109 (206)   N29° 38.58'   W07° 13.52'
Cut a corner on Olaf by heading SE to a
cairn on a hill about 1km away. The piste
from Tata joins around here.

110 (205)   N29° 37.85'   W07° 12.84'
Rejoin Olaf and head NE with cairns
every 5m or so.

111 (204)   N29° 38.46'   W07° 12.31'
Fork right following cairns on mounds.

111.5 (203.5)   N29° 38.79'   W07° 12.28'
Oued Mellah just before it joins Oued Draa
on the border. Cross the oued to the east.

112.5 (202.5)   N29° 39.03'   W07° 11.96'
Leave the oued and err to the NE passing
over a patch of soft grey sand.

113 (202)   N29° 39.43'   W07° 11.80'
Top of a low pass, pointing east. Follow
the track east past Dakar mounds.

118 (197)   N29° 39.33'   W07° 09.49'
Cross a broad chott marked with cairns.

121 (194)   N29° 39.94'   W07° 07.50'
A corrugated track. Observation post on
the hill 500m to the SE.

125 (190)   N29° 41.42'   W07° 06.16'
Two rocks on either side of the track with
'CS' painted on them. A nice passage fol-
lows; could be an OK camp spot.

131 (184)   N29° 40.97'   W07° 02.87'
Track rises out of a oued onto a stony
hamada. Head NE.

132 (183)   N29° 41.64'   W07° 02.35'
The track drops into a side oued, does a
squiggle and then continues NE over
another oued.

137.5 (177.5)   N29° 43.49'   W07° 00.00'
Cross 7°W on hamada (a chance to position yourself on a map with gridlines).
Nothing to south, jebel to the north and
the Iriki chott ahead.

146 (169)   N29° 43.90'   W06° 55.67'
Heading east you cross a second north-
south track with another in 1km. Soon
small dunes appear.

153 (162)   N29° 43.41'   W06° 50.92'
A piste marked on some maps and Olaffed
heads SE but stops. Continue east.

158 (157)   N29° 43.50'   W06° 48.12'
Track rises over a small pass with dunes
to the south; possibly another nice camping spot.

168 (147)   N29° 43.21'   W06° 41.72'
Jebel Zguilma visible not far to the south.

174 (141)   N29° 43.23'   W06° 38.37'
The track now turns NE and soon even
NNW for a bit as it crosses western Lac
Iriki.

180 (135)   N29° 45.05'   W06° 35.52'
Key point. Having crossed a oued you
reach a fork. Take the route with cairns to
NNW. East leads onto Lac Iriki and
Chegaga dunes to rejoin this route at
around KM251, a distance of about 60km.

184 (131)   N29° 47.59'   W06° 36.87'
Bump along the western edge of the
lakebed heading NNE with some sandy
patches. After a while pass flat-topped
Jebel Nouhsour to the west.

190 (125)   N29° 49.64'   W06° 38.12'
Sandy passage over a oued. If you keep
up speed here there's no need to air
down.

192 (123)   N29° 50.47'   W06° 37.76'
Having picked up a track joining from the
left you now curve NE then east following
Dakar mounds across the lake.

195 (120)   N29° 51.51'   W06° 35.85'
Leave the lake bed and head through a
pass with a shack on the left and a tyre
marker soon after.

MS – SAHARA

197 (118)   N29° 52.49'   W06° 34.73'
Tracks join from the right as you head north towards the fort.

199 (116)   N29° 52.75'   W06° 34.60'
Pink fort and checkpoint. From here a smooth track runs to Zaouia Sidi Abt.

217 (98)   N29° 58.20'   W06° 26.00'
Zaouia Sidi Abt en Nebt. A few buildings, a mosque and the mausoleum (zaouia). In 1km leave to the ESE over a stony track, a bone-shaking 30km stage that can take up to two hours.

224 (91)   N29° 58.57'   W06° 21.98'
Pass a village with an '*Ecole Nomade*'.

229 (86)   N29° 57.89'   W06° 19.17'
Unmanned checkpoint on a hill with a **well** to the south. In 3km go straight, not right.

249 (66)   N29° 54.29'   W06° 08.48'
Forking right here might be better.

251 (64)   N29° 53.06'   W06° 07.23'
Junction; a piste runs SW to a fort and tourist dune camps. Pass an auberge soon. Stony section mostly over.

256 (59)   N29° 52.67'   W06° 04.51'
Early junction for the piste heading to Tagounite. Right is for Mhamid.

258 (57)   N29° 52.55'   W06° 03.54'
Cross the Oued el Rharg. Directly south of

here at N29° 50.95' W06° 02.65' there may be a **waterhole** in the oued.

263 (52)   N29° 52.19'   W06° 00.54'
Junction with a track splitting NE to Tagounite via a gap in Jebel Bani at N30° 03.12' W05° 44.42' and overall the same distance. For Mhamid head SSE. It may help to stick KM290 in the GPS and just 'Go to' on the best track.

276 (39)   N29° 50.22'   W05° 53.02'
Metre-high dunes begin here as you near Mhamid.

279 (36)   N29° 49.80'   W05° 51.39'
Work your way along generally heading east towards KM290.

290 (25)   N29° 50.25'   W05° 45.24'
After a very sandy stage you get to the corner of a grubby-looking campsite. Carry on SE towards town.

294 (21)   N29° 49.68'   W05° 43.72'
Join the tarmac in Mhamid, passing a few cafés and touristy shops.

295 (20)   N29° 49.49'   W05° 43.21'
Mhamid roundabout surrounded by all the fruits of desert tourism. There are plenty of plush, palm-shaded kasbahs a few kilometres up the road.

315   N29° 59.38'   W05° 35.08'
Tagounite ZIZ fuel station on the north side of town.

MS9   OUARZAZATE – TAZENACHT   77KM
November 2008 ~ Yamaha Ténéré

Description
Not really a true desert route but a handy short cut from Ouarzazate through low hills towards the Foum Zguid, Sirwa or Anti Atlas routes. It sets off following a road to the turn-off at KM25. Soon after this point and from the 1612m high point and onwards you get great views of the Sirwa massif.

Off road
The inter-village section between Imidar and Tisslite gets a bit rough but nothing a **4WD** or even a loaded adv bike can't manage. On a **mountain bike** it would be a pretty full day's ride as the final road section from near Anezal down to Tazenacht is hilly and twisty so not a great place to be riding in the dark. If you need it, there's small *gîte* in Anezal.

Route finding

Out of Ouarzazate the road that cuts through directly south via Ighels to near Tazenacht may confuse you until you turn off it at KM25. From here an old Olaf traces or parallels this route, but in places is imprecise. The only traffic you're likely to see on this section are the Ouarzazate–based bike tour operators. The route **map** is on p130-1.

Fuel and water

Fuel at each end and maybe at Anezal; water in the wells, the creeks and the two main villages on the piste.

Suggested duration

Allow about two hours on a bike or up to three in a car to Tazenacht.

0km   **N30° 53.97' W06° 54.66'**
Mobil fuel at the southside **Ouarzazate** junction; one of a few around here. Take the south Ouarzazate bypass.

2.2 (74.8)   N30° 54.41' W06° 55.97'
Pass the Olaf left turn (it joins up later) and at a roundabout turn left on a road. In 2km cross another roundabout.

8.5 (68.5)   N30° 51.33' W06° 57.12'
Possibly leave the new road here for the direct route to the palmy village of Taguenzalt. In 8km Olaf joins from left near Taguenzalt. Follow the track or the new road south along a oued.

25 (52)   N30° 47.30' W07° 04.01'
Turn right for Imidar.

26.5 (50.5)   N30° 47.65' W07° 04.76'
Near **Imidar** continue straight along the oued, not into the village. Recross the oued a couple of times and pass through a defile into a valley. The track gets thin and is little used until you reach Tisslite.

29 (48)   N30° 46.99' W07° 05.76'
Exit the oued out to the right and ascend to the SW.

30 (47)   N30° 46.68' W07° 06.60'
High point at 1612m. The possibly snow-capped peak of 3305m Jebel Sirwa is visible ahead. From the pass drop back down onto the next valley.

33 (44)   N30° 46.49' W07° 07.98'
Pass a refuge and then drop into a oued

and follow it for a while. It can get sandy.

36.5 (40.5)   N30° 45.68' W07° 09.32'
Another goat fold and adjacent shelter.

44.5 (32.5)   N30° 45.55' W07° 12.71'
Fenced off pink huts by a oued and near-by cultivation with a ruin like a mine-head over the creek. The track detours around a small wash-out.

45.5 (31.5)   N30° 45.43' W07° 14.26'
Pass a **well** north of the track just after crossing the oued again as you curve south and uphill.

46.5 (30.5)   N30° 44.82' W07° 14.12'
Enter **Tisslite** village (Tamassine on old maps) from the north.

47 (30)   N30° 44.71' W07° 14.17'
In the middle of the village turn right and head west. You'll pass a football field and follow power lines as the track improves.

52.5 (24.5)   N30° 44.90' W07° 17.13'
Join the N10 just over a kilometre south of **Anezal** and turn south for Tazenacht. This is a scenic drive in its own right, with large flat lay-bys popular with free camping campervans and a great **viewpoint** south into the desert at around KM65 (N30° 38.84' W07° 16.28') following the 1715m **Tizi-n-Bachkoum** pass.

77   N30° 34.69' W07° 12.34'
Shell fuel on **Tazenacht's** north edge. There are a few hotels and restos in town. For more on Tazenacht see box p189.

For MS10 THE DESERT HIGHWAY *see p114*

MS11 AOUFOUZ – MERZOUGA   134KM
March 2012 ~ BMW F650GS

Description
An adventurous way of reaching the erg from the north. Once you're on the plateau at KM31 it's slow going over gnarly limestone, but within an hour there are pleasingly smooth episodes and great viewpoints off the edge of the Bine El Korbine escarpment down to the erg. By the time you drop steeply off the plateau at KM77, just short of the Algerian border, the route's already getting sandy and is about to get sandier as you pass the watchtowers before the oued running down to the Chebbi plain. From around KM104 set off on your own way to an auberge of your choice or cut 20km across to Rissani.

Off road
No problems for a 4WD, drop the tyres at KM87 where regular cars will need some gusto. Anything bigger than a 650 moto may be in for a shock in the sands and a pushbike will indeed be pushing in places.

Route finding
Easy enough as even where Olaf thins out it's clear as a bell and once within sight of the erg you can head on cross country. For the map see pp152-3.

Fuel and water
Fuel at each end. Water from nomads' tents or wells early on. On a big bike it could be hot work in the sands.

Suggested duration
Half a day will see you there.

0km
ZIZ at the south end of palm-clad Aoufouz.

15 (119)
Turn off left just before a oued. In 200m cross that oued and pick up the track running east, hooking up with Olaf.

26 (108)   N31° 36.55' W04° 05.57'
Well on the right with a bucket.

30 (104)   N31° 37.24' W04° 03.95'
Just after another **well**, as you cross a small creek the mystery of the small granite memorial on the left from Citroën to Marius-Louis de Bouche ('1898-1933'?) has been solved. In 1933 the Casablanca car dealer was ambushed and killed here.
   With that thought you take a rocky climb out of the valley.

31.5 (102.5)   N31° 37.04' W04° 03.13'
Important crossroads where ME2 comes down from the north. You turn east, possibly passing a tea tent.
   After 40km (N31° 35.72' W03° 58.35') Olaf thins out but the track remains clear and fast south all the way to the rim.

58 (76)   N31° 28.73' W03° 52.70'
Cliff edge and maybe fossil vendors. You might make out Erg Chebbi 30km to the south and a couple of hours away.

67 (67)   N31° 27.19' W03° 46.15'
A low sandy rise.

74 (60)   N31° 26.58' W03° 43.29'
A gorge head cuts in right by the track – shelter if you need it. The going now gets sandier as you turn south.

77 (57)   N31° 25.04'   W03° 43.13'
Edge of a military zone with a clear sign
back to Erfoud if coming the other way.
Descend steeply off the escarpment.

82.5 (51.5)   N31° 24.33'   W03° 45.75'
Olaf returns at a checkpoint and passport
check. There are several military installations on the hilltops around here.
  In just over a kilometre keep right, left
leads to a hilltop fort. Drop into a valley,
cross a oued northwards then west and
finally SW again.

87 (47)   N31° 24.08'   W03° 48.33'
Oasis with palms ahead and maybe
nomads to the north. You may want to
reduce tyre pressure here. Olaf passes to
south, which may be less sandy.
  I rode around the northside of the trees
into thick churned sand and hacked my
way back to Olaf a kilometre later.

97 (37)   N31° 22.71'   W03° 53.66'
More palms and last sandy stretch ahead.

104 (30)   N31° 20.74'   W03° 57.57'
Low dunes, nomad camps and many
more tracks. You can leave Olaf here and
have much more fun making your own
way south or SW along or between any
number of tracks.
  You may pass close to *Auberge Yasmina*
at the top of Erg Chebbi from where
auberges proliferate all the way to
Merzouga, about 25-30kms to the south.
It's fun to cruise the gravel plains eyeing
up a comely auberge.

134   N31° 08.13'   W04° 03.11'
Eventually you'll need fuel. Here it is.

MS12 MERZOUGA – MECISSI   138KM
March 2012 ~ BMW F650GS

Description
I've always thought this intriguing zone north of MS6 – known to some as the
'**Black Rock Desert**' – was a blank spot in the Moroccan Sahara region so set
out to find a way through from Taouz towards Alnif. No lateral pistes were
evident on maps new or old, though sat images defined plenty of tracks, none
which seemed to quite link up.
  If it all got too complicated I knew I could bail south to MS6 or north to
Rissani before the Rheris crossing – or even *because* the Rheris was uncrossable.
I now had Olaf in a *satnav* not a GPS (see box p23) which meant formerly
unseen 'thin Olaf' routes became more evident and were used to help string
together a route which followed my ideal planned course. Only the finale
along a piste mashed to a pulp by convoys of mine trucks took the edge off a
great ride.
  Note I did this on a windy day with visibility down to a mile at times, so
some obvious landmarks may have been missed.

Off road
There's enough going on to give you your money's worth here, but nothing
too challenging. A regular car would struggle in places as would a fully loaded
big bike, no matter what tyres it's running. This is all amplified by the fact that
from KM48 to 108 there are no villages, very few nomads, and any mines are
miles away. The crux is of course the Rheris river crossing at KM84. If you're
alone and the water is flowing hard it could be too much of a gamble. When
you hit a soft patch the 3km crossing of the Ziz flood plain just out of Taouz as

well as the similar basin of salt-capped mud at KM72 are not without their moments either. Compared to the potential of that ending badly, the sands around KM100 are a piece of cake.

Route finding

Where a track or simply the best way to ride diverged from Olaf, I followed that, even if it meant riding cross-country for a while. (As it was, some Olafs didn't relate to any nearby track and may have been plotted on a map, not actually logged on the ground.) On this route you'd do well to adopt a similar strategy; don't slavishly follow a thin Olaf, instead use it as a guide to a presumably plausible route. The point where I crossed the river at KM84 was off Olafs but this was where clear tracks led to an easy crossing. For the map see pp152-3.

Fuel and water

Fuel at each end only. Wells just after the Rheris crossing, and a few along the mine truck track at the end, plus of course the river.

Suggested duration

It's not far but you'll want a full day. Alnif has the nearest hotels at the end.

0km
AFRIQUIA fuel 5km north of Merzouga junction. Head south to Taouz alongside the Ziz.

28 (110)   N30° 54.52' W03° 59.65'
Tiny village of **Taouz** (what a difference an erg makes). Before the village centre turn west on a track across the Oued Ziz assuming it's reformed after the last flood. I took my own way across the dried mud, but it's best not to linger on this surface or to get too near the deepest fresh ruts.

31.5 (106.5)   N30° 55.54' W04° 01.34'
Once on the other side you may want to make a quick detour to a cluster of **pre-Islamic 'keyhole' tombs** at N30° 54.51' W04° 02.27', about 3km SW. These Neolithic relics are a common sight across the Sahara overlooking similar riverside locations, but rarely survive in Morocco. A keyhole tomb is a ring pierced by a passageway which almost always points towards the sunrise.

Otherwise, head WNW erring right at 600m and via N30° 57.37' W04° 03.43'.

40 (98)   N30° 58.49' W04° 04.33'
You join a piste (Olaffed) heavily used by mine trucks whose tyres have pulverised the sand into powder and dust. Turn left, west.

42.5 (95.5)
Now turn north off the dusty truck piste towards a gap, crossing an awkward rock bar. Soon you come to an abandoned village with a dry well in the oued.

Carry on north, then west then NW; other tracks may join from the east.

48 (90)   N31° 00.72' W04° 07.74'
The main track continues north through a gap; you take the track splitting left into the 'Black Rock Valley', a fast wide piste rolling west. It occasionally braids on itself.

55 (83)
Cross a north–south piste and carry on west, leaving Olaf and winging it as necessary, though there are tracks all over.

64 (74)   N31° 00.45' W04° 16.62'
Cut north over a small rise (nomad camps nearby) then carry on west. Olaf is off to the north.

66.5 (71.5)
The valley ends as you enter a 1500-m sandy passage and follow it through into the Oued Rheris basin.

68 (70)   N31° 00.42'   W04° 18.85'
Emerging from the passage, the main track curves south and then SW. Leave it and carry on west any way you like. In 3km you'll cross more north-bound tracks leading about 40km south to KM162 on MS6; a way out if the river further on is flowing and too deep.

About 2km further on you may find yourself on that nasty 'chalky' surfaced dried mud again so err south to the edge of the basin along the base of the hills.

77 (61)   N31° 00.40'   W04° 24.37'
Short cut across a reassuringly solid rocky rise then enter into the main floodplain, thick with vegetation and sandy hummocks. Follow whatever main tracks you find; mine led to...

82 (56)   N30° 59.74'   W04° 26.47'
... this point on a high sandy bank overlooking river channel below. If you arrive here too and are unsure of the crossing, first walk down the steep sand bank to inspect the river as once down some vehicles may not have enough room for a run back up. Other crossings, including Olaf to the south may be easier.

The bank on the far side is flat but rises gradually along a sandy gully so think about dropping tyre pressures. There's more soft sand later.

83.5 (54.5)   N30° 59.84'   W04° 27.25'
Estimated position of a well (15m) and trough soon after the crossing. There are cleared 'fields' and more pre-Islamic tombs on the slopes to the south.

Carry on west along a sandy valley.

94 (44)
Cross north–south tracks and carry on WNW. In a couple of kilometres you divert north around a line of small dunes which lie across the valley.

100 (38)   N31° 01.77'   W04° 35.63'
Emerge from the 'Black Rock Desert', such as it was, at a formed track heading SW to Tafraoute (KM134 MS6). You want to go west but there are dunes that way and soft sand all around.

The actual track can be worse than either side; I hacked SW for a bit until the way west opened up. Once on the gravel plain head cross-country to the next waypoint at the base of the jebel; there is no single clear track. You might want to connect with other routes such as KM180 MS4 which is about 20km WSW of this point.

114 (24)   N31° 01.87'   W04° 42.93'
Join a fat Olaf just north of a building, although you can pick up this piste anywhere you like. It comes up from Foum Mharech, 35km to the south near Tafraoute on MS3/6.

From here the fun part is over and all that remains is to follow the procession of dust-clad Isuzu haul trucks shuffling their ore NW to the road. At times the *feche-feche*-like ruts they make are a foot deep but traction in the powder is actually quite good. You pass a few gardens and a well or two. It's a dreary end to a great route.

138   N31° 12.81'   W04° 49.52'
Mecissi: pass along a lane between walls to the N12. The *Ziz* is just to your right.

ANTI ATLAS

Outline of the Anti Atlas region

The exact point where the Anti Atlas ends and High Atlas begins is hard to define on the ground but for this book it's the N10 highway between Taliouine and Tazenacht. Geologically the Anti Atlas is actually part of a much older formation and today experiences a drier climate. This makes it a good proposition when the High Atlas may be snowbound or you're trying to shake off the rain.

Running down close to the Algerian border as far as Assa, many 'MA' routes are mountain desert tracks which are satisfyingly long while also combining a cultural element, all the while being accessible in a rental from Marrakech or Ouarzazate. In essence this area is the western extension of the MS Sahara zone, but with the addition of canyon and mountain routes and with far fewer tour groups it all adds up to the best of southern Morocco.

MA Routes

MA1	Tafraoute – Aït Herbil	106KM	P175
MA2	Aït Herbil – Igmir – Tafraoute	97KM	P178
MA3	Akka – Timkyet – Tafraoute	201KM	P180
MA4	Fask – Taghjijt – Timoulay	71KM	P184
MA5	Ousemlal – Amtoudi – Aït Herbil	119KM	P184
MA6	Tazenacht – Issil – Tata	171KM	P188
MA7	Foum Zguid – Issil – Taliouine	174KM	P190
MA8	Tafraoute – Tazalarhite – Igherm	135KM	P192
MA9	Tata – Akka Ighern – Foum Zguid	169KM	P197
MA10	Ousemlal – Foum el Hassan – Assa	195KM	P198
MA11	Taliouine – Tata – Igherm	266KM	P199
MA12	Foum Zguid– Assaragh – Taliouine	190KM	P201
MA13	Taliouine – Agadir Melloul – Tata	252KM	P203

MA1   TAFRAOUTE – TIZERKINE GORGE – AÏT HERBIL 106KM

April and November 2008 ~ Mazda pickup, Yamaha Ténéré

Description

A satisfying way of getting back to Aït Herbil if you came up MA2. You climb steeply out of Tafraoute and at Tleta Tasserirt (not all maps show it, or in the right place) you break off to the east along a wide track. It soon turns into an old asphalt road near Taraout, but once it enters the upper Tizerkine Gorge this abandoned road becomes potholed and in places has been washed away. Not that you mind much as descending through the gorge is most agreeable as the oil-bearing argan trees give way to desert palms.

By the time you reach Tizerkine village the palms are dense as you join Route MA3 and follow it down to Afella (among its many other names). Here, in the town's forded oued, you turn south to follow the wide stony canyon of the Assif-n-Int, passing some prehistoric engravings and a couple of nomad goat camps along the way. While it's fun to drive along a riverbed, the Assif lacks the adjacent MA2's villages and dramatic ascents, although with no other southbound sealed roads for miles, it's a relatively quick way of getting down to the N12 road and the desert around Akka and Assa.

Off road

There are no tough off-road ascents or drastic clearance issues, so **any vehicle** showing a bit of daylight around its ankles could manage. The Tizerkine stage would be fun on a **mountain bike** but the unremitting shingle along the Assif canyon would be less so; you may as well reverse MA2 which is prettier.

Route finding

Once off the sealed roads, which aren't busy apart from the haul truck stages (see KM49), you won't see any traffic and it's hard to get lost. Note that Souk el Had d'Afella-Ihrir is what appears on most paper maps but it's also known as Souk el Had Issi, Talate-n-Yssi on old maps and Google, or just plain old 'Yissik'. 'Afella' is the name I use. This route is **mapped** on p186-7.

Fuel and water

There is fuel at each end (not always at Aït Herbil) and probably in Afella too if you ask around. Once on the piste there are several wells along the oueds.

Suggested duration

Half a day. From Afella to Aït Herbil (54km) takes about two hours in a car.

0km   N29° 43.20'   W08° 58.30'
AFRIQUIA fuel station in **Tafraoute** town centre. Head south out of town.

3 (103)   N29° 41.77'   W08° 57.74'
At this junction keep left.

7 (99)   N29° 39.80'   W08° 57.63'
Right for Izerbi past the Painted Rocks of artist Jean Verame, from 1984. You keep left and commence a 500m climb.

19 (87)   N29° 36.80'   W08° 55.14'
Junction and a milepost in Arabic and a wide track leading left to the nearby village of Tleta Tasserirt. **Take the dirt road** through the village.

22 (84)
Fork right here for the Gorges de Tizerkine. Left (Olaffed) leads north onto the plateau and back down to MA3.

On the way to Tizerkine you soon get

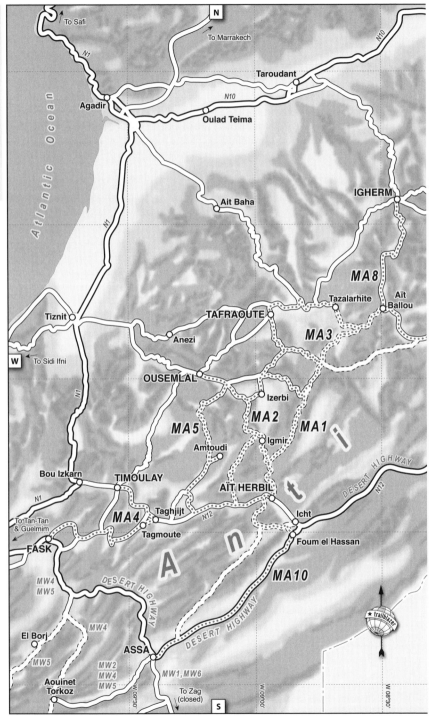

Anti Atlas (MA)
Routes Overview

MA1 Tafraoute – Gorge – Aït Herbil
MA2 Aït Herbil – Tafraoute
MA3 Akka – Tafraoute
MA4 Fask – Timoulay
MA5 Ousemlal – Amtoudi – Aït Herbil
MA6 Tazenacht – Issil – Tata
MA7 Foum Zguid – Issil – Taliouine
MA8 Tafraoute – Tazal' – Igherm
MA9 Tata – Akka Ighern – Foum Zguid
MA10 Ousemlal – Foum el Hassan – Assa
MA11 Taliouine – Tata – Igherm
MA12 Foum Zguid – Assaragh – Taliouine
MA13 Taliouine – Agadir Melloul – Tata

to the village of **Taraout** after which the wide track becomes an old broken road.

32 (74)
Deep but dry well on the left.

36 (70)   **N29° 35.12'   W08° 48.02'**
Tizerkine village where the broken road turns into a rubbly track. Carry on winding through the thick palmerie.

40 (66)   **N29° 34.37'   W08° 46.32'**
Turn right and join MA3 for the short distance to Afella.

48 (58)   **N29° 31.48'   W08° 48.03'**
An Olaffed track joins from the left, coming from KM50.5 on MA3.

49 (57)   **N29° 30.10'   W08° 49.07'**
The **tarmac junction** at an elaborate milepost. The tarmac goes NE (left) 16km to the Akka gold mine and on to KM50.5 on Route MA3.
    You carry straight on and soon get to **Afella**. On the right, is a basic café.

52 (54)   **N29° 29.89'   W08° 49.28'**
Drop down to the oued and **leave the road**, south, into the Assif-n-Int oued. Initially this track is a diversion around the town for the haul trucks.

56.5 (49.5)   **N29° 27.85'   W08° 50.41'**
At a sign: '*Graveurs 7km*' turn left off the haul track. Enter a shallow canyon along which winds a stony oued which you'll-follow just about all the way to Aït Herbil.

61 (45)   **N29° 26.05'   W08° 50.96'**
A track goes off to the left for the engravings. The *Rough Guide* has some details with promises of elephants and rhinos.

68.5 (37.5)   **N29° 22.62'   W08° 52.59'**
Pass two **wells** on the right and in about 5km pass a dry well.

77 (29)   **N29° 18.82'   W08° 54.15'**
A valley joins from the right near some goat nomad camps.

84 (22)   **N29° 16.36'   W08° 57.06'**
Pass a **cistern** on the left.

89 (17)   **N29° 14.79'   W08° 58.79'**
Don't turn left here to take a short cut, it gets too rough. Keep straight ahead to join the main route or road in 250m at N29° 14.78' W08° 58.92'. Here you meet Route MA2 heading north and this is where you turn left, south, for Aït Herbil.

96 (10)   **N29° 12.04'   W08° 59.32'**
If it hasn't already, the tarmac starts near Imouzlag village and soon rises above the oued with great views of the settlement below. Just before you reach the N12 highway there are a couple of shops.

106   **N29° 07.99'   W08° 57.92'**
The basic ZIZ fuel station of **Aït Herbil** on the N12 highway. The nearest place to stay is the *Igmir Guest House*, 32km back up MA2.

MA2 AÏT HERBIL – IGMIR – TAFRAOUTE   97KM
March 2008 ~ Mazda pickup

Description
Even though there is talk of improving the road, this is still among the best short routes in the Anti Atlas, and whichever direction you do it in you're in for a wonderful, winding traverse along the gorge of the Oued Smouguene through the eastern ranges of the Anti Atlas. On the way you pass cliff-side Berber villages followed by palm-shrouded Berber villages as far as Igmir, where the route suddenly climbs fit to burst your radiator's cork out onto the highlands and Berber hill villages along the tarmac to Tafraoute. At the very start of the route there's a chance to inspect rock engravings at Aït Herbil, though if you've seen examples in Algeria and Libya you may not be that impressed.

Off road

This route was originally done in 2004 in a clapped-out Mercedes 190 (see the website) so anything with more clearance will manage fine. The stony ruts and oued crossings through the gorge will make riding a moto while enjoying the scenery a bit tricky. Mountain bikers may find this route a better proposition in the opposite – and no less impressive – direction, as from Igmir you may be walking or pedalling at walking pace much of the time.

Route finding

On the lower sections the route is clear, though flooding may wash away parts and lead to stony detours. For some reason this well-established and popular route is not depicted on any of the paper maps of Morocco, although the much less used MA1 sometimes is.

Note that in the narrow, palmerie trails you may have to back up so others can get by. The **map** is on p186-7.

Fuel and water

Fuel at Aït Herbil (supplies can be intermittent) and Tafraoute with water from the many villages along the route.

Suggested duration

Allow half a day, though camping around KM29 or spending the night at the Igmir guest house (KM35) is more fun and gives you a chance to meet the locals and appreciate the evening/dawn light on the gorge walls.

0km   N29° 07.97'   W08° 57.93'
Aït Herbil fuel station on the N12 with a basic café. The **rock carvings** as described in the *Rough Guide* are at N29° 08.9' W08° 56.4', about 3km off route.

4.5 (92.5)
Pass by **Aguerd** where the road rises above the village with impressive views. Soon the road drops down to the oued and crosses it via a concrete ford.

10 (87)
Tarmac may end, though there's talk of improving the road.

17 (80)   N29° 14.79'   W08° 58.79'
Junction with MA1 which comes in from the right, along the oued from Afella.

19 (78)
Cross a oued and re-enter it soon. As you pass walled gardens by the piste at around N29° 16.02' W08° 59.23', the very

scenic 10km section of this route begins, initially along the narrow oued and passing the village of **Tamesoult** (N29° 16.2' W08° 59.5').

23.5 (73.5)   N29° 17.13'   W08° 59.58'
Leave the narrowing oued up the bank to the right. Out the other side turn left uphill into the village where you'll see a couple of hand-painted signs at a junction (N29° 17.23'   W08° 59.58') showing distances to Igmir and Tafraoute. Follow the signs left out of the village below the cliffs. Soon you're back in the stony oued bottom or alongside it.

26 (71)   N29° 17.54'   W09° 00.31'
Anywhere around here is a great place to camp or have a break among the shady argans. The pressing of argan nuts (once they've been digested and passed on by goats) makes a highly-prized and nutty-flavoured oil, available at Igmir and widely sold in and around Tafraoute.

31.5 (65.5)
Leave the oued as you encounter walled enclosures and pylons on the outskirts of **Igmir**. Pass under an avenue of trees. Soon you get to the *Igmir Guest House* (N29° 20.03' W09° 00.14') on the other side of the oued.

You now leave the **Smougeune** valley, taking a very steep 5km ascent with great views of the track snaking back down into the valley to Igmir.

40 (57) N29° 20.71' W09° 02.43'
The piste forks at a detailed sign. Go right (north) for Tafraoute ('53km'). Left and south gets pretty rough; part of MA10.

47.5 (49.5) N29° 23.84' W09° 04.29'
Fork right off the old route to Tafraoute along the newer track.

50 (47) N29° 25.04' W09° 03.61'
Pass a track leading right, east down to **Agoujgal** (where a mine haul track leads north to Izerbi) and **Aoukerda** (10km) which is marked on some paper maps and which can also be reached by walking up from Igmir; ask at the guest house.

52.5 (44.5) N29° 26.40' W09° 03.44'
Turn left at this junction towards **Tahwawat** village.

53.5 (43.5) N29° 27.08' W09° 03.74'
Join the **sealed road** just east of Tahwawat at a yellow sign for the Igmir Guest House. Right for Izerbi and Tafraoute.

60 (37)
Izerbi, with some striking private villas.

66 (31) N29° 29.97' W09° 00.68'
Junction right to Afella on Routes MA1 and MA3. Carry on north and in a couple of kilometres cross a junction, signed left for 'Tiznit 90'. Carry on over the 1200m Tizi ou Manouz pass and into the Ameln valley of Tafraoute.

94 (3) N29° 41.77' W08° 57.74'
At this junction turn left for Tafraoute, right is MA1.

97 N29° 43.20' W08° 58.30"
Fuel station in **Tafraoute** town centre next to the *Hotel Tafraoute* (more details at the end of Route MA3).

MA3 AKKA – TIMKYET – TAFRAOUTE 201KM
March 2008 ~ Mazda pickup

Description

Two hundred kilometres of action and spectacle that'll leave you wishing you had eyes in the back of your head to take it all in. You start on the desert floor out of Akka and head north up into an orogenic wonderland of Berber mountain villages where brightly-dressed womenfolk attend to the chores among buildings shrouded in their own rustling palmeries. The kids here are not averse to some *stylo* action, but living where they do who can begrudge them the distraction. While the chances are that in a car you'll complete this route with mild whiplash from the relentless jolting, you'll be able to use the recovery time to process the many wonders you saw and the encounters you had.

The scenery ranges from never dull to mind-boggling. From the 'Desert Highway' (see p114) you pass through Akka's extensive palmerie and scoot up a piste to meet the R109. Once you leave this road at Tizgui ida ou Ballou village (KM69.5) the drama comes in fast and doesn't let up until you emerge on the high plains (still at the same bone-shaking speed), only to have it return with a dazzling drop into Aouklid. From here you spin down through another string of palm-clad villages jammed alongside a gorge before you reach the tarmac for a well-earned and soothing hour's drive over to Tafraoute.

Off road

The piste from Akka is a piece of cake but once you leave the R109 at Tizgui ida ou Ballou this isn't the place to be towing a caravan full of badly packed Ming vases. Even something like a Range Rover or a VX will need to have their tyre sidewalls if not their very sides watched carefully in the gorge. Many times in the riverbeds you'll see stone width-markers giving guidance to the clearance ahead. Unless you're leading a donkey piled up with hay, continue in anything wider than an average 4WD at your peril.

Heavy bikes may also struggle on this part of the route. To keep your balance, directional stability and on the look out for bigger rocks in the riverbeds you need to move too fast to enjoy the spectacle. As with bigger cars, wide alloy panniers and wide bikes will require careful positioning. And the descent into Aouklid at KM112 will require judicious front braking on the loose stones.

This particular descent too may govern the direction in a regular car. Attempting MA3 in reverse it's possible a regular car won't manage this loose ascent; the climb up onto the plateau from the other end (the direction of this route description) is concreted on its steepest stages.

Any sort of storm down here doesn't bear thinking about. The run-off would rush off the bare rock slopes into the gorges and surge through them in minutes. My impression was this route is too stony for all but the hardiest **mountain biker**. You'd be much better off walking.

Route finding

This route, with many branches besides, is 98% Olaffed. As for paper maps, once off the R109 nothing in print gets close. The widely-depicted route from near Aït Ballou down to 'Bou Zarif' and back up to Timkyet doesn't exist with the prominence shown (but see KM50.5 and KM69.5).

Once you leave the Tazegzaoute gorge (where this route continues clearly, despite what maps show), Timkyet will be the first village that relates to any modern map, although they haven't kept up with the many new roads between here and Tafraoute.

Note that Souk el Had d'Afella-Ihrir is what appears on most paper maps but it's also known as Souk el Had Issi, Talate-n-Yissi on old maps and Google Maps or just plain 'Yissik'. I settle on 'Afella'. Once off the highway at either end you may see a couple of local vans close to the tarmac. No local traffic seems to go over the top if it can help it. Where's the **map**? Page 194-5.

Fuel and water

In Akka look for the green *Afriquia* sign at the west end and north side of the main street. The guys here have fuel out of drums slightly above national rate. In Tafraoute you drive straight into a modern *Afriquia* forecourt soon after you enter town from the south.

There are plenty of villages and some handy **wells**, complete with bucket and pulleys on this route. The high well at KM100 looks like a good place to fill right up.

Suggested duration

A day will do you all the way to Tafraoute. Or start late and camp out.

0km   N29° 23.39'   W08° 15.58'
Akka fuel (see p181). Leave town to the west, passing under the arch. In just over a kilometre (N29° 23.05' W08° 16.08') turn north **onto the piste** at a sign: 'Imitek 33'. You're heading up the west side of the settlement towards a gap in the Jebel Bani range filled with Akka's palmerie and satellite villages.

4 (197)   N29° 24.57'   W08° 16.00'
Pass south of the first village of Aït Antar and then north of Tagadirt with the big palmerie below you.

7.5 (193.5)   N29° 26.26'   W08° 16.13'
Cross the main oued running through the gap by a pool. Here you can take a diversion a couple of kilometres to the NW to try and locate some **rock engravings** by some old barracks. Otherwise continue straight on northwards for Imitek on a wide, rubbly piste.

25.5 (175.5)
Top of a 720-metre pass.

34 (167)   N29° 38.59'   W08° 16.33'
A good double-bucket **well** with water at 30m. The white hut you can see up ahead is a checkpoint on the road and they may be watching you.

35 (166)   N29° 38.97'   W08° 16.25'
Join the R109 **tarmac** near the observation hut just west of **Imitek**. Turn left or west.

50.5 (150.5)   N29° 38.73'   W08° 25.24'
Pass a sign to the SW for 'BRPM' mine and 'Izgoui ida Oubaloul 62'. This is the way 'Bou Zarif' (a name not found locally) and

In the Tazegzaoute gorge.

the mine is Iourirne signed at KM140.5 and so a good way to come back.

Along the R109 you'll observe many spectacular examples of crumpled anticlines (folded rock strata) to the east. It's about to get a whole lot more impressive.

69.5 (131.5)   N29° 44.65'   W08° 31.01'
Tizgui ida ou (or just 'Aït') Ballou village with a sign left for Tazegzaoute. This is the main route option through this area.

70 (131)   N29° 44.53'   W08° 31.39'
Junction by a oued with a **well** not far to the left. Turn right, SW.

73 (128)   N29° 43.57'   W08° 32.47'
Fork right here to take the high track above the oued rather than the stony track through it, to the village of Sidi Al Haj Ou Ali. Up ahead you'll see the striking zig-zag erosion pattern of twisted and near-vertical strata (on the cover of the last edition) which even the pylons can't spoil.

76 (125)   N29° 42.95'   W08° 33.97'
Cross the oued at the end of the village. As you wind along the track look back; you'll soon see the ruins of an old agadir (fortified storehouse) perched on a spur. Carry on below the ranges into the narrowing gorge. On a big or loaded bike you'll need to concentrate intently for the next 20km along the river bed.

80 (121)
The palmerie smothering the villages along this narrow gorge begins.

87 (114)   N29° 40.38'   W08° 34.92'
The gorge opens out with a **well** on the right. Right on cue there are some trees for a shady break.

93 (108)   N29° 40.54'   W08° 37.03'
Finally after what feels like hours in wonderland, leave the oued near the village of Ifassras and less than 200m later at N29° 40.55' W08° 37.10' fork left for Timkyet. Right here also leads up onto the plateau; KM49 on Route MA8, which is 2km north of KM108, below. The climb begins.

97.5 (103.5)   N29° 39.27'   W08° 37.96'
After a slabby oued crossing, on a bike or in a car you may get into third gear for a

few hundred metres. It's something definitely worth noting. Then, within a kilometre of this point, you get to a cleared sportsground by the side of the track.

99 (102)   N29° 38.28'   W08° 38.41'
The village of **Aït Alha**. Turn right out of the oued where an out-of-place *Coke* sign reminds you what century it is. Keep right up the valley. The track gets very steep at times. In about a kilometre (N29° 38.36' W08° 38.77') you get to a **well** (10m) on the left with a bucket. There are a couple more **wells** soon after.

101 (100)
You've climbed 200m out of the gorge in just over 2km, at times on concrete slabs. The sage bush plateau now around you is comparatively bleak and dreary, but you may spot gazelles. For cars at least, the going still remains slow. In less than a kilometre (N29° 37.88' W08° 39.64') you pass a lone farmhouse on the right.

108 (93)   N29° 40.54'   W08° 41.47'
Key junction. Straight on (NW) leads to Tafraoute reversing Route MA8, you turn left, signed for Aouklid and Timkyet. In 400m at N29° 40.45' W08° 41.71' another sign promises 'Aouklid 7km' and to the right 'Tafraoute 43' (MA8). Within a kilometre of this sign you pass the abandoned village of Idouwayghd and soon after a track 'triangles' in from the right (ie: also from Tafraoute along MA8).

111.5 (89.5)   N29° 39.01'   W08° 42.45'
You pass the 1862m **high point** of this route and the steep, loose descent into Aouklid begins.

114.5 (86.5)   N29° 38.06'   W08° 42.72'
Although it's not marked on any maps this is Aouklid . From here there's a line of mostly unmapped villages with adjacent gardens all the way to the tarmac.

116.5 (84.5)   N29° 37.54'   W08° 43.30'
Don't go right, below the mosque here; keep left in the oued.

122 (79)   N29° 37.14'   W08° 44.60'
Enter a palmerie and the gardens of Timkyet; you're back on the paper maps.

124.5 (76.5)   N29° 36.44'   W08° 44.91'
Turn right and head to the next village.

127.5 (73.5)   N29° 35.55'   W08° 45.84'
Tamegroute village with a shop opposite a squat mosque or shrine.

131.5 (69.5)   N29° 34.37'   W08° 46.32'
Keep left for Afella. Coming in from the right is Route MA1 from Tafraoute (40km) along the lovely Tizerkine Gorge.

137 (64)   N29° 32.18'   W08° 47.53'
Pass a left turn by some gardens and buildings but go straight on.

140.5 (60.5)   N29° 30.71'   W08° 48.79'
At an elaborate milepost join the tarmac from the gold mine at Iourirne (16km) and eventually back to KM50.5 for Tata.

Within a kilometre you reach 'Afella' with a basic shop on the right before you cross the oued where MA1 leads south.

For Tafraoute head west on good tarmac and over a pass on a road that only features (well, most of it) on Google Maps until you reach…

170 (31)   N29° 29.97'   W09° 00.68'
… the junction with the Izerbi–Tafraoute road which does feature on maps. A sign proclaims: 'Tafraoute 32' to the right. In a couple of kilometres you get to a junction, signed west for 'Tiznit 90'. Carry straight on and over the 1200m pass of Tizi ou Manouz and down into Tafraoute.

194 (7)   N29° 39.80'   W08° 57.64'
MA1 joins from the right.

198 (3)   N29° 41.77'   W08° 57.74'
At the junction turn left for Tafraoute.

201   N29° 43.20'   W08° 58.30'
Fuel station in **Tafraoute** town centre. The *Hotel Tafraoute* is a cheapie right next to the petrol station forecourt where you can park. It's not the quietest location but what town centre is?

Campsites seem to be mostly about 6km out of town up the Ameln valley.

This road, the R106, continues via Igherm to Taliouine (170km) and is a great ride on a motorbike or bicycle along remarkably quiet country roads.

MA – ANTI ATLAS

MA4   FASK – TAGHJIJT – TIMOULAY   71KM
March 2008 ~ Mazda pickup

Once a rough piste and now a scenic drive open to all, MA4 links the
Guelmim–Assa road with the N12 along some windy valleys past
the occasional nomad camp, folds of rock and a village or
three. The valleys and jebels in this region are not in the
usual linear arrangement but curl and loop around each
other and the creek courses, and so the road follows the
same detours to cover the relatively short distance
between the highways. At the far end the villages and
palmeries of Tagmoute and Taghjijt are both nice places
for a wander, and if you're coming up from the 'MW'
region, you're lined up nicely for the 'MA' Anti Atlas routes.
There's fuel at the east end of Fask and Timoulay, as well as
Aït Herbil to the east and Bou Izkarn to the west. It's also available at Taghjijt
if you ask around. There's water in a couple of wells along the route as well as
the villages.

A kilometre out of Fask turn left at a bend then leave the road and follow
it north up the valley and round to the village of Igherm Iguezzoulene with a
white-domed zaouia (shrine). Soon after at KM23 you reach a junction with a
road going directly north to Timoulay. Carry on east towards the Adrar
Touzannaga then as you curl round the Adrar pass the village of Ksaba Aït
Moussa ou Daoud.

The road bypasses Tagmoute and joins the N12 at KM50 (N29° 04.48' W09°
26.14') about 2.5km north of Taghjijt and its dense palmerie. Turn north-west
for the basic SHELL in the strung-out village of Timoulay. There's a cashpoint
and another SHELL in Bou Izkarn down the road on the N1 coastal highway, but
after a quick look around, that's just about all it's got going for it. The map is
on pp184-5.

MA5   OUSEMLAL – AMTOUDI – AÏT HERBIL   119KM
April and November 2008 ~ Mazda pickup and Yamaha Ténéré

Description
MA5 is another way of dropping down onto the desert floor from the north,
but fuel and a couple of shops are all you'll find at either end of this route, so
realistically you'd want to start from **Tafraoute** or thereabouts and consider
wild camping at the far end (a few miles after KM88 down Route MA10 would
do, or on the sand sheet east along the N12 past Icht). Being a short route
between fuel stations, MA5 may well work better combined in a loop with
Routes MA1, 2 and 10 based out of the guest house at Igmir halfway up Route
MA2, certainly on an unladen moto.

The route itself may be nothing special but the highlight is the visit to
Amtoudi where a finely restored fortified stone storehouse or 'agadir' is
perched over the escarpment above the canyon-bound settlement. You can
easily walk or be carried by mule up to the top and enjoy a fascinating guid-
ed tour of the interior by the guardian. You'll find storage rooms, beehives, a

small museum and of course great views down the valley from where you came. Outside the walls ancient petroglyphs suggest – as is so often the case with these places – that the locale has been occupied for millennia.

From Amtoudi you head south across the plain to the N12 and turn east for Aït Herbil.

The fortified storehouse at Amtoudi.
© Peter Hartleb.

Off road

For your suspension the wake up call comes around KM30 south of Ouafka as you rise up onto the plateau. Here you join the southbound track linking a village or two and drop down a short gorge towards the Amtoudi junction where you rejoin the road. This can be easily done in anything you've got.

Route finding

No great dramas await you as long as you can follow these instructions. There are villages all along the route, so as far as passing traffic goes you shouldn't be stranded for long. The **map** is on pp186-7.

Fuel and water

Fuel at each end and a couple of wells in the villages on the way through.

Suggested duration

A couple of hours' driving or riding time, but you'd want to spend as least as long exploring the environs of Amtoudi.

0km   N29° 31.57' W09° 14.73'
PETROMIN fuel on the west side of **Jemaa Ida Ousemlal** to give it its full title; a few shops. Fill up and head east through town towards Ouafka.

11 (108)   N29° 30.10' W09° 08.49'
Junction in **Souk Khemis de Aït Ouafka or just 'Ouafka'. The** road to the NE comes down from Tafraoute – an alternative start for this route. Turn right or south at the crossroads and follow the road up into the hills.

30 (89)   N29° 24.36' W09° 15.27'
After passing through a few villages, at the apex of a hairpin just after a village ('Aghoudid' on old maps) you turn left and SE **onto the piste**. After three kilometres and a bend to the south you pass through Aït Ali ou Hamad with its

distinctive crenellated mosque. Continue SSE along a broad track.

37 (82)   N29° 21.17' W09° 13.46'
After a hut on the left, soon the short descent into the valley begins, passing a small, stepped waterfall and deserty cacti on the way.

43 (76)   N29° 18.97' W09° 12.87'
Six kilometres later you've dropped 300m and enter the village of Targa Oukhadir alongside its oued. In a kilometre and a half you pass the ruins of old Oukhadir.

56 (63)   N29° 13.27' W09° 13.50'
Join the road by a sign to the villages you've just come from (Ouafka is out by 10km) and a building on a hill. Turn sharp left or north for 4km to Amtoudi which is shown on some maps as 'Id Aissa'.

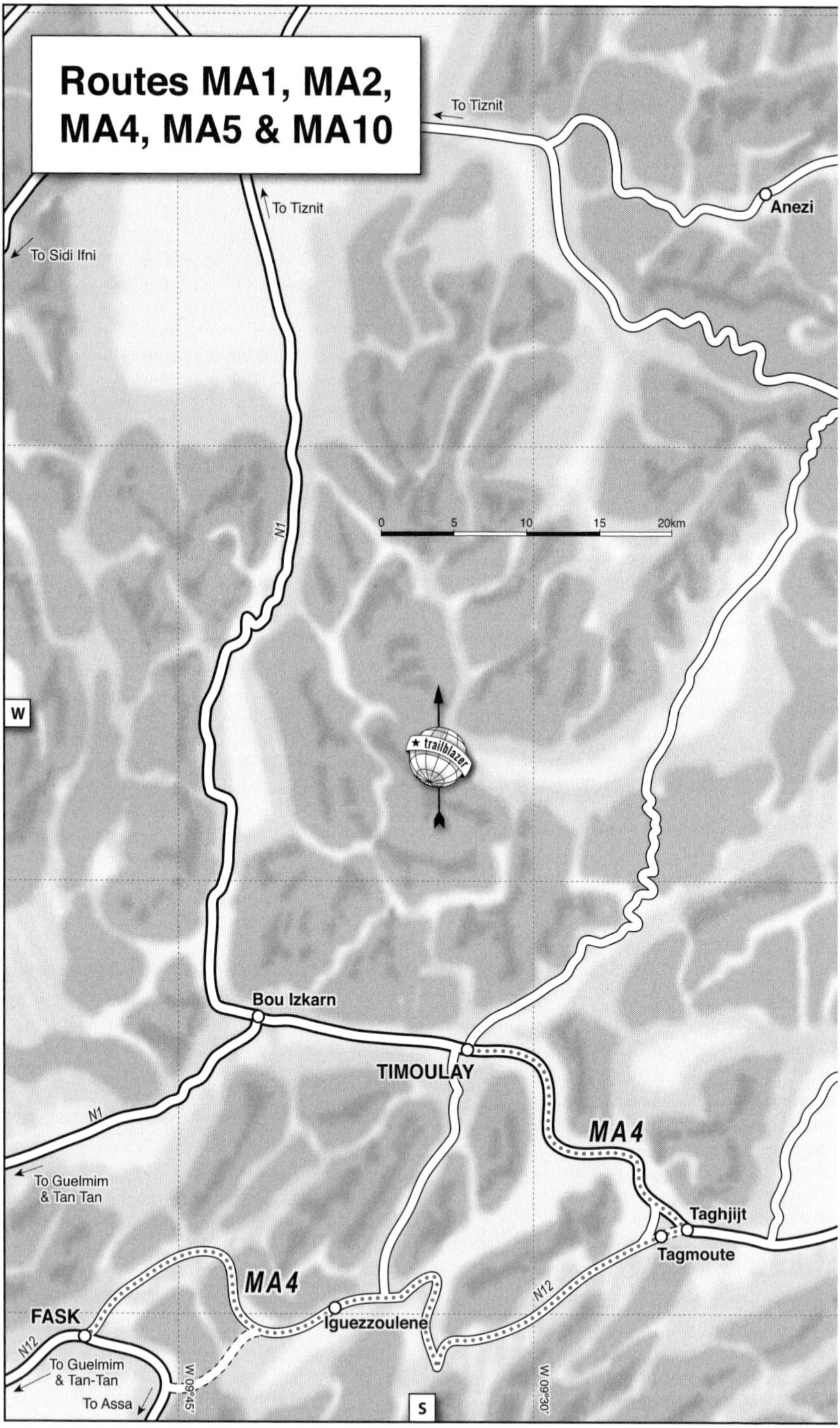

Routes MA1, MA2, MA4, MA5 & MA10

MA – ANTI ATLAS

To Tiznit

Anezi

To Tiznit

To Sidi Ifni

N1

0   5   10   15   20km

W

★ trailblazer

Bou Izkarn

TIMOULAY

MA 4

N1

To Guelmim & Tan Tan

Taghjijt

Tagmoute

MA 4

N12

FASK

Iguezzoulene

N12

To Guelmim & Tan-Tan

To Assa

W 09°45'

W 09°30'

S

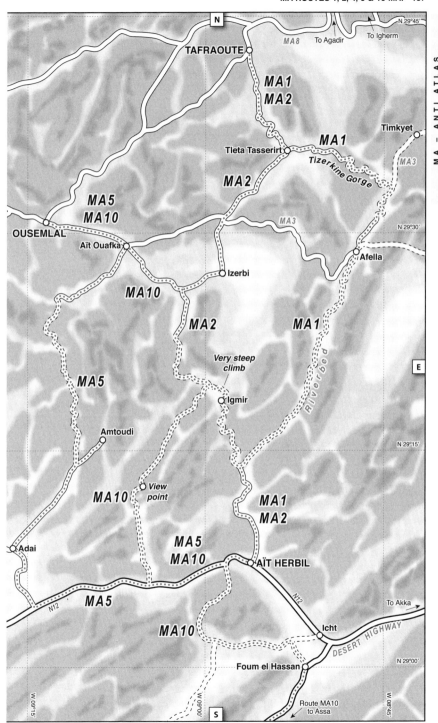

As you reach Amtoudi the sealed road ends by a basic auberge and coach park. I drove onwards for another kilometre or so, over and along the oued and parked by some houses below the agadir (N29° 14.65' W09° 11.11'). From here I walked straight up the gully and picked up the mule path; about 25 minutes' effort to get to the top where the old guardian was waiting for me, key in hand. Allow up to an hour for a good look around inside. You pay the guardian what you like.

According to the guidebooks there's another auberge in the village and another even more dramatic agadir perched a little further up the valley as well as a palm-filled canyon. If you like these sorts of places but aren't planning to overnight then allow at least half a day to explore Amtoudi's agadirs and canyon.

When you've had your fill, turn back south past the point where you joined the road and carry on 11km to the village of ...

77 (42)
. . . Souk Tnine Adai (to give one spelling; and note that the cumulative distances from here on assume you took the 10km round trip to Amtoudi). Here bear left at the road bollard and head SE around the hill and across the plain for the N12.

86 (33)   N29° 04.89' W09° 15.64'
At the N12 turn east for Aït Herbil. In about 15km at N29° 06.53' W09° 07.53' just before some trees, you pass the point where MA10 comes down from the north.

119   N29° 07.97' W08° 57.93'
Aït Herbil fuel station with a basic café but not much else.

For somewhere to stay the *Igmir Guest House* is 32km up Route MA2; allow an hour to get there.

MA6   TAZENACHT – ISSIL – TATA   171km
March 2008 ~ Mazda pickup

Description
Depending on where you start and where you want to end up, both this and Route MA7 take a diagonal route up and over the main southern range of the Anti Atlas, known here as the **Jebel Timkouka** and which separates the desert from the temperate northern plateaux. Both routes inch their way along canyons and past villages that barely feature on any map.

Once you leave the N10 highway a side road runs nearly all the way to Issil, with the 2000m Jebel looming ahead. There you climb to a U-shaped groove on the horizon and commence a dramatic descent to the valley floor. You'll be back on tarmac before Akka Ighern but leave it soon after on a track to Akka Iguirn on the N12 just west of Tata. You can extend this route in all directions by mixing in parts of MA7, 12 or 13.

Off road
Getting up to the Timkouka Pass is not so hard; getting back down the south side is slow but once at KM60 the roughest stage is over. A **robust 2WD** ought to manage it as little low-range crawling is required and with the absence of sand, **bikes** large and small can just stand up and let the suspension do its job.

Route finding
Although nothing accurate or detailed appears on paper maps, there's little chance of getting lost in the mountains as long as you keep close track of your orientation. Beyond Issil don't expect any traffic until Ighern Warfaln at KM80 by which time the sealed road may be near. The map is on p194-5.

Fuel and water
Tazenacht and Tata for fuel. There aren't so many wells between the villages but they're close together in distance if not time.

Suggested duration
Do-able in a day but better to slow down, camp out and carry on next day.

0km   N30° 34.39'   W07° 12.56'
AFRIQUIA fuel at the west end of **Tazenacht**. Head west out of town.

13.5 (157.5)   N30° 29.90'   W07° 18.84'
The original turn south through Zaouia Sidi Abdallah passing a shrine and water tower. Or continue to a tarmac junction.

20 (151)   N30° 26.81'   W07° 20.51'
Route MA7 (or tarmac) joins from the right. In a couple of kilometres you'll pass a water tower on the left near Zawyat Taliza, and at KM25 is Tiwiyine (N30° 24.79'   W07° 18.76'). Continue south through a couple more villages to Issil.

40 (131)   N30° 17.95'   W07° 17.50'
Junction. Issil is visible 1km to the SE (on MA7). Keep right and head SW for Jebel Timkouka.

43 (128)   N30° 16.62'   W07° 19.19'
Well with a bucket.

45 (126)   N30° 16.28'   W07° 20.04'
The village of Wantkou at the base of the jebel. Pass through and ascend the ridge westwards on a rough track towards the pass with great views to the north.

48 (123)   N30° 16.31'   W07° 21.28'
The windy 1830m Timkouka Pass with a grave in a walled enclosure. Should you do this route in reverse the view over the plain will creep up and be as mind-blowing as KM78 of MA7.

To the south a canyon unwinds down to the desert floor; a slow stage in a car. (The fork right around KM51 leads only to a radio mast.)

60 (111)   N30° 13.39'   W07° 22.73'
The 700m descent is over; cross a oued.

64 (107)   N30° 12.07'   W07° 23.23'
Leave another oued and head west into the hills, passing a deep, but dry, well as you exit a branch oued 1500m later.

68 (113)   N30° 11.09'   W07° 25.42'
Crest a rise, a valley opens up ahead with straight tracks leading SW.

76 (95)   N30° 09.46'   W07° 29.05'
Junction with an oil-drum-lid sign in Arabic indicating '80km' (Tata or maybe Taliouine?). Turn left. Straight on is an Olaf dead end.

77 (94)   N30° 08.75'   W07° 29.47'
Junction; turn left, SW. Straight on goes to the 'green cairn' crossing of routes MA12/13 where you can follow MA12 up to Assaragh or MA13 south along a parallel valley to meet this route at KM96.

TAZENACHT

Tazenacht has a few hotels, cafés and no fewer than four fuel stations and is also well known for its **carpets**; you'll see them displayed all over the main road, but there doesn't seem to be any of the accompanying hassle you may get in the cities. It makes a great place to browse and even buy without pressure, and potentially at better prices too. The carpets are the work of local Berber co-ops and the sheep you may pass out on the Issil plain provide the raw material you'll see dyed and drying in some village backyards.

If you're serious, the time to get here is very early for the Friday or Saturday morning souks. Northern dealers come down to fill their vans for the tourist souks of Marrakech, Meknes and Fes where a gullible or indifferent customer can easily pay ten times what they would down here.

79 (92)   N30° 08.11'   W07° 29.00'
Cross to the south side of the palm-lined oued. Here a new bypass (possibly a road now) runs east and across the oued; MA12 coming up. If it looks clear it could be a simpler way. Otherwise continue SE to Ighern Warfaln.

80 (91)   N30° 07.75'   W07° 28.28'
Enter 'Ighern Warfaln'. After 150m curve right and head another 150m SW, then turn left for 150m ESE and get to N30° 07.58'   W07° 28.19'; a oued passing through the middle of the village. Turn left down this oued over bare rock slabs; it doesn't feel right but it's the right way (see sat map image on website), passing finely-built stone buildings and a ruined ksar. Turn right out of the oued and continue south and east over the hills.

87 (84)   N30° 06.27'   W07° 27.18'
Cross a big oued by some pylons, joining MA12 coming up from Agmour. A stone signpost nearby features various unrecognisable village names. In just over a kilometre you cross back over a ford.

94 (77)   N30° 03.47'   W07° 27.06'
If not already then join the tar road and turn right for Akka Ighern. Left is for Agmour; MA11 in reverse. In 1km pass the new road running east about 90km to Foum Zguid (MA9).

105 (66)   N29° 59.69'   W07° 31.77'
Junction in **Akka Ighern** with the road from Taliouine (Route MA11). A few cafés,

shops and a barber. Turn left here, SE, for Tata.

111.5 (59.5)   N29° 58.64'   W07° 32.59'
Leave the tarmac by a pylon branch line and turn right or west for Akka Iguirn.

113.5 (57.5)   N29° 58.29'   W07° 33.65'
By a wall leave this track to Tiskamoudine and turn right to follow a track SW.

114.5 (56.5)   N29° 57.66'   W07° 34.17'
After crossing a water channel, a track joins from the left from a water tower.

118 (53)   N29° 56.04'   W07° 34.88'
Track joins left from Issarghine village.

126 (45)
One of many tracks leading NW to Targant village. Continue SW.

133.5 (37.5)   N29° 49.64'   W07° 40.34'
A **well** (15m with a rope and a bottle) and trough on the north side of Oued Targant. In less than 1km you drop off the stony hamada into a small oued running west.

138 (33)   N29° 48.41'   W07° 42.24'
Join a big oued south to Akka Iguirn.

143 (28)   N29° 45.84'   W07° 42.03'
Pass through Akka Iguirn village, join the N10 highway and turn west.

171   N29° 44.31'   W07° 58.42'
Fuel stations on the SW edge of **Tata**. For more see the box on p193.

MA7   FOUM ZGUID – ISSIL – TALIOUINE   174KM
April 2008 ~ Mazda pickup

Description
A spectacular and isolated transit from the desert floor along a serpentine canyon track passing through villages hidden in a tectonic crumple zone and lost to any map maker. Up and over the Jebel Timkouka you crawl at little more than a hobbled donkey's pace to emerge above the Issil plain wondering what day it is while surveying a viewpoint from *One Million Years BC*, but sadly without the fur bikinis.

No maps really can do this route justice and you'll end the day in Taliouine grinning at a steaming tajine which will probably grin right back. This is one of four great routes here for lighter bikes and adds up to southern Morocco in an argan nutshell.

Off road
In a 4WD the 40km off-road section will include hours of inching round steep hairpin turns, several villages and some palmeries. As long as you nurture your tyres and rims, a trail bike will be great fun on this route, a loaded mountain biker will have a tough time but won't forget it in a hurry. Without low range a 2WD may struggle in places.

Route finding
Not on any map but pretty well Olaffed and with little opportunity to go wrong. Just sit back and enjoy the ride. The route **map** is on p194-5.

Fuel and water
For fuel you have Foum Zguid plus two or three places on the N10 before Taliouine itself, and for water there are a couple of wells and the villages. (I think I've used that phrase before.)

Suggested duration
With tarmac at Issil now it's easily do-able in a day as long as nothing breaks.

0km   N30° 05.40' W06° 52.66'
AFRIQUIA fuel on the north side of **Foum Zguid**. Go north.

18 (156)   N30° 14.90' W06° 51.05'
Turn west onto a tarmac road. There's a big roadhouse just up the road.

37 (137)   N30° 13.37' W07° 01.80'
The **tarmac ended** here in 2012, turn north for Tlite.

40.5 (133.5)
Cross the oued into **Tlite** and then turn back down into the oued by a ruined ksar, passing an old graveyard by a palmerie.

44 (130)   N30° 16.21' W07° 03.74'
Pass the old village of Tawrirt-n-Tilas on purple stone dust. You now rise out of the valley with the pylons and a water tower towards a radio mast on the ridge.

46 (128)
Pass a ruined ksar on the right by a palmy oued and in 1km pass above Aghgoumi village, heading for the gap in the ranges. Once you're through the gap you pass lush palm gardens on the right.

48 (126)   N30° 17.60' W07° 05.44'
Fork right out of the oued as the blue arrow on the rock suggests and proceed steeply up into the pass.

50.5 (123.5)   N30° 18.24' W07° 05.98'
Crest pass at 1150m and descend again.

53.5 (120.5)   N30° 19.11' W07° 06.64'
An inter-range basin opens up with the small village of Amtezguine tucked in alongside its gardens.

55.5 (118.5)   N30° 19.71' W07° 06.99'
Keep left and head into the oued through a wall-lined palmerie on both sides, not into Amtezguine. At one point you're on a concrete embankment.

56.5 (117.5)   N30° 19.82' W07° 07.30'
At another blue arrow turn right and then steeply hairpin left out of the village (rejoining Olaf which went through it). Leave the village heading SW and rise up over a gorge. In 1km cross a shingly oued and continue uphill, passing a perfectly cleared area on the left soon after. Some tight hairpins follow as you crawl west in first gear above the valley below.

63 (111)   N30° 19.69' W07° 09.47'
You're at 1495m after a long, slow, but dramatic ascent.

65 (109)
The track improves a bit as you see buildings and the parched terrace plots of Zawyat Ainas ahead.

70 (104)   N30° 17.68'   W07° 12.17'
High point at 1724m, and '15km' from Issil, according to a sign. At the top Olaf goes left, you go right and join up in a couple of kilometres.

72 (68)
Running SW now, a track crosses and in 1km another track joins from the right at N30° 16.85' W07° 12.56'.

76 (98)   N30° 16.15'   W07° 12.87'
Pass a lonely village with a pink mosque.

78 (96)   N30° 15.81'   W07° 14.74'
Cross a 1635m pass as a canyon opens out to your left. Within 500m you round a bend and suddenly the Issil plain opens up before you, dotted with isolated outcrops: a dramatic Saharan vista which the late afternoon light won't spoil at all. You're finally out of the mountains which have absorbed you for hours.

81 (93)   N30° 16.62'   W07° 15.57'
Pass a well on the left and head for Issil.

85 (89)   N30° 17.57'   W07° 17.18'
Issil with a store but not much else. By now a tarmac road will lead north to the N10.

111 (63)   N30° 28.87'   W07° 21.58'
The distance and position may be out a bit but you join the N10 and turn west for Taliouine. Soon you'll pass a lone ZIZ just before heading up a pass, as well as a basic SHELL about 22km before Taliouine after the village of Tinfat where Route MH9 comes in from the north.

174   N30° 31.49'   W07° 53.22'
ZIZ on the west end of **Taliouine**, a few kilometres from the town centre where there are several auberges. See the website under Updates for a link to accommodation information.

MA8   TAFRAOUTE – TAZALARHITE – IGHERM   135KM
November 2008 ~ Yamaha Ténéré

Description
This is a version of Route MA3 in reverse, a great transit up through the Ameln valley and Tazalarhite on the edge of the Tizkhit plateau, uninhabited apart from a couple of plucky farmsteads. On the far side you drop off steeply into the deep canyon of the Oued or 'Assif' Oumdar. Here ensues a slow but fascinating passage along the riverbed past a string of palm-choked villages and lush gardens labelled as Tazegzaoute on the maps. Then, as the canyon opens out an hour or so downstream, the dramatic angular erosion of the cliffs is unlike anything you've seen in Morocco. Soon you're back on the highway, heading north. As a place to celebrate a great day on the piste, Igherm is a bit of an anticlimax, but give yourself another hour and you could be in Tata, Taroudant or Taliouine.

Off road
In good weather the only restriction on this route is the 23km passage along the Assif Oumdar (KM60-83) and possibly muddy stages up on the flat plateau top. Apart from the need for good brakes to get down to the riverbed, something like a big Land Cruiser will have to watch the width on some of the narrow passages in the gorge. In the riverbed you'll see **stone width-markers** giving guidance to what can pass ahead; push past them at your peril.

Motorbikers may find the riverbed section hard work. Depending on how your bike is set up and its load, to keep your balance and directional stability in the shingle-filled riverbeds you'll need to ride too fast to appreciate it all.

Lowering tyre pressures would help but risks punctures on the sharper rocks; with harder tyres you can take the hits at the speed you need to maintain. On a big, loaded bike, riding this tricky 23km stage without a break will take forearms like Popeye. Finally, whatever you're on or in, if black clouds are gathering and grumbling overhead, the bed of the Assif is no place to linger.

Route finding
On road or track there are several junctions to get right, so plan ahead and read carefully. Both times I took this route I was the only vehicle on the piste apart from a local pickup or two at the easy ends. For the **map** see pp194-5.

Fuel and water
Fuel at each end only and water from a couple of wells on the plateau and on the steep descent into Ifassras.

Suggested duration
Easy to do in a day, though ending it in Igherm may not be too thrilling. Once back at the road at KM89 you can head down to more tourist-agreeable Tata (see box below) or take the mountain route down to Tata once in Igherm (the end of Route MA11 in reverse). Camping out on the plateau would be windy and bleak, and in the gorge most probably the opposite.

TATA

Tata is the provincial capital, as big as a place gets down here and dubbed the 'Siena of the Sahara' on account of its hundreds of sienna-daubed colonnade arches shading the sidewalks.

It has two **fuel stations** facing each other on the far side of town on the road to Akka. Coming from the east down the wide boulevard, when you get to a T-junction in town just past the barracks, most of the town and the municipal **campsite** are to the right or north; the road to Igherm. For the two main **hotels** and fuel turn left. The Rough Guide has a handy map, *al hamdullilai*!

The **campsite** (N29° 44.84' W07° 58.39') used by long-term RV-ers is pretty much in the middle of town by a yellow 'Pigier' sign on the town's main road which carries on to Igherm. There are also a couple of hotels along this street: the *Essalam* and the *Sahara* a few doors down. Neither may be too flash upstairs but both are great places to eat: you can get half a roast chicken with salad, chips, plus a drink or two for around 65dh.

Just after dusk is the time for *le promenade* when, market days excepted, the town briefly becomes energised. In an hour it's all

over and they're back home watching dubbed Brazilian soaps.

I usually stay in the tiled interior of the near-empty *Hotel Renaissance*, five minutes walk from the town centre and which you'll pass on the way to the fuel stations. A storage room over the road for the bike was offered without asking. Half board was 250dh with an en suite room and access to the roof to cool off if need be.

Just down the road next to one of the fuel stations is the flashier *Hotel Tata, Relais des Sables*. With a name like that you know they're ready for cheched-up tour groups. We ate there once which for some reason took them by surprise.

Based in Tata, scenic drives and desert pistes lead off in all directions: tracks run north-east through the Jebel Timouka to the N10; south-east of town along the Algerian border to meet MS8 on its way to Chegaga and westwards there's more of the same towards Tafraoute.

Sticking to the road, touring bikes and motorhomes or bicycles can enjoy tranquil transits along MA9 or MA11 or the 'Desert Highway' MS10 running towards the ocean.

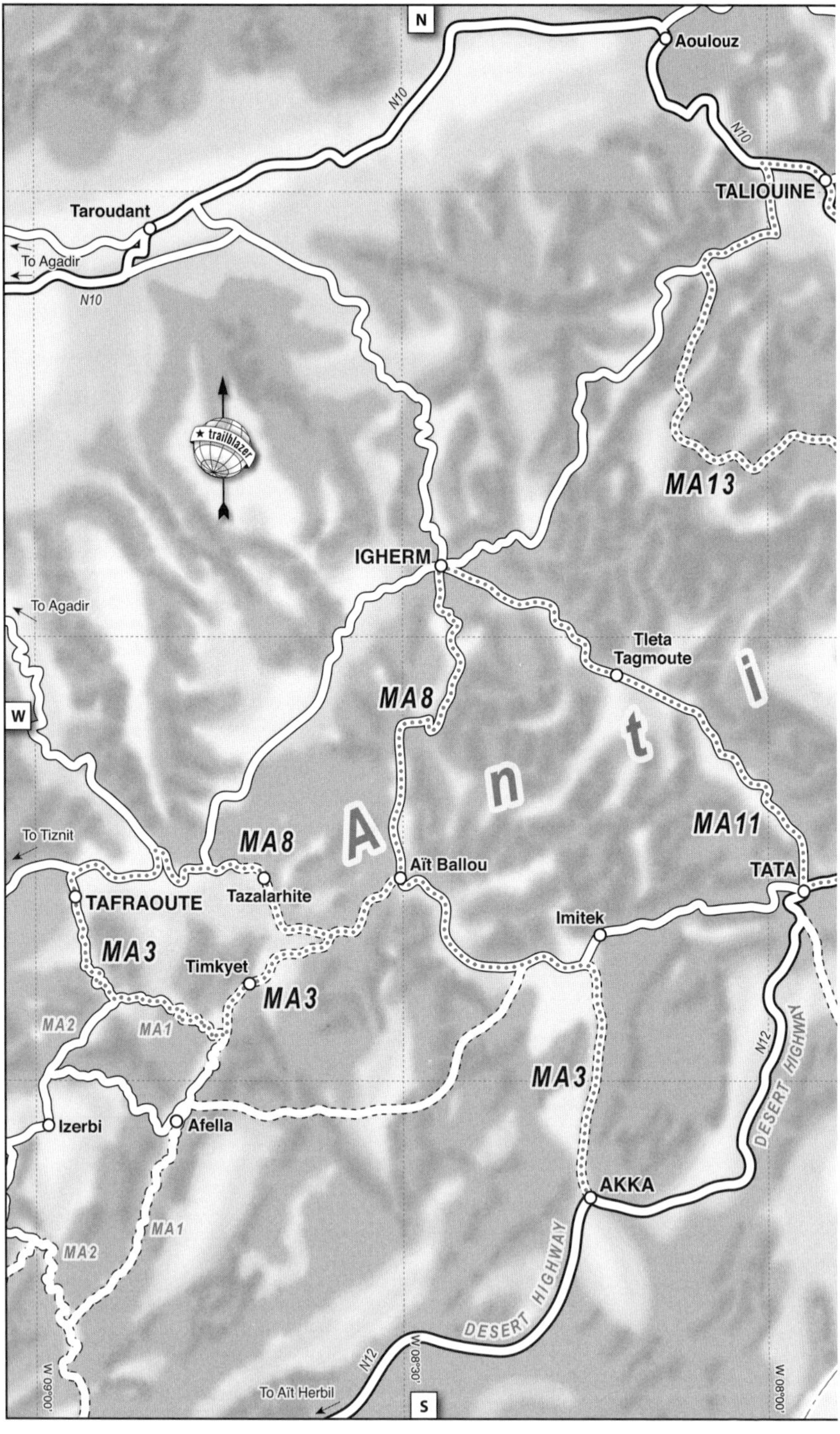
N
Aoulouz
N10
N10
TALIOUINE
Taroudant
To Agadir
N10
trailblazer
MA13
IGHERM
To Agadir
Tleta
Tagmoute
W
MA8
Anti
MA11
To Tiznit
MA8
Aït Ballou
TATA
TAFRAOUTE
Tazalarhite
Imitek
MA3
Timkyet
MA3
MA2
MA1
MA3
N12
DESERT HIGHWAY
Izerbi
Afella
AKKA
MA1
MA2
DESERT HIGHWAY
N12
W 09°00'
W 08°30'
W 08°00'
To Aït Herbil
S

N

To Ouarzazate

N10

TAZENACHT

To Agdz

DESERT HIGHWAY

N 30°30'

MA11
MA12

MA6

MA7

N10

Issil Plain

MA6
MA7

Jebel Timkouka

Issil

MA7

MA7

MA11

MA12

Assaragh

MA6

MA7

To Zagora

Agadir
Melloul

MA13

MA6

El Mhamid

N12

Foum Zguid

MA9
MA12

N 30°00'

Akka Ighern

MS7

E

MA6
MA11

Tissint

MA9

Jebel Bani

MS8

DESERT HIGHWAY

N12

DESERT HIGHWAY

N12

Akka
Iguirn

MA13

Mrimina

MA6
MA9
MA11
MA13

Jebel

MS8

To Tagounite

N 29°30'

0   10   20   30km

W 07°30'

W 07°00'

MA – ANTI ATLAS

Routes MA3, MA6, MA7, MA8, MA9, MA11, MA12 & MA13

0km   N29° 43.20'   W08° 58.32'
AFRIQUIA fuel in **Tafraoute** town centre by the *Hotel Tafraoute*. Head north out of town along the main road.

4 (131)   N29° 45.14'   W08° 57.89'
Junction; turn right for the Ameln valley and the road to Igherm. Head east up a valley past campsites and other auberges below the 2300m Jebel El Kest; it's a long ascent. At the head of the valley, as you go round a sharp left-hand hairpin, the road shown from here on many maps to Agard, just south of Tafraoute (and seemingly a more direct route), doesn't exist, at least with the prominence it's given.

22 (113)   N29° 44.53'   W08° 49.90'
Soon after the hairpin mentioned above leave the Aït Baha road and turn right for Igherm, passing through the village of Titeki.

33 (102)   N29° 46.51'   W08° 46.79'
Village of Azgour with ox-blood red painted houses. As you go uphill, just after a like-coloured mosque on the right, turn right or SE onto a track. There is a white block inscribed with Arabic. About 1km down this track fork left for Afasfass and Tazalarhite.

37 (98)
Pass through Afasfass as you climb east and then south up the hill side.

41 (94)   N29° 45.06'   W08° 43.74'
Top out at nearly 1900m at the mining village of Tazalarhite; its old town perched on a rock with newer houses spread around below. To the north you may also see snow capping the western end of the High Atlas as it drops towards Agadir.

Pass round the west side of the village, heading SE. In 1km keep right at a fork. And the same again in less than another kilometre; keep right at KM42 (N29° 44.61' W08° 43.33'). These tracks off to the left look like they're associated with the mine.

You're now setting off to traverse the treeless 1800m Tizkhit plateau dotted with a sagey scrub and rocks. There's the occasional pastoral enclosure and maybe the odd gazelle bounding away from you at high speed.

47 (88)   N29° 42.57'   W08° 42.36'
A lone farm with a **well**, surrounding cultivation and a few trees.

49 (86)   N29° 41.53'   W08° 41.39'
Arrive at a plastered block. Turning left or SE here leads down to Ifassras at KM66 below, possibly via the village of Mazdal, taking one side of a triangle. This route carries on straight south.

51 (84)   N29° 40.53'   W08° 41.47'
Meet Route MA3 at another stone block. MA3 runs SW for Timkyet and Afella. You carry straight on, or SSE.

58 (77)   N29° 38.22'   W08° 39.32'
Having turned NE and passing the other lone plateau farmhouse on the left, at this point you drop off the plateau and commence a very steep descent. You'll appreciate the places where they've concreted ramps over the track.

60 (75)   N29° 38.28'   W08° 38.41'
Brake hard for the village of Aït Alha or you'll end up in someone's living room. Once through the village turn left into the oued.

66 (69)   N29° 40.54'   W08° 37.03'
Arrive at the village of Ifassras and pass the junction at N29° 40.55' W08° 37.10' where the track from KM49 comes down. You now set off to crawl along the shingly riverbed of the Assif Oumdar towards Tazegzaoute and Aït Ballou; great fun to crawl along in a car listening to the birds and the bees and the *stylo* pleas, a bit more demanding on a moto.

You pass through thick palmeries and gardens jammed in below a string of villages perched above the banks; it's hard to know which one is actually Tazegzaoute or where it starts or ends. Whatever, it's worth taking a break now and then from the rattling vehicle just to take it all in.

79 (56)   N29° 41.66'   W08° 34.63'
The palmerie ends and the gorge opens out below distinctively eroded zig-zag formations on the left. From now on towards the highway, look back to see them at their best.

83 (52)   N29° 42.95'   W08° 33.97'
Cross the oued at the west end of the village of Sidi Al Haj Ou Ali and pass some striking villas built by prodigal sons who've done well up north. Many towns and villages in this part of Morocco have such lavish-looking dwellings set among the more traditional mud-brickery.

86 (49)   N29° 43.57'   W08° 32.47'
After switch-backing down from a high point with a great view behind you, meet a track coming up from the oued on your right and carry on NE.

88.5 (46.5)   N29° 44.53'   W08° 31.39'
Cross the Oumdar oued one last time and on the north bank turn towards the village of Aït Ballou visible just ahead.

89 (46)   N29° 44.72'   W08° 31.04'
Having passed around the north side of Aït Ballou, you **join the R109 highway** at a white stone block with many village names and head north for Igherm, passing a village with a ksar or fortress on the right with a couple of restos.

135   N30° 05.26'   W08° 27.67'
Igherm SHELL just before the crossroads and by the little souk. If you're wondering where to go next, a winding tarred road leads right at the crossroads by the basic *Hotel Anzal*, down to Tagmoute and Tata.

MA9   TATA – AKKA IGHERN – FOUM ZGUID   169KM
April 2012 ~ Yamaha TTR250, BMW F650GS

By now it's very likely this route has been sealed end to end, making a great alternative to the N12 'Desert Highway' to the south. A former Dakar Rally piste, you leave the N12 after 50km near Kasba el Joua and cross the plain 21km north to Akka Ighern. In the middle of town turn right and follow the new road north-east towards Agmour. You turn right in 10km where in 2012 the next 50km was prepared for asphalt.

This newly oriented road joins the old piste from Akka just before a ford where it sets off north-east along the jebel-bound valley. This road has been in preparation for many years and during that time new fords waiting for the tarmac were being ripped out by floods. As anywhere in this part of Morocco, there's nothing to suggest this couldn't happen again which may mean short gnarly detours that could be a stretch for low-slung vehicles. After some 72km you're back on tar at the R111 junction coming from Tanenacht. There's a roadhouse just to the north, or **Foum Zguid** (pronounced 'Zgyd' not Zgoo-id; also with fuel) is through a gap or 'foum' in the ranges, 18km to the south. Coming through the gap and with the desert ahead you won't be surprised to learn that it's almost exactly 1000 miles as the crow flies to Timbuktu on the south side of the Sahara, crossing just one road on the way.

The *Restaurant Chegaga* in the town centre on the corner is a good spot but not so cheap. For somewhere to stay carry on down the road and you'll soon get to the small campsite on the right which was OK if a bit pricey too. The *Auberge Iriki* a bit further on the right has a spacious locked yard though on my last visit the food was ordinary and the place a bit noisy. Last time we stayed out at the deserted *Sable d'Or* camping auberge just out town 250m past the arch which had basic rooms and ablutions but plenty of space to camp and even a pool in summertime. The route map is on pp194-5.

MA10 OUSEMLAL – FOUM EL HASSAN – ASSA   195KM
November 2008 ~ Yamaha Ténéré

Description
Another way of getting down off the Anti Atlas to the desert, but as with Route MA5, nothing can quite match the wonders of MA2 up the Oued Smouguene. This route follows MA2 along its less impressive upland stage before splitting off to cross the plateau to the west, a rough track, enlivened not inconsiderably by the impressive viewpoint at KM66.

From here you drop down, cross the plain below and head east a short distance along the N12 to pick up a track which winds in and out of the jebels. You reach Foum el Hassan, passing nomad camps along the way and where you follow the 'Desert Highway' south-west to Assa.

Off road
After the block at KM46 where the track splits for Igmir (Route MA2), the piste you follow is little-used and so soon becomes rough up to the KM66 viewpoint before the big descent. The second section is in better shape and won't give an off-road vehicle any trouble; even regular cars could manage it and it's short enough to be a fun taster or indeed a quiet place to camp out. Mountain bikes will enjoy this stage more too, but from Foum el Hassan – no oasis despite the palms – it's a long road ride to anywhere else.

Route finding
The first piste stage is straightforward with little to confuse you. The winding route of the second section requires a bit more concentration. On these piste sections you're unlikely to come across any traffic other than the mule caravans of the nomads. The **map** is on pp186-7.

Fuel and water
Ousemlal and Assa only for fuel, though Aït Herbil is a short detour from KM88. No wells were noted on the piste apart from at KM113, but there must be some out there. Otherwise try the villages.

Suggested duration
End-to-end in a day is not difficult, but breaking it up with a camp out north of Foum el Hassan would be more fun.

0km   N29° 31.57'   W09° 14.73'
PETROMIN fuel on the west side of **Jemaa Ida Ousemlal** to give it its full title. The town has a few shops. Fill up and head east through town towards Ouafka.

11 (184)
Junction on the east side of Souk Khemis de Aït Ouafka. The road to the NE comes down from Tafraoute – an alternative start for this route. Carry on east.

32 (163)   N29° 27.08'   W09° 03.74'
Take the piste which is being improved and which leaves the sealed road to the south, just east of Tahwawat village at a yellow sign for the Igmir Guest House. In about 1.5km at N29° 26.40' W09° 03.44' turn right and follow this track south towards Igmir.

On the way you may notice a track joining from the right and another leading off left, but the main way is clear. (Full details of the turn offs are in Route MA2).

46 (149)   N29° 20.71'   W09° 02.43'
The piste forks at a detailed sign block.
Turn right (SW) and wind slowly into a
shallow valley. Left leads 8km down to
Igmir on Route MA2.

60 (135)   N29° 15.27'   W09° 05.56'
Although it's a very unlikely prospect,
according to some maps right here leads
SW to Amtoudi just 10km away (MA5). I
gave it a go for about half an hour but
soon got confused in a maze of mineral
exploration tracks heading off in all directions. There was no clear sign of a single
through-route to Amtoudi, or indeed anywhere useful.
    Back on Route MA10, in 4 or 5km you
pass the **high point** at around 1112m.

66 (129)   N29° 12.69'   W09° 06.82'
Viewpoint where the escarpment drops
dramatically towards the N12 and the
jebels beyond.
    The track switchbacks down to the
plain without too much difficulty. Once
you've dropped 350m and are back on the
flats, head directly south, passing tracks
leading east to the villages of Talilit and
later Tagigalt, close to the road.

78 (117)   N29° 06.55'   W09° 07.55'
Join the N12 highway close to two cairns
just west of some trees. Turn left, or east.

88 (107)   N29° 07.37'   W09° 01.87'
Leave the road again south down a track.
(Olaf starts about 3.5km further on, just
after some Armco on a bend.)

92.5 (102.5)   N29° 05.22'   W09° 01.36'
Olaf joins from the east – an extra 7km.

100 (95)   N29° 02.47'   W09° 01.14'
Curve south then SE then east round the

Jebel Tastaft. At this junction keep
straight; east. Right here picks up the Olaf
mentioned below.
    About 1.5km later pass a building
before a oued crossing.

104 (91)   N29° 02.12'   W08° 58.84'
A bigger track joins from the SW by some
ruins. It's Olaffed and after some 50m
joins the Assa road 24km from town at
N28° 43.30' W09° 13.53'. It looks washed
out and little used these days.

110 (85)   N29° 01.97'   W08° 55.40'
Head into a oued then cross back to the
north bank and continue NE, leaving
Olaf.

112 (83)   N29° 02.48'   W08° 54.36'
Arrive at a junction of a track coming
down from near Icht. Turn south into the
main oued. The shingle and ruts can be
tricky on a heavy bike.

113 (82)   N29° 01.95'   W08° 54.37'
Pass a **well** (6m) high on the east bank of
the oued by some big trees.

115 (80)   N29° 01.04'   W08° 53.59'
Join the tarmac at a concrete ford on the
west side of Foum el Hassan. Turn SW for
Assa.
    Despite its long outdated prominence
on maps and road signs, Foum el Hassan
is a poor border village with some stores
and a basic hotel somewhere. In colonial
times it was a garrison (as it is today) on
the long-abandoned road to Algeria, via
the mysterious 'Tour de Merkala' – probably a natural formation.

195   N28° 37.05'   W09° 27.05'
ZIZMO at the west end of Assa. For a hotel
in town see the end of Route MW2.

MA11 TALIOUINE – TATA – IGHERM   266KM
November 2008 ~ Yamaha Ténéré

There's a direct road route from Talliouine to Igherm,
about 100km through the hills to the south-west along
the R106. Although nearly three times as long, this
route takes a big arc to the south-east, over the crest of
the Anti Atlas to the desert floor and back up again; the

sort of scenic drive you want to discover in Morocco. Only sealed in the last few years, not all maps classify this route as tarmac or even depict it at all, but barring heavy rains it'll be open to all vehicles large and small, and **bicycles** especially will find it a great ride, certainly as far as Tata (fuel and hotels) before the big climb back up to Igherm. See pp194-5 for the **map**.

Route description

Kilometre zero is at the auberges at the east end of **Taliouine**. Head east, away from town past the turn off for the mountain road up to Askaoun (another great 50km drive but a dead end unless you have the clearance). Back down below, you pass the old kasbah to the south, cross the oued and pass a Ziz a couple of kilometres out of town. Here starts a steep climb up to 1500m where, around KM15, you leave the N10 to the south and head for the ranges. The road climbs slowly up across the plateau to the small town of Agadir Melloul at KM48 (a few shops and a café). A couple of kilometres on, the road peaks around 1860m at the Tizi-n-Ounzour and then rolls off the Anti Atlas crags through a short narrow canyon. You emerge in a narrow valley as the metres tumble away and your ears creak. Suddenly the air is warmer and the scenery more arid.

The stone-clad village of Tisfriouine crops up on a bend at KM71, a desert settlement with an old shrine by the mosque. Four kilometres later, your arrival on the desert fringe is underlined by a dense roadside palmerie. After crossing 30°N the road takes a turn to the north-east to circumvent the spur of a ridge and the start of the Admal valley, as agreeable a place to lunch as anywhere along this route. Even with a low-slung road vehicle it's not hard to get off the road and enjoy a break, or even out of sight beneath the jebels to enjoy a night out in the desert at around 1000m.

Back on the road, at KM116 you arrive at **Akka Ighern**, a small town with a couple of cafés and a shop as well as surrounding palmeries and market gardens. Set at the edge of a flat basin surrounded by mountains, at the roundabout by the trees, many other MA routes head for the hills (including the MA9 scenic drive) while you turn south across the floodplain to the N12 'Desert Highway' and at KM137, just after **Ksaba el Joua**, turn west for Tata.

Behind the Jebel Bani ridge the Sahara rolls away unbroken for a thousand miles to Timbuktu, and as you drive down the boulevard into laid-back **Tata**, the biggest town for miles around, you'll find the two better hotels and fuel (KM186) to the left (see box p193). Turn right for the main street with several cafés and hotel restaurants, as well as ATMs and a centrally located campsite.

Continue up this street, through the town's palmerie, over the Oued Tata and north out of town for the final stage back up into the ranges and Igherm. Initially you follow the valley upstream, passing striking, twisted rock strata and distant nomads' tents until you emerge at another rim-rocked basin. On the far side at KM225 is **Souk Tleta Tagmoute** and at the town centre (a couple of shops), bear right and wind on through the settlement. Soon you'll pass the *Gite Tagmout* and the remains of the old town. The valley narrows and the road may be washed-out as it crosses and re-crosses the oued past more palmeries jammed alongside the banks.

The climb begins as the road folds back on itself, away from the desert and back up into the scrubby heights of the Anti Atlas. Winding north and then west, it flattens out and suddenly at KM266 you're at the crossroads that is Igherm town centre right by the basic *Hotel Anzal*. For the SHELL and the shops turn left. Should you have a few miles left in you this road, the R109, continues with no less drama for just over 100km back down to Tata.

MA12 FOUM ZGUID – ASSARAGH – TALIOUINE   190KM
April 2012 ~ BMW F650GS; Yamaha TTR250

Description
Although the off-road section on this route is short (and probably shorter still since we did it), it's still another great variation on the MA6 and 7 and 13 routes; if you like this area you'll want to try them all. It crosses the wide arid floodplain separating the edge of the Anti Atlas from Jebel Bani and the Sahara beyond, before rising up into the hills via a village-lined canyon.

If you really want to give your suspension a damn good thrashing split north onto MA7 at KM37, cross the range and drop into the Issil plain, rise out of it again and south along MA6 as far as KM107 of this route and keep going to see how far you get. On a bike you might make it to the gîte at Assaragh which will be a perfect end to a spectacular day's off-roading. The subsequent section over the plateau to the Taliouine road is relatively tame; reversing MA13 over Adrar Tingagouene is more sporty.

Off road
There's nothing here to confound a big bike or a regular car, especially if you avoid the Agmour village section and the steep ascent at KM109. Rain and storms will of course cause havoc in the gorges, whether the roads are sealed or not.

Route finding
A knot of roadbuilding got us in a muddle around Agmour but once on the plateau the main piste north-west is clear. The **map**'s on pp194-5.

Fuel and water
Fuel only at each end though you can ask in the bigger villages where there's bound to be water too.

Suggested duration
You could make Taliouine in a day but unless you're camping it's more satisfying to stay in the two auberges in Aguinan and Assaragh.

0km	**N30° 05.40' W06° 52.66'**	**38 (152)**	

0km   **N30° 05.40' W06° 52.66'**
AFRIQUIA fuel north side of **Foum Zguid**. Leave to the north.

18 (172)   **N30° 14.90' W06° 51.05'**
Turn west onto a tarmac road. There's a big roadhouse just up the road.

38 (152)
In 2012 the tarmac ended at the Tlite turn off (MA7). A wide track with embedded stones and corrugations continued west.

At 53km pass Tigmassine to the north and at KM70 is a dead end piste to the north.

The descent at around KM110.

79 (111)   N30° 01.78'   W07° 21.62'
With confusing roadworks and pistes, just
before a ford (just after is easier) we
turned north up the oued to Agmour.

You can simplify things by continuing
11km along the main track/road to a T-
junction, turn right and in 2km turn left
(KM93). It's about the same distance.

88 (102)
Agmour. Go SW on a new road.

93 (97)   N30° 03.48'   W07° 27.05'
Junction, turn right, north (Olaf) on new
blacktop or alongside a cleared roadbed
primed for surfacing any day.

99 (91)
After crossing a oued reach a junction
with an aged red signblock daubed with
blue paint. Leave Olaf (MA13) and follow
the right arm (below the course of the
forthcoming road) to Tamsoult.

101 (89)
Tamsoult village. If not on the new road,
work your way round the SW side of the
village to the NW. Up the track you'll see
Ighern Warfaln (on MA6, MA13) and its
impressive ruined citadel or agadir on the
other side of the palm-filled valley.

106 (84)   N30° 08.02'   W07° 28.89'
Rejoin Olaf from KM99 on the west bank
of a wide valley dotted with palms.
Continue NW. In 1km MA6 comes in from
the NE.

108 (82)   N30° 08.55'   W07° 30.02'
T-junction by a few buildings where a pile
of stone blocks have Arabic directions

daubed in green. NE leads to a side oued
which turns NW to join up.

In the right vehicle you go left (SW) to
turn right in 1km to take a rougher, high
level pylon track steeply over a cone
mountain. It's more fun and about 1km
shorter.

112 (78)   N30° 09.09'   W07° 31.25'
Join the low level track coming around
from the east and carry on upstream,
bending left and right. In about 2km
there's a big shady lunch tree on the left.

120 (70)   N30° 11.06'   W07° 31.49'
Ouedside well (25m) in Tinzourine village
with another well soon. You then leave
the oued and cross a spur passing a
zaouia (shrine) built among older ruins
and a graveyard.

126 (64)   N30° 12.39'   W07° 33.72'
Gîte on a fork right by the track at the
north end of **Aguinan**. Head down into
the dense palmerie and then climb very
steeply at times up the cliff to the petrified
waterfalls (tufa).

131 (59)
Junction. Assaragh gîte is 1km to the east.

133 (57)   N30° 13.75'   W07 35.68'
Junction. Left for Agadir Melloul (MA13,
not Olaffed and rough), right for
Taliouine. Follow the track north, cross a
oued in 3km and in another 3km (KM139)
in Timdrart village, turn left or west to
ascend the hillside to nearly 2000m.

150 (40)
Junction, keep left. Thin Olafs potentially
lead north to the N10.

162 (28)
Join the Agadir Melloul road (MA11) and
turn north, passing Tagadirt village with
more tufa formations and old storehouses
built into the low cliffs.

At KM178 reach the N10 and turn
west, dropping down some sweeping
bends towards Taliouine.

190
Zɪz Taliouine eastside. The town with several auberges is another 2km on.

MA13 TALIOUINE – AGADIR MELLOUL – TATA   252KM
April 2012 ~ BMW F650GS; Yamaha TTR250

Description
This route initially leads you into the relatively populated but not so dramatic hills south of Taliouine on mostly good tracks. Once you join and quickly cross the road (MA11) at Agadir Melloul, a gnarlier and so more interesting stage leads over the 2000-metre Adrar Tingagouene to the head of the canyon, reversing MA12 for a while. You then leave that canyon over the cone mountain and traverse an unoccupied parallel valley before meeting the road built in 2012 to Akka Ighern and so the N12 to Tata.

As mentioned on MA12, you can turn this route into a protracted off-road excursion by detouring to MA6 and 7 via Issil to end up in Foum Zguid. That will take a couple of days covering a distance of 280km with around twenty-five percent on tar.

Off road
Apart from heavy rains of course, only the 32km stage across the Adrar Tingagouene is likely to give any pause to a regular car, although it ought not be enough to put off a smoothly ridden adventure touring bike.

Route finding
Just about all of this route is Olaffed and even where it's not over the Adrar, it's still clear enough to follow. The **map** is on pp194-5.

Fuel and water
Fuel at each end only and with no viable short cuts. Water from the wells and villages as listed.

Suggested duration
You could do this in one long day but you'll have more fun overnighting at the auberges in Assaragh or Aguinan. Wild camping would best be done in the canyon well south of there or better still on the cone hill or the valley beyond KM160 but before the road.

0km   N30° 31.91' W07° 55.33'
SHELL fuel in Taliouine town centre. Head west and in about 11km cross a bridge in a town (more fuel) and turn south onto the R106 Igherm road.

31 (221)
Turn south off the R106 and in 6km you might like to bypass the town of Amzaourou (leave Olaf) spread out on the other side of the oued, and take the track to the right.

Follow the oued upstream passing a couple more villages, some with wells.

52 (200)
Start of a switchback ascent. Once on top carry on climbing eastwards then curve back west and south, passing a hut at about KM57.

61 (191) N30 14.79 W8 07.24
Junction in the middle of Aït Azzi village. at a white sign block with Arabic writing; thin Olafs head south and west. You follow a little used track westwards, soon passing another southward junction. The track gets narrow and rough as it winds around a hillside.

67 (185)

As you pass through a village and cross a oued to go uphill the track widens and improves. Thin Olafs run south and NE. You curve to the south until you arrive at...

74 (178)   N30° 12.82' W08° 01.69'

... a junction by a village with a post office. A short section of tarmac runs east. It soon ends but a broad well-formed track rolls west and north up over 1600-metre passes and past villages.

105 (147)

The road (MA11) just north of Agadir Melloul. Head into the village centre and soon turn left, east, opposite a shop and the mosque (N30° 14.01' W07° 47.79'). The rougher and more interesting stage across the 2000-m Adrar Tingagouene starts here.

108.5 (143.5)

Sign for nearby Issa village left, you go right and SE for Tayfest and Assaragh.

119 (133)

A bit less than 1km after Tayfest village there's a steep climb with scenery reminiscent of Jebel Sarhro.

125 (127)   N30 13.31 W7 39.71

A 1934m pass with great views east. As you drop you'll see the old way down to the left. In 3km keep left at a junction and another 1km on keep left again and drop down to a oued with a garden (N30° 13.27' W07° 38.25'). Cross it up towards Taltgmoute. Use the pylons as a guide.

130 (122)

Pass buildings on a hill with Taltgmoute village centre to the north.

134 (118)

Keep left at this junction as you drop downhill to the main piste.

135 (117)

Arrive at a main piste and turn right towards nearby Assaragh. In 500m you cross the KM133 MA12 junction and continue southwards.

137 (115)

Edge of Assaragh. Turn off left for the village and the gîte, or continue south (picture right) for Aguinan, taking an impressive drop down past the petrified waterfall.

Go through the palmerie in the oued, passing the gîte on the way out and follow the oued south, reversing MA12.

156 (96)   N30° 09.09' W07° 31.25'

Reach the junction in the oued where the high track rises over the cone mountain to the right of a low track which stays in the oued and comes round the hill.

158.5 (93.5)   N30° 08.30' W07 30.00'

Having come over the mountain you're at the KM109 MA12 junction which goes left. You turn right or SW, off Olaf.

160 (92)   N30° 07.82' W07° 31.04'

Just after the track curves south is an easily missed fork for a little used track (seemingly 'virtualised' on Olaf) to the back of Bou Soummoum, about 14km away and a short distance NW of Akka Ighern. Coming the other way you'd leave the Akka road at N30° 02.13' W07° 35.29' and head over the oued into Tinrhourine and NE.

You, on the other hand, follow the wide valley southwards.

164 (88)

Approach what looks like a semi-abandoned village with cultivation down in the oued. There's a stone tower here and large paved terraces, possibly for drying. Follow the piste southwards.

170 (82)   N30° 02.64' W07° 27.70'

Join the Akka road which should be open to traffic by now and turn right for Akka Ighern.

183 (69)

Akka Ighern town centre. Right for the café, left for Tata.

204 (48)

Turn right onto N12 highway for Tata.

252

Tata: fuel on the SW side of town.

WEST

Outline of the West region

This small region north of the Mauritanian border adds up to half a dozen routes either side of the **Oued Draa** valley. Being a long way to go it's probably the least-visited region in this book. The routes and terrain are again Saharan in character but without the full elevation of the Anti Atlas or the tourists and the associated infrastructure found further east. Chances are you'll see no one on these pistes apart from the ancient Landrover 'mules' transporting the Saharawi ('Saharans') who you'll meet out in the desert and the villages; former nomads of Arab Bedouin rather than Berber origin, now relegated to tending flocks of goats and sheep for the army garrisons and coastal resorts.

North of the Draa, MW3 is a great run. South of the Jebel Ouarkaziz (Routes MW1 and 6) you could meet military patrols so it's best not to stray any nearer the border than these routes do. With the open terrain you could make your own adventurous cross-country links between the key points and roads to the west.

In winter the **weather** here ought to be at its best; reliably cool, rain-free and so a good time to be in the desert. As noted on Route MW6, even disregarding the 40°C-plus temperatures, storms in summer or at any time can be sudden and violent, and temporarily cut off routes.

MW Routes

MW1   TAN-TAN – JEBEL OUARKAZIZ – ASSA   268KM
April 2008 ~ Mazda pickup

Description
This is a desolate traverse inland to Assa, following the south side of the **Jebel Ouarkaziz**. Running north-east with barely a break for nearly 300km, the ridge made a natural barrier during the 1980s' war with the Polisario. At the handful of passes in the range there are still defensive walls and trenches with gun emplacements built to plug the gaps.

You pass through the first of these 'mini berms' at KM76, head out into the former Polisario badlands and then turn in again towards the end of the route at KM225. These installations can make you understandably anxious about the presence of mines which are said to exist elsewhere along the Moroccan borders, but these walls are wartime relics compared to the main militarised **Berm**, further south which today marks the de facto border, dividing the Western Sahara between Morocco, and the so-called Polisario Free Zone inland (see the map on p222; it's best to shield this map from army types).

With the jebels distant and low and no palm-ringed settlements to speak of, the scenery here lacks the variety of the best of Morocco, but it's a satisfyingly long desert run rarely visited by tourists or, it seems, by anyone else.

Off road
The narrow valley stage after KM78 is a bit of a crawl and may filter out the average **road car**, but is not characteristic of what lies ahead. If you make it to KM94 you're back out in the open and on your way. On a **motorbike** there's no problem other than the long hammering and possibly the fuel range. For **bicycles** MW1, lean as it is on known wells, is too long. There are more enjoyable routes to pedal around here.

Route finding
Most of the time the Ouarkaziz ridge or parallel formations lie close to the north. Things can get muddied around KM150 for a bit, but keep plugging away just north of east and you'll eventually get somewhere useful. With no villages after Mseid and even nomadic tents unseen mid-route, this is a lonely track as you wind through small passes and across dusty chotts. After Mseid I saw no vehicles until Assa, although I did follow recent Land Rover tyre tracks most of the way. Olaf thins out at KM90 and stops around KM110 but I managed – so can you.

If you think it all might be over too quickly, you could string this route out by reaching down for Labouirat on Route MW6 at KM135 and then following MW6 one way or the other. The route **map** is on pp218-19.

Fuel and water
Fuel at each end with nothing between. Water is from just a couple of tanks and wells as marked.

Suggested duration
You could bang this out in a day but it's best commemorated with an overnight stop in the middle of nowhere. Have I said that already?

0km   **N28° 26.03'   W11° 04.75'**
Tan-Tan east fuel station. Head into town but after 400m turn left at the sign 'Lemseid 68km'. Follow the road inland.

27 (241)
Tilemsen village. In a few kilometres the road rises over a ridge with good viewpoints back and ahead at KM37.

58.5 (209.5)   N28° 04.30'   W10° 52.79'
Possible turn off to the east to pick up Route MW2.

68 (200)   N28° 00.90'   W10° 48.88'
The **tar ends** in **Mseid** ('Lemseid'), a small village at the base of the Jebel Tassout by a big gap in the range. Drive into the village, turn right and head south through the wide pass.

69 (199)   N28° 00.48'   W10° 48.88'
Just as you come through the pass, by some solar panels and a **well** pump, turn east along the back side of the Jebel Tassout, passing some tents and buildings. There are many tracks here going to various nomad encampments. Make your way any which way to KM74.
   Carrying on south here may well lead to KM180 or maybe KM219 on MW6.

74 (194)   N28° 01.06'   W10° 46.26'
Key point: a small cairn in the oued with a **well** 500m to the north. At the cairn turn right, south, out of the oued towards a low berm you'll have seen running across the valley, looking like a buried pipeline.

76 (192)   N28° 01.26'   W10° 45.27'
Cross over the berm, and again a kilometre later as you head up to a pass.

78 (190)   N28° 01.01'   W10° 44.40'
Pass through the Jebel Ouarkaziz. On the other side turn east and head along a narrow, stony valley. It's slow going but doable without resorting to low range. There may be various deviations to get round washed-out sections.

80 (188)   N28° 00.61'   W10° 43.32'
Well (20m).

87 (181)   N28° 01.68'   W10° 39.89'
Palms. Always nice to see some palms.

90 (178)   N28° 02.26'   W10° 38.43'
Olaf thins out but carry on NE as you emerge from the valley – a clear track continues.

94 (174)   N28° 03.75'   W10° 36.27'
Fork right to the east. The terrain finally opens up and the track speeds up.

104 (164)   N28° 05.92'   W10° 31.45'
Having done a dog-leg down to some standing stones, a track joins from the right (marked on old French maps).

110 (158)
Some tall cairns. Continue NE.

113 (155)   N28° 08.75'   W10° 27.80'
Hassi Tagueleimet, now a **cistern** with water inside. This is the last known water on this route until the pass at KM227.

115.5 (152.5)   N28° 09.47'   W10° 26.56'
Possible early split to the south for **Labouirat**. You continue east around the north of a hill to enter and follow a oued.

125 (143)   N28° 11.22'   W10° 21.93'
Semi-abandoned camp with domed mud ovens.

128 (140)   N28° 11.36'   W10° 20.46'
Remains of a very old truck.

135 (133)   N28° 12.09'   W10° 16.38'
Junction. There's a white building just to the south by a pass, probably the track as marked on the Michelin map as the 'P1600' to **Labouirat**, about 75km to the SE. (KM118 on Route MW6). You continue east.

137 (131)   N28° 12.15'   W10° 15.04'
Fork right to the SE towards a big chott. In a kilometre at N28° 11.64' W10° 14.64' head east into a pass and cross a oued with palms and bluish rocks. Could be a nice spot to camp.

145 (123)   N28° 10.62'   W10° 10.38'
Fork left here; up ahead is a shallow pass out onto the Aster chott to the east. From this point the terrain looks like a wide open run SE for about 40km to Labouirat on MW6 via a couple of low passes.

MW – MOROCCO WEST

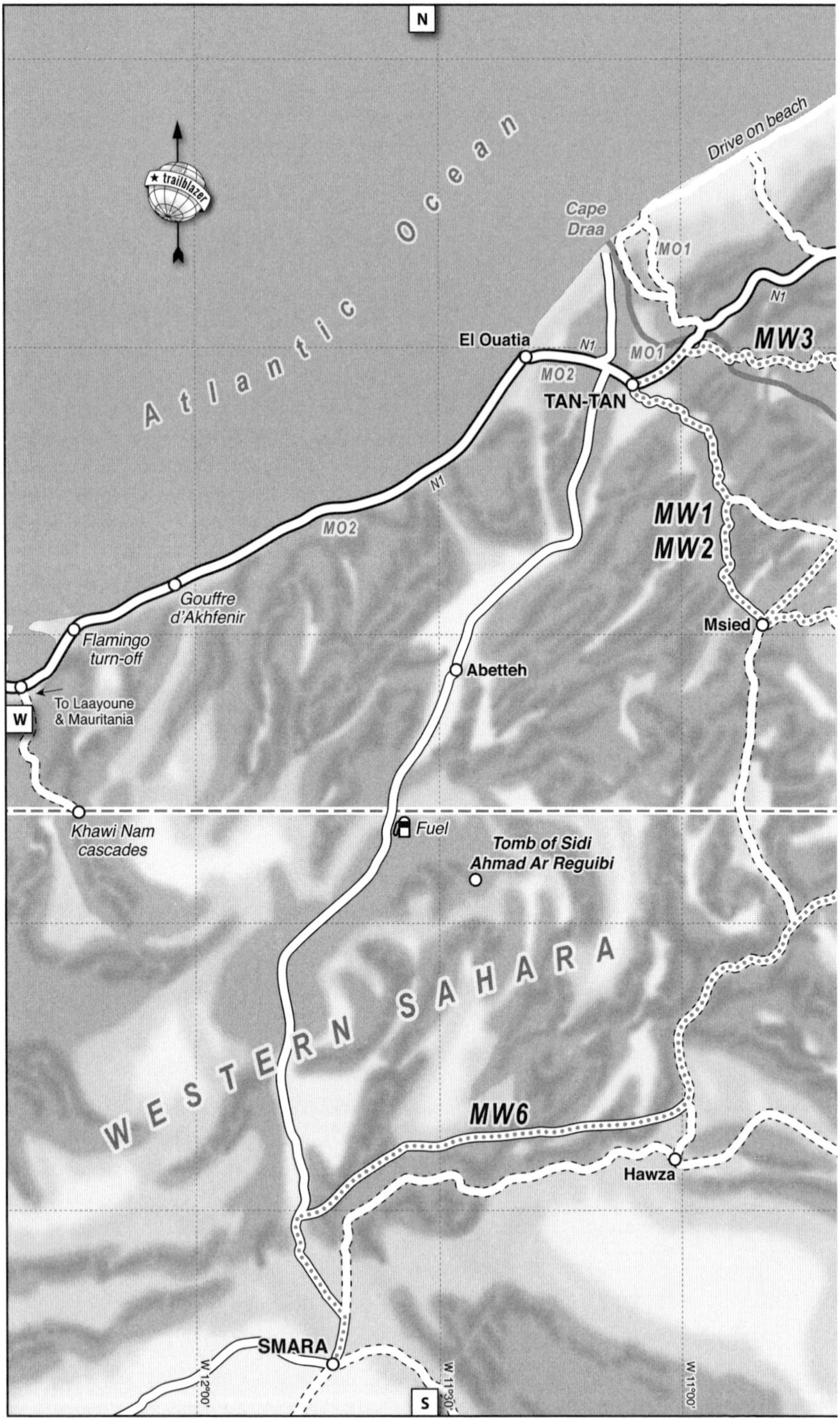

MW – MOROCCO WEST

N

Atlantic Ocean

Drive on beach

Cape Draa

MO1

El Ouatia

N1

MO2

MO1

TAN-TAN

N1

MO1

N1

MW3

MO2

MW1
MW2

Gouffre d'Akhfenir

Flamingo turn-off

Msied

← To Laayoune & Mauritania

W

Abetteh

Khawi Nam cascades

🔒 Fuel

Tomb of Sidi Ahmad Ar Reguibi

W E S T E R N   S A H A R A

MW6

Hawza

SMARA

W 12°00'

W 11°30'

W 11°00'

S

West Region (MW)
Routes Overview

MW1 Tan-Tan – Ouarkaziz – Assa
MW2 Tan-Tan – Assa
MW3 Assa – Tiglite – Tan-Tan
MW4 Fask – Aouinet Torkoz – Assa
MW5 Guelmim – El Borj – Assa
MW6 Assa – Smara

146.5 (121.5)   N28° 10.60' W10° 08.97'
Former camp with more charcoal ovens and a kilometre to the east, a crumbling block marked with Berber writing and bullet holes. A track seems to lead north from here although there's no break in the Jebel Ouarkaziz. It could be to 'Amon' or 'Amot' as marked on some maps, possibly a well.

150 (118)   N28° 10.26' W10° 07.09'
A large, stone-cobbled circle with an arrow on the ground, pointing east – a desert air strip? Around here you start heading NE. The tracks multiply and become ill-defined as you pass along the Oued Tigzert.

159 (109)   N28° 12.00' W10° 02.86'
After possibly blundering around for a bit, pick up a track heading NE. The track winds over the bumpy, dried mud of the Oued Tigzert. After a while you notice an unusually long and straight line of trees to the south, marking a oued line.

171 (97)   N28° 14.51' W09° 57.34'
Fork right.

188 (80)   N28° 16.41' W09° 47.68'
Turn NE through a small pass. Continue NE, then NNE.

202 (66)   N28° 18.34' W09° 39.40
Cross a oued, possibly a good camping place. Up ahead, nomad tents may appear as the terrain opens out.

Behind the hills visible 50km to the SE is **Zag** on the closed border road to Smara. You don't want to go there, but you'll easily meet MW6 on the way.

212 (56)   N28° 19.12' W09° 33.31'
The track drops down into a camp-worthy oued with some trees.

221 (47)   N28° 20.24' W09° 28.94'
Pass a **white tank** south of the track.

222 (46)   N28° 20.46' W09° 28.89'
You join a prominent and now well-formed northbound track. This is KM48 on Route MW6 to Labouirat, 64km away, and Smara, about 338km to the south.

225 (43)   N28° 22.04' W09° 29.14'
Pass through a defensive wall across the first gap in the Jebel Ouarkaziz since Mseid and head into the pass.

227 (41)   N28° 22.87' W09° 29.40'
In the pass there's a **well** to the right as well as crumbling gun emplacements.

228 (40)   N28° 23.44' W09° 29.49'
Emerging from the pass, fork right and follow this inter-jebel valley eastwards. This is KM42 on MW6.

235 (33)   N28° 25.90' W09° 24.75'
A deep **well** (35m) just after a pylon.

236 (32)   N28° 26.07' W09° 24.46'
Join the **Assa–Zag highway** at a broken rusty sign saying 'El Arbouyet 68'. From here it's 32km to Assa fuel, crossing the Oued Draa on the way.

268   N28° 37.05' W09° 27.03'
Assa fuel and café at the west end of town. For directions to the **hotel** see the box over the page.

MW2   TAN-TAN – OUED DRAA – ASSA   238KM
February 1999 ~ Toyota HJ6; part updated April 2008 ~ Mazda pickup

Description
Part of an old Dakar route from the late 1990s, this version of Tan-Tan to Assa is a relic from the first edition of *Sahara Overland* and not as interesting as it looks as, depending on your suspension and tyre pressures, the bumpy terrain gets tiresome. The piste passes through typical south Moroccan scenery, crossing stony hamada and for a while passing along the terminal stages of the **Oued Draa** as it flows west between parallel mountain ranges.

Off road

Doing it in a cart-sprung **Land Cruiser** didn't leave the best impression but this is a rough, stony trail, churned up by run-off feeding the Draa. **Motorcycles** will be less affected, but **mountain bikes** will get a migraine.

Route finding

Jammed between the ranges and at times boulder fields, route finding doesn't present many variables, though you'll have to wing it along the undriven stage from KM58.5 to KM67. Once you pick the trail of 'Dakar' cairns built up on mounds of bulldozed earth (up to KM189), a single track leads you clearly north-east to Aouinet Torkoz and the road to Assa.

  This route doesn't appear on any map until you near Aouinet Torkoz, yet it's one of the best-marked pistes in the Sahara. There are so many cairns on this route that you could almost stumble from one to the next blindfolded. You won't see much traffic other than the odd nomad's 88" Landrover. For the route **map** see pp218-19.

Fuel and water

Fuel at Tan-Tan and Assa with several wells along the way as marked.

Suggested duration

With an early start you can easily get to Assa in a day.

0km   N28° 26.03' W11° 04.75'
Tan-Tan east ('north') fuel station. Head into town but after 400m turn left, inland.

37 (201)
Having passed **Tilemsen** village at KM27, the road crests a ridge.

58.5 (179.5)   N28° 04.30' W10° 52.79'
Turn off, noted in 2008. The next way-point and the route description up to KM170 date back to 1999.

67 (171)   N28° 05.50' W10° 48.30'
A piste crosses at right angles. Turn NNE up the valley.

80 (158)   N28° 10.70' W10° 43.30'
Following a bumpy section, head out across smooth clay pans with frequent cairns either side of the track. After a few kilometres you're near a ridge on your left.

90 (148)   N28° 14.20' W10° 38.80'
In a kilometre you enter some churned up chotts with lots of scrubby vegetation.

93 (145)   N28° 15.20' W10° 37.60'
The piste becomes very stony and starts to rise over low hills. In a few kilometres you

come north through a pass and soon see white buildings to the left and right. Stay on the right-hand track, following the cairns. The track runs ENE.

97 (141)
Pass a building to the right.

99 (139)
The track crosses a broad, vegetated oued. On the other side the track forks: go right, following the cairns into the hills, ESE, seemingly crossing back into the valley you've just come from.

100 (138)
Emerge into a parallel valley.

105 (133)   N28° 18.20' W10° 32.20'
Pass a **well** on the right just before a oued Over the next few kilometres there are several very stony oued crossings.

110 (128)   N28° 18.60' W10° 29.60'
Head east across a wide gravel valley. In 3km head into another valley and soon pass a concrete building with a green door on the left of the piste. It's very stony going for a few hundred metres.

120 (118)   N28° 19.70' W10° 24.20'
Waypoint. In a kilometre you see a distinctive strip of red rock on an outcrop to the left.

You're now entering the course of the **Oued Draa** as it takes a northern turn through the Jebel Amermerdene. The track becomes even stonier, making progress very slow for a while.

132 (106)   N28° 21.40' W10° 19.80'
After turning south for a bit cross a oued with a palmerie enclosed by a stone wall.

133 (105)   N28° 21.50' W10° 19.50'
Fork right following cairns heading east with occasional stony patches and minor diverging tracks.

140 (98)   N28° 20.40' W10° 16.10'
Still on a stony plain with occasional rough oued crossings. Continue east.

144 (94)
To the left is a building with two red doors. The terrain is becoming sandy with a few trees as the pace speeds up. Anywhere in the next few kilometres would make a good spot to camp.

150 (88)   N28° 21.10' W10° 10.20'
Waypoint. Still a fast smooth surface with some... the only word is 'stony' – patches.

164 (74)   N28° 22.70' W10° 02.40'
Pass a building to the right as the terrain manages to get rougher.

170 (68)   N28° 22.90' W09° 59.30'
Fast going over a clay pan. Around this point you meet tracks coming down from routes MW3 and MW5.

177 (61)   N28° 23.92' W09° 55.41'
Clay pan ends but the good surface continues.

180 (58)   N28° 24.06' W09° 53.81'
Fork left here, away from the oued.

181 (57)   N28° 24.48' W09° 53.46'
Head for this waypoint and continue NNE for Aouinet Torkoz.

190 (48)   N28° 29.00' W09° 51.20'
Enter the old western quarter of Aouinet Torkoz with possibly a couple of stores.

Drive east over the oued to the newer side of town where the **tarmac starts** and where MW4 comes in from the north. Follow the tarmac east to Assa, passing a couple of roadside **wells** on the way.

236 (2)
On arriving at the 'teapot' roundabout on the outskirts of **Assa**, the town centre is straight ahead and there's a hotel to the right (see box below).

For fuel, turn left at the roundabout, follow the road round to the north and at the main road turn left, passing Assa Park (see below).

238   N28° 37.05' W09° 27.05'
Ziz fuel and café at the west end of Assa.

ASSA

A focal point for nearly all the routes in this region, **Assa** is a clean and, in parts, prosperous-looking town with more money spent on municipal street furnishings than many other places down south. Maybe the mayor was owed a favour.

Both guidebooks ignore Assa and don't even show the sealed roads which run through, between Foum el Hassan and Guelmim, an impressive stretch of the 1500km-long 'Desert Highway'.

Check out the well-tended **town park** on the main road near the fuel station. Above the beds of seasonal flowers, it includes a witty life-sized diorama of gazelles browsing innocently on an outcrop while a cunning jackal stalks, ready to pounce.

Then just down the road on the way to Aouinet Torkoz is the '**teapot roundabout**' where a jaunty trio of oversized jugs dispense a brew. According to Wikipedia, the next nearest teapot roundabouts are both in Algeria, over 1500km away. One is in the old oil town of In Amenas close to the Libyan border, the other opposite the *Air Algerie* office in Tamanrasset.

South-east from the roundabout, the *Hotel Nidaros* is the only **hotel** for at least 100km in any direction.

MW3   ASSA – TIGLITE – TAN-TAN   231KM
April 2008 ~ Mazda pickup

Description
A great run through the western end of Jebel Bani to the coastal ranges, fin-
ishing off right in the reeds of the **Oued Draa** as it nears the sea. It's all here:
deserted desert blacktop, palmy gorges with inviting waterholes, fast tracks
over bleak uplands passing more hidden gorges, cosy valleys and brightly-
painted villages against the dun backdrop of the Sahara.

Off road
Just about do-able in a **2WD** with bent up bumpers and some bridging planks.
After rain things could get muddy in the Oued Draa towards the end (there's
an alternative escape route), or in the deep gorges converging around Tiglite.
    Providing the rider has been on a prolonged spinach diet and isn't over-
loaded, this route could be done on a big bike. Just make the most of the restful section up to Tiglite; after that you'll need some stamina to reach Tan-Tan.
    On a **mountain bike** this would be a tough three- or four-day haul. But
with enough water on the way and places to rest, if you're on top form, give it
a go. Just remember the end stage may wear you out and there's not much
traffic to depend on.

Route finding
Easy enough, Olaf is by your side to all but the bitter end at KM198. At worst
just hammer your way westwards until you hit the coastal highway or expire
from the effort. Options include starting from Fask via El Borj (see MW5). You
may come across a local car or two as far as Tiglite but I saw no moving cars
on the route. The **map** is on pp218-19.

Fuel and water
Assa and Tan-Tan for fuel plus maybe villages like Tiglite and Aouinet
Ighoman. There are many wells and waterholes as listed, plus villages and
doubtless more sources unseen.

Suggested duration
Overnight in a 4WD, two full days in a regular car or a day on a fast moto.

0km   N28° 37.05' W09° 27.05'
Assa ZIZ westside. Head into town but
turn right, south, after 500m. Follow the
road round to the teapot roundabout and
take a right for Aouinet Torkoz.

39 (192)   N28° 27.94' W09° 46.11'
Well by the road.

47 (184)
At Aouinet, drive straight over a crossroads where MW4 comes in from the
north and over the oued to the old side of
town. **The tar ends**.

48 (183)   N28° 28.99' W09° 51.20'
Leave town and head SSW.

58 (173)   N28° 24.48' W09° 53.46'
Fork left down to the oued.

59 (172)   N28° 24.06' W09° 53.81'
Once near the oued head out onto a
smooth clay pan and at KM62 follow old
Dakar Rally cairns across the pan.

66 (165)   N28° 23.89' W09° 58.25'
The northern split from KM58 joins right
as you near the western edge of the pan.

67 (164)   **N28° 23.84' W09° 59.01'**
Another track joins from the right. Soon
you reach a **well** (4m) and may see some
nomad tents to the north. Various tracks
run in from the left but your destination is
clear: the gap in the range directly ahead.

73 (158)   **N28° 24.55' W10° 02.60'**
The main junction; head north.

76 (155)
Taskala village.

76.5 (154.5)   **N28° 26.19' W10° 03.21'**
Leave Taskala at a **cistern** by a pink hut.

78 (153)
A track goes off to the right. Not for you.

82 (149)
The winding ascent into the gorge begins.
After a few kilometres and some hairpins
you may pass some deep **waterholes** in
the riverbed, right.

87 (144)
Cross a small oued with pink oleanders
(in April at least). In a couple of kilometres you're out of the gorge and on a 500m
plateau.

91.5 (139.5)   **N28° 30.87' W10° 01.18'**
If you're in a mad rush take the fork left
here, it rejoins the track at KM96.5, cutting
off the elbow and saving a couple of kilometres.

94 (137)   **N28° 32.32' W10° 00.29'**
A track joins the bend's 'elbow' from the
east, possibly a direct route from Aouinet.

95 (136)
'Blue bag' junction with the track from El
Borj and Tadalt (routes MW4 and 5). In
700m or so you cross a dense, palmy oued
with more pink flowers and frogs in the
pools. It's a shady spot for lunch.

96 (135)   **N28° 32.33' W10° 01.28'**
Main junction where you join the El Borj-
Tiglite track. Tabayoudet mountain is
ahead and in a few hundred metres at
N28° 32.51' W10° 01.45' the short cut
from KM91.5 probably joins from the left.
    The track now becomes smooth and
fast, and in 2008 was marked by stone

cairns stuffed with blue plastic bags
(hence 'Blue bag' junction). It could be
due for sealing, though there was no sign
of it in late 2012.

121 (110)
The Oued El Merked below right becomes
a deep gorge.

124 (107)   **N28° 28.51' W10° 15.08'**
The southern outskirts of Tiglite in the
wide canyon of the Oued Tiglite. The fast
section is over, but the surface continues
to be good for a bit. Turn north through a
gap in the range.

131 (100)   **N28° 28.23' W10° 18.89'**
Near one of Tiglite's palmeries keep right.
Follow the track north and east through
the settlement until the next waypoint.

133 (98)   **N28° 29.20' W10° 17.91'**
Don't cross the oued, but keep left and
take the steep, well-graded track out of
the canyon.

138 (93)
You're now out of the canyon on a
plateau. There's a good flat spot for a
camp hereabouts.

142 (89)   **N28° 30.18' W10° 19.37'**
Buildings ahead and pylons. Go right or
keep straight; the tracks join up.

145 (86)
Follow the track and usually the pylons.
Side tracks lead off to nomad camps.

161 (70)   **N28° 30.04' W10° 31.28'**
Aouinet Ain Oussa (or Aouinet Ighoman
on the Michelin map). Go left at the junction as you come into town and head for a
palmerie and old mosque on the west
side, towards the pass.

163 (68)   **N28° 30.10' W10° 32.22'**
You're on the way out of Aouinet, passing
through the gap in the range with a wide
basin ahead bordered by the Jebel Rich to
the south.

164 (67)   **N28° 29.90' W10° 32.80'**
Three pistes diverge, the right Olaf track
may be best, but whichever way you go,
aim for the next waypoint.

174 (57)   N28° 28.72'   W10° 38.81'
Join Olaf at this point if you're not on it already. The village of Kheneg el Adam is visible to the NW.

176.5 (54.5)   N28° 29.30'   W10° 40.22'
Junction with white stones. Go straight (west) here to pick up the waypoint at KM185.

Then again, if you've got time on your hands, turn north to explore the abandoned village of El Ayoun du Draa (as it's known on some maps: N28° 30.14' W10° 40.71'; water) then make your way to KM185 via another occupied village.

185 (46)   N28° 29.20'   W10° 44.21'
On the main track heading west. In 1km another track joins from the left and from here on you'll need clearance.

188 (43)   N28° 29.52'   W10° 46.16'
Cistern with water at arm's reach, and another one soon after. Within a couple of kilometres coastal scenery and vegetation begin to emerge.

195 (36)   N28° 29.51'   W10° 49.74'
Well to the south. Olaf is running parallel along an old track to the north.

196 (35)   N28° 29.69'   W10° 50.33'
Join Olaf at a pass where the track swings right around a wash-out ahead. Cacti and coastal vegetation increase. A village is visible below.

198 (33)   N28° 30.28'   W10° 50.84'
Cross the oued in the village of **Ain Kerma** with gardens. After the descent, out of the village take the left split if you're heading for Tan-Tan.

If you want to head north to the N1 then Olaf sets off that way to reach the coastal highway in about 12km at N28° 35.75' W10° 51.48'. From this waypoint you're about 96km south of the next fuel at Guelmim.

199 (32)
Back on the Tan-Tan route, head westwards into rolling hills which lead along a narrow, shaley gully for a couple of kilometres.

202 (29)   N28° 30.19'   W10° 52.78'
The gully opens out with hills all around.

203 (28)   N28° 29.85'   W10° 53.14'
Pass the deep **Guelta ez Zerga** in the Oued Draa; a good place for a swim or a wash. Out of the oued turn right, with pylons visible ahead.

207 (24)   N28° 30.90'   W10° 54.69'
Pass through a flood-worn defile alongside the Draa's possibly grassy banks. Within half a kilometre or so, N28° 30.92' W10° 55.21' could be a short cut on the way to KM212. In a bit you pass under the big pylon cables straddling the wide riverbed.

209 (22)   N28° 31.27'   W10° 56.17'
If you didn't try to follow the short cut above you must turn left here, even though you can see cars being stopped on the Draa Bridge checkpoint less than a kilometre ahead.

Fun though it would be to drive out of the Draa and onto the N1 like the Creature from the Black Lagoon, when I tried it, the way along either bank was blocked by trees or muddy pools, and even if you could make it, it's possible the police at the checkpoint will spot you scurrying about in the reeds before you can adequately explain yourself.

212 (19)   N28° 30.51'   W10° 56.16'
Having followed the winding track, come round a bend to a dam. Here turn right, steeply up a rubbly hill to overlook your route. Or staying down at the dam level and crossing it to the left may work too, as the highway is so near so you can try anything.

215 (16)   N28° 30.43'   W10° 57.58'
Join the N1 about 16km north of Tan-Tan and a couple of kilometres south of the Draa Bridge by some painted bollards and just north of some Armco.

231   N28° 26.04'   W11° 04.72'
Tan-Tan fuel on the east side of town with two more in town. For a bit more on the town, see the end of Route MO1.

MW – MOROCCO WEST

MW4 FASK – AOUINET TORKOZ – ASSA   121KM
April 2008 ~ Mazda pickup

Description
An easy desert run with just 39km of piste over the hills to the Draa valley and
east to Assa. The highlight is rising up above the gorge as you pass over the
watershed and begin your descent to Aouinet Torkoz. You can extend this
route into a loop by picking up MW5 out of Aouinet and reversing it back to
the junction below at KM33; a great day out in either direction.

Off road
Barring the usual calamities there are no difficulties to speak of on this route
for anything with wheels bigger than a BMX bike.

Route finding
Easy, but you won't see much traffic between El Borj and Aouinet. For the map
see pp218-19.

Fuel and water
Fask and Assa for fuel, plus there are a few wells along the route as detailed.

Suggested duration
You can do this one in just a couple of hours or spin it out with other local
routes to make a day of it.

0km   N28° 59.12' W09° 49.57'
Ziz and café in **Fask**. Head SE for Assa.

22 (99)   N28° 50.35' W09° 43.33'
Turn south for Tadalt.

32 (89)   N28° 45.78' W09° 45.90'
Cross **Tadalt** oued. Soon the **tarmac ends**.

33 (98)   N28° 45.26' W09° 45.79'
Fork left here and follow a stony track
towards the ridge. Right is MW5.

49 (72)   N28° 38.61' W09° 43.34'
Very deep **well** (50m +).

53 (68)   N28° 37.28' W09° 45.10'
A **tank** with a bucket and water at just 3m.
After KM59 the track and scenery im-
prove as you rise over the gorge.

60 (61)   N28° 34.79' W09° 47.86'
Drop down to the riverbed and cross the
stony oued a couple of times.

65 (56)   N28° 32.98' W09° 48.94'
Deep **well** (50m).

69 (52)   N28° 31.53' W09° 50.86'
Rough sign pointing right for 'Bord Six
swimming pool' less than 3km away. In
2008 it was unoccupied.

71 (50)   N28° 30.78' W09° 51.43'
Rejoin the tarmac north of **Aouinet
Torkoz** (called something else as you near
town). There's not much in Aouinet.

74 (47)   N28° 28.97' W09° 50.87'
Turn left in the village centre and head for
Assa.

119.5 (1.5)   N28° 36.40' W09° 26.81'
Teapot roundabout. Turn left for the fuel
station, straight ahead for the town centre,
right for the only hotel for miles.

120.5 (500m) N28° 36.97' W09° 26.79'
Turn left here at the main road, pass
Assa's park and in 500m you get to the
Ziz.

121   N28° 37.05' W09° 27.03'
Fuel station and café. For more details on
Assa, see the box on p212.

MW5   GUELMIM – EL BORJ – ASSA   196KM

April 2008 ~ Mazda pickup

Description

An interesting way of getting from Guelmim on the coastal highway inland to Assa that's less demanding than say, MW3 in reverse. Like MW4, this is a great route to get the feel of your **new adventure bike** if you've never ridden it on real dirt before. You pass through Asrir and at Tighmert (called versions of 'Ait Bekkou' on paper maps) where you can wander through the palmerie or surreptitiously enjoy the *Facomtour Hotel*'s range of semi-erotic artworks.

The road stage is no eyesore, but things get interesting as you leave the Assa highway and even more so once the tar ends. The highlight is the passage through Jebel Bani down a palm-lined gorge and the saltpans south of the village of Taskala. Within 28km you're back on the tarmac at Aouinet Torkoz.

Neither guidebook is too positive about **Guelmim**, most probably because it may have oversold its claim to be another of Morocco's 'Gateways to the Sahara' with all that entails. It is indeed the last big town before the sands of the Western Sahara, and if you need to buy or do something, this is the place to do it. But be warned, the weekly 'camel' market is now said to be a sham put on for day trippers out of Agadir. It's also the most likely time and place you'll bump into 'Blue Men' who despite the widely-parroted belief, are no more 'Tuareg' than George Clooney in a denim kaftan, though they may well be Saharawi 'Bedouin'.

Off road

Manageable in a **regular car** or two-up on a **big bike**. For pushbikes and road vehicles, the only rough section might be the descent from Jebel Bani through to Taskala on the desert floor.

Route finding

Straightforward, you won't need GPS though you'll want to know your east from your elbow. There are a few piste junctions south of Taskala village but if you get in a pickle it's less than an hour east-north-east to Aouinet Torkoz where most tracks are destined anyway. You'll see a few cars up to the Tadalt turn-off. Beyond El Borj you might see a local Landrover or two. The route **map** is on pp218-19.

Fuel and water

Guelmim, Fask and Assa have fuel stations plus there are a few wells.

Suggested duration

A slow day. With pedals or time to spare camp out in the hills south of El Borj.

0km   N28° 58.70'   W10° 04.61'
Guelmim SHELL on south side of town. Follow the road NE into town. At 1.5km cross the bridge over the oued and turn right. Fork immediately left and follow this road SE to a roundabout. Cross the roundabout and curve right and then left

getting to another roundabout and a kind of square by the town's main market. Leave town to the SE.

6 (190)   N28° 57.97'   W10° 01.84'
Turn right for Asrir.

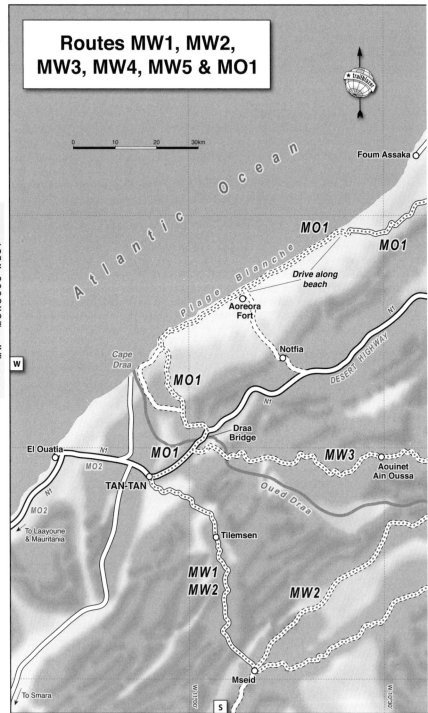

MW – MOROCCO WEST

11.5 (184.5)   N28° 55.31'   W10° 00.80'
Piste heads SW, as shown on maps.

13 (183)
Turn right and bypass most of Asrir.

19 (177)   N28° 56.75'   W09° 57.35'
Turn right here for **Tighmert** and right again into the *Facomtour Hotel* where Yamaha launched the XT660Z Ténéré in 2008. You can camp in the front yard or take an en suite room.

The hall has a stage for re-enacting the legendarily seductive *guedra*, a local belly dance performed by Berber women and which may explain the saucy paintings.

21 (175)   N28° 57.16'   W09° 55.52'
Back on the road heading east, fork left and then turn left (north) to soon rejoin the main Guelmim–Fask R103 road.

33 (163)   N28° 59.10'   W09° 49.61'
Ziz fuel and café on the far side of Fask.

54 (142)   N28° 51.11'   W09° 43.79'
Pass a **well** on the right.

56 (140)
Turn right for Tadalt and El Borj.

66 (130)
Pass Tadalt village on the right.

67 (129)   N28° 45.26'   W09° 45.79'
Soon **the tarmac ends** and shortly the track forks. Go right into a wide valley heading SW. Left is MW4, a shorter and easier alternative to this route.

83 (113)   N28° 39.51'   W09° 53.04'
El Borj village with an arch. Once in town fork left and left again up the hill.

84 (112)   N28° 39.21'   W09° 53.16'
Leave El Borj to the south then SW, following pylons. In 10km you cross a 600m pass with another pass 2km later.

101 (95)   N28° 32.92'   W10° 00.16'
Junction at a oued with shady trees on the right: fork left here. Straight on leads to Tiglite and Tan-Tan (Route MW3).

102 (94)   N28° 32.45'   W10° 00.77'
Junction; turn left. Right soon joins MW3.

104 (92)   N28° 31.57'   W10° 00.94'
A track joins from the right (see Route MW3). Within 2km drop off the 500m-high plateau to a winding, palmy gorge.

109 (87)   N28° 29.88'   W10° 02.71'
Possible **waterholes** in the creek.

118 (78)
Track joins from the left.

120 (76)   N28° 26.19'   W10° 03.21'
Pass a **cistern** and enter the small nomadic settlement of **Taskala** sat in a gap in Jebel Bani. Up ahead the desert opens out with distant ranges and MW2 comes in from the west.

123 (73)   N28° 24.55'   W10° 02.59'
Fork left.

124 (72)   N28° 24.27'   W10° 01.92'
Fork left again.

129 (67)   N28° 23.84'   W09° 59.01'
Pass a **well** by the piste (4m) and possibly some nomad tents to the north. Fork right.

131.5 (64.5)   N28° 23.89'   W09° 58.24'
Start of a smooth, fast clay pan.

135 (59)   N28° 23.92'   W09° 55.41'
Cairns run across the pan for 2km.

138 (56)   N28° 24.06'   W09° 53.89'
Fork left.

139 (57)   N28° 24.48'   W09° 53.46'
Head NNE to Aouinet Torkoz.

148 (48)   N28° 28.10'   W09° 51.20'
Aouinet Torkoz village. Head east to the newer side of town and **the tarmac.** At the crossroads MW4 comes down from Tadalt (38km) Assa is east down the road.

194.5 (1.5)
On arriving at 'teapot roundabout', Assa centre is straight ahead, a hotel is to the right, for fuel and the café turn left.

196   N28° 37.05'   W09° 27.05'
Ziz fuel station and café on the west side of Assa. For more on Assa see the box on p212.

MW6   ASSA – SMARA   385KM
Part updated April 2008 and April 2012

Description
Running down to the **Saguia el Hamra** in the Western Sahara, MW6 has all the ingredients of a real Saharan route with mountains, reg (stony desert), fast sections, numerous oued crossings, rocky piste and your old friend, corrugations – all in all a satisfyingly remote setting rarely seen in 'mainland' Morocco.

The region was the scene of Polisario wars in the 1980s, and today you may spot the *raïmas* (tents) of Reguibat nomads by the route.

Off road
The terrain is rocky between KM190 and KM240. On a bike the only problem is the range and on a **big motorbike** the sandy sections. For any vehicle this is a remote piste by Moroccan standards and best **not done alone**.

Route finding
There is now a graded piste from the R103 south of Assa to Labouirat from where it's said the only waypoint you may need is KM260 south of the chott. The **map** is on pp208-9.

Fuel and water
Assa and Smara have fuel. Water at the village of Labouirat and at Hawza base (off route). In between there are at least four wells along the piste.

Suggested duration
It's hard to imagine doing this route without at least one night out in the desert.

0km   N28° 37.05'   W09° 27.05'
ZIZ in **Assa** westside. Head east into town.

3 (382)   N28° 36.70'   W09° 25.90'
Just before KM3 where the main road heads east, turn right for Zag. On the way cross a bridge over the Oued Draa.

32 (353)   N28° 26.10'   W09° 24.50'
Leave the road to the right before the gap in the Jebel. Pass a deep **well** in 500m. Carry on west along the valley.

42 (343)   N28° 23.40'   W09° 29.50'
Junction; turn south to another gap in the Jebel Ouarkaziz. In the pass there's a **well** on the left as well as defensive walls.

48 (337)   N28° 20.46'   W09°28.89'
Route MW1 heads off to the west here about 70km to Mseid and on to Tan-Tan.

56 (329)   N28° 17.10'   W09° 32.40'
Junction with the former Dakar track. If

not already then you're now on a broad graded track running all the way to Labouirat.

112 (273)   N27° 57.20'   W09° 57.40'
Labouirat. Leave the village to the west. You're between hills on fast reg.

143 (242)   N27° 53.00'   W10° 14.60'
The sandy Oued Gnifida Tarf with An-Nous hill to the south. Bearing SW.

164 (221)   N27° 45.10'   W10° 24.50'
Buildings: Sidi Ahmed al Kenti. Sandy.

185 (200)   N27° 37.00'   W10° 31.30'
Cross the Oued Afra with a **well** on the far side and head SW!

195 (190)   N27° 32.80'   W10° 33.60'
Ascend onto a plateau along a rocky track.

MW – MOROCCO WEST

208 (177)   N27° 29.00'   W10° 38.90'
Crossing with other pistes. Head south.

219 (166)   N27° 24.28'   W10° 39.77'
A Dakar track heads to Mseid on MW1.

231 (154)   N27° 17.20'   W10° 39.00'
Follow the oued west. In 4km you'll pass
a **well** (N27° 16.9'   W10° 43.8'). Climb
onto a plateau before a descent with great
views.

245 (140)   N27° 15.80'   W10° 45.00'
Fast section follows as you cross a chott.

260 (125)   N27° 09.37'   W10° 53.83'
SW corner of the flat and fast chott. You
might see tarmac ahead.

275 (110)   N27° 06.70'   W10° 57.90'
Hawza base and checkpoint (but south of
the tarmac road from Smara).

Stuck near KM231. Full story at 🖥 west
africa2006.blogspot.co.uk. © David French

363 (22)   N26° 54.10'   W11° 46.20'
Junction (estimate). Go south for Smara,
north to Tan-Tan with fuel in 80km.

385   N26° 44.65'   W11° 41.25'
Smara fuel just after a roundabout.

Western Sahara and the Berm

Some tracks pass through
restricted military zones

OCEAN

Outline of the Ocean region

The two routes here add up to a short excursion along the desert's oceanic edge, partly right on a tidal beach – and a much longer transit down the N1 highway south to the Mauritanian border. One could be considered a beachside novelty, the other the start of a trans-continental adventure.

The other continental shelf.

The maritime influence here means the climate along Morocco's Atlantic coast is less extreme than elsewhere in the country. In summer temperatures along the coastal strip remain moderate, so that undertaking the Atlantic Route at this time need not necessarily be the stifling effort that you'd experience further inland.

Of course as soon as you move away from the coast at this time, (as you will do in Mauritania when you follow the sealed road to Nouakchott or take the 'railway piste' to Atar) temperatures will soar back up to the 40+°C norm of mid-summer, with associated sandstorms. Winter of course is a much more agreeable time to be cruising past the Atlantic shore.

MO Routes

MO1   SIDI IFNI – PLAGE BLANCHE – TAN-TAN   194KM
April 2008 ~ Mazda pickup

Description
Sidi Ifni is a former Spanish enclave (like today's Ceuta and Melilla) where a dead-end coastal road leads past the turn-off for an inland track to the ruins of Fort Bou Jerif and the nearby tourist lodge ('FBJ'). A piste here leads back to a sealed road between Guelmim and Plage Blanche on the Atlantic. Guelmim (see p217) is an alternative start if you want to get straight to the beach.

Once off the beach you'll pass the clifftop shacks of fishermen as well as some impressive viewpoints over the crashing surf below. On leaving the coast, multiple tracks complicate the inland run but eventually you'll pass the spectacularly-located *Ksar Tafnidilt* hotel near the highway and so Tan-Tan.

The scrubby inland coastal scenery around here is not so enthralling, but cruising by the surf or looking down from the sea cliffs certainly is.

Off road
Driving or riding on a tidal beach is always a lottery, but on firmer sand you can get away without reducing tyre pressures. Of course, desperately deflating four tyres at once with the tide lapping around your ankles you may think otherwise. Ideally don't start this stage more than an hour after low tide. Ask around or try somewhere like ⌨ easytide.ukho.gov.uk, search ('Predict') under 'Sidi Ifni' and then subtract about 10 minutes for **Plage Blanche**. Note that tide table times may not match the actual **local time**. If you do strike vehicle trouble on the beach (see box p225), as long as you can get onto the low dunes above the high-tide mark you'll at least have some time to work it out.

The crux is getting off the beach through the soft sand ruts at KM112 and up the sandy ascent soon after. A 4WD won't have much trouble, but because this track rises *and* curves it's hard to take a controlled run up on a big bike or in a road car or van. Reducing tyre pressures will do the trick. Beyond this point there's not much to stop you apart from some dunes around KM160.

Route finding
It gets thin away from the cliffs and I saw no traffic other than a car on the beach and some army cars on the cliff top. The route **map** is on pp218-19.

Fuel and water
Sidi and Tan-Tan for fuel with a few wells as marked.

Suggested duration
You can do this route in one long day assuming the tides match up, or overnight in comfort at Fort Bou-Jerif or Ksar Tafnidilt.

0km   N29° 22.71'   W10° 10.57'
Sidi Ifni fuel. Head up hill and turn right at the junction.

3 (191)
Turn left here at the sign for 'Tan-Tan'. Right goes to the port.

17 (177)   N29° 16.35'   W10° 15.28'
Pass a sign – one of many sometimes confusing ones hereabouts, but just keep on the tarmac and head straight on past Sidi Oarzrik whose low dome mosque you'll soon see by the sea.

33 (161)   N29° 10.69' W10° 20.82'
Sign indicating 'FBJ 12km'. Turn left here
onto a wide track. Straight on leads 8km
to Oued Noun where the road ends and
tracks to uncertain destinations start. In
1500m on a left-hand bend turn right
(south) onto a smaller piste (N29° 09.88'
W10° 20.59') passing three wells close to
the track with water at a few metres.

40.5 (153.5)   N29° 06.99' W10° 19.57'
Sign just after a building. Turn right for
FBJ. The track can get washed out.

43 (151)   N29° 05.76' W10° 20.12'
Crest a rise and get a view of the huge
Fort Bou Jerif ruins dating from the 1920s.

45 (149)   N29° 04.92' W10° 19.88'
Fort Bou-Jerif tourist camp near the ruins.

Not really an overlanders' meeting point
as some guidebooks suggest, although the
food is great. Out of FBJ turn left (or just
drive straight past) and fork right and follow white painted cairns to the road.

54 (140)   N29° 00.42' W10° 20.70'
Road from Guelmim, turn right.

84 (110)   N28° 57.78' W10° 36.23'
Arrive at Plage Blanche, a few buildings
with antennae and maybe some hardy
motorhomers. Drop into the oued and
work your way round to the beach.

85 (109)   N28° 57.80' W10° 36.92'
On the beach. I've read warnings of nail-
filled planks and getting strangled in fishermen's lines, but saw nothing other than
pure off-white sand here and one 4WD.

THE SHIPWRECK FROM HELL

I didn't know what exactly the deal was with
Plage Blanche, where it started and where it
ended and the staff at FBJ weren't helpful.
Their literature suggested the Plage was
some 40km long, but not to go beyond the
shipwreck. So I figured once I got on the
beach I'd watch for the wreck or 40km on the
beach. I was already pushing my luck with
the timing, getting on the beach 45 minutes
after low tide, but how long does it take to do
forty clicks on flat beach sand?

Around KM27 and maybe half an hour
on the beach I noticed some soldier-looking
guys cavorting in the surf and a fort on the
clifftop, but carried on regardless into suddenly softening sand.

I'm no stranger to nice, dry desert sand,
but sinking on a tidal beach has a much more
menacing quality. I steered towards the surf
and then up to the beach searching for a
firmer surface. This didn't feel right. Then up
ahead rusting on the beach lay the Shipwreck
from Hell like a skull on a stick. Was this the
wreck from the *FBJ* notebook but only at
KM30? I figured it must be and turned round
with difficulty to head back and ask the guys
on the beach.

I powered back along my already soggy
tracks, pushing hard in low range when suddenly a BANG exploded from somewhere.
Puncture? Burst radiator hose? A con-rod
making a dash for the Canaries? Already
stressed and wanting to get back to the

proper desert, suddenly my mouth became
very dry as I hopped out to inspect the tyres.
All was well.

Looking under the lid I'd guessed close
enough. Incredibly – or maybe not – while
pushing at near full throttle in low range the
huge induction pressure had blasted a hose
off the Allisport intercooler. I looked right at
the surf, now just 20 metres away, crammed
the hose onto the scalding spout and grabbed
a 10 mil from the tool roll under the seat,
tightened the clip and hoped it would stay
there. It's remarkable how focussed you
become at these high-pressure moments with
quite a lot at stake. Your own mental 'intercooler' kicks in.

The car started fine and trying not to
push too hard in low 2nd, I crawled back
along the beach to the firmer sand, appalled
to see my tracks from just 10 minutes ago
had already been washed over by the incom-
ing tide.

The bathing soldiers were from the fort
I'd seen on the cliff top which of course was
Aoreora. I turned up the oued mouth and
breathed a sigh of relief once I got safely
beyond the high-tide mark.

Just as the first day's work on the original edition of *Sahara Overland* had nearly cost
me my vehicle in a flooded river (by then
already in a replacement car!), so it seemed
the first route for *Morocco Overland* had also
required a fiery baptism.

MO – OCEAN

Don't overshoot the Aoreora fort exit in 27km, although at the lowest tide it's said you can get up to 10km past Aoreora.

112 (82)   N28° 50.76' W10° 50.79'
Aoreora fort on the hilltop. Turn inland crossing soft sand ruts and into oued which you hope is dry.

113.5 (80.5)   N28° 50.44' W10° 50.14'
A track continues up the oued to Notfia and the N1 highway, but at this point you turn back to take a steep and loose sandy ascent right (NW) out of the oued.

114 (80)   N28° 50.26' W10° 50.37'
Top of the ascent, turn right to the fort.

115 (79)   N28° 50.43' W10° 50.67'
Fork near the fort, turn left (SW). Tracks get faint and diverge but it's hard to get too disorientated with the cliffs sometimes right by your side.

124 (70)   N28° 48.49' W10° 55.43'
Some shacks and an observation tower.

127 (67)   N28° 48.09' W10° 56.91'
More fishermen's shacks, great views over the sea and white cairns. Possibly an army checkpoint and a **well** too.

131 (63)   N28° 47.00' W10° 59.11'
Fork, keep right passing a hilltop grave-yard. Within 1km the track follows the cliff edge with great views.

137 (57)   N28° 45.76' W11° 02.21'
Several shacks and tents – a chance to buy a fresh fish?

141 (53)   N28° 44.61' W11° 04.07'
Pass a pink fort with radio masts.

142.5 (51.5)   N28° 43.80' W11° 04.40'
I turned inland here but on reflection should have carried on to the **Draa estuary** and then gone inland. Doing that you'd meet this route at KM155 and will cover about the same distance.

147 (47)   N28° 42.12' W11° 03.02'
Crossroads, head SSE.

148 (46)   N28° 41.59' W11° 02.82'
Junction. Continue straight.

153.5 (40.5)   N28° 38.69' W11° 02.95'
Track rises up onto a small plateau.

155 (39)   N28° 37.85' W11° 03.05'
A junction marked with stones where the **Cape Draa** route joins from the right.

155.5 (38.5)   N28° 37.63' W11° 02.87'
A basin and the Oued Draa ahead. An old track used to curve round the basin's eastern rim; this direct route drops into it and crosses it to the south-eastern rim.

160 (34)   N28° 36.20' W11° 01.26'
Far side of the basin with mesas all around. The old rim track soon joins from the left. Descend into a valley; the terrain gets a bit more demanding from here on.

160.5 (33.5)   N28° 36.10' W11° 01.05'
Ease down a rocky descent. Dunes appear and this could be a nice place to camp. In 2km crest a small dune.

165.5 (28.5)   N28° 33.54' W11° 00.53'
The Oued Draa is visible to the west just before a stony drop in and out of a oued.

167 (27)   N28° 33.01' W11° 00.31'
A stony rise by a palm tree. Pylons ahead.

168.5 (25.5)   N28° 32.51' W10° 59.78'
T-junction, turn left (NE) towards the old fort of Tafnidilt.

169 (25)   N28° 32.77' W10° 59.57'
Ksar Tafnidilt hotel on a hillside looking over the old ruined fort of the same name. A great location and if it's that time of day it could be better than anything you'll find in Tan-Tan.

From the *Ksar* the track braids east-wards to cross a oued by a washed-out bridge just before meeting the old coast road. Turn right and soon you reach…

175 (19)   N28° 31.97' W10° 56.56'
… the highway with a 'Ksar Tafnidilt' sign. Turn right (SW) and soon you'll get to the Draa Bridge checkpoint.

194   N28° 26.04' W11° 04.72'
Tan-Tan fuel with two more in town. Once you pass the famous twin camel gateway there's not much to Tan-Tan, but it's best to find this out for yourself.

MO2   THE ATLANTIC ROUTE TO MAURITANIA   1147KM

Based on material from José Brito and Tim Cullis.

The N1 highway through the **Western Sahara** to Mauritania is now sealed all the way and can be covered in three days. Along with the inland scenery, the towns are nothing special and it can take some effort to find diversions from the unending blacktop; the most obvious being dramatic sea cliffs coming close to the road at regular intervals. **Laayoune** is the regional capital and a military base surrounded by the *bidonvilles* (shanty towns) of the displaced Saharawi nomads. As you head south, traffic progressively thins out, especially once past Dakhla.

The so-called 'Atlantic Route' to Mauritania opened up to tourists in the 1990s by which time the trans-Sahara routes through Algeria were unsafe. Although security threats in the Western Sahara from the Polisario Front had diminished by this stage, until 2002 a military convoy of dubious value escorted vehicles twice a week from Dakhla to the Moroccan border post.

These days all traffic flows unescorted along the coastal N1 highway and as far as tourists are concerned the southbound transit of the Western Sahara is limited to this road. South of Smara off-road excursions inland are possible as long as you stay clear of the heavily-militarised series of trenches, walls, minefields and natural barriers known as 'the **Berm**' (see map p222). At around 2000km long, the de facto border runs unbroken from Guerguarat close to Mauritania's Atlantic border up to the Jebel Ouarkaziz east of Assa.

Because of this, the seemingly plausible alternative route to Mauritania from Laayoune to Bir Mogrein via Galtat Zemmour is not possible. You'd need to pass through the off-limits Berm and into the Polisario Free Zone before getting to Mauritania; something the Moroccans won't permit. Sure, in its last decade in Africa, the Dakar Rally annually entered northern Mauritania via Galtat (or latterly Smara), but this probably involved well-established arrangements and incentives with local officials. In recent years smuggling operations, as well as possibly related deadly attacks on army bases and patrols in northern Mauritania mean that the coast road to Mauritania remains the only option and for years has been entirely safe.

Western Sahara history

With the old horizontal border south of Tan-Tan still identified on most maps (much to Morocco's irritation) the Western Sahara comprises the former late-19th-century colony of Spanish Sahara made up of two territories: the **Saguia el Hamra** and **Rio de Oro** to the south. Following successful wars of independence right across Africa in the 1950s and '60s, this marginal colony was abandoned by Spain in favour of Morocco, rather than the mostly nomadic indigenous population. Calling themselves the **Saharawi** ('Saharans'), in 1973 they formed the **Polisario Front** (Popular Front for the Liberation of Sequia al Hamra and Rio de Oro) who in February 1976 announced the independent Saharawi Arab Democratic Republic (SADR).

Morocco's response was the 'Green March' in November of that year when about 350,000 unarmed Moroccans marched into the territory.

Annexation by Morocco followed in 1979 and so came war with Polisario guerrillas – supported by Algeria and for a time, Mauritania.

A UN ceasefire was finally agreed in 1991 on condition of a referendum to decide the legal status of the territory. This referendum repeatedly gets postponed while Morocco continues to encourage migration from the north to help outnumber the Saharawi in any referendum, entrench its occupation and develop the territory. While the Polisario cause is viewed by some in the West as a struggle for self-determination akin to Tibet, realistically it has about as much chance of succeeding.

Geography

Away from the coast the Western Sahara is an **arid limestone plateau** covered with small bushes, local dunes, low outcrops and escarpments, and shallow water courses. Elevation is generally around 200m, meeting the sea in cliffs up to 60m high. The highest point is 701m near **Galtat Zemmour**, the lowest is the **Sebkha Tah** salt pan at -55m (KM211) and with only one major oued: the **Saguia el Hamra** ('Red Canal'). Like its northern counterpart the Oued Draa, the Saguia rarely flows, but unlike the rest of the Sahara, the influence of the Atlantic gives the Western Sahara a less extreme temperature range. Humid oceanic winds help create a relatively **mild micro-climate** with fog delivering moisture up to 30km inland. Because of this, the coastal band constitutes a 'corridor' between sub-Saharan and Mediterranean ecosystems, supporting northern species like the hare, African wildcat and Egyptian mongoose as well as porcupines, honey badgers and striped weasels from sub-Saharan regions.

Compared to the mixed and Berber population of Morocco, the indigenous people of this region are distinctively Arabic or Moorish in appearance and manner, and nomadic by tradition. The Reguibat and the Delim are today the dominant tribes of the Saharawi confederation, but as elsewhere in the Sahara, the desert's lean resources along with the collapse of the nomadic lifestyle (formerly based as much on raiding and hostage-taking as pastoralism) has moulded a less outgoing temperament than you'll find among the Berbers of the more fertile north.

Full-blooded Reguibat nomads like to trace their lineage back five centuries to a legendary Yemeni holy man, Sidi Ahmad al Reguibi. His still-venerated shrine is about 105km south of Tan-Tan alongside the Oued Chbika (N28° 00.4' W11° 25.1') in a region also noted for its many pre-Islamic 'antennae' tombs. The French aviator and writer Antoine de Saint-Exupéry described many edgy encounters with the fearsome Reguibat in books like *Wind, Sand and Stars*. Earlier, European mariners shipwrecked or lured onto the western Saharan shore were much less lucky, as Dean King's book *Skeletons on the Zahara* vividly and gruesomely describes while dispelling any quaint notions of nomadic chivalry or hospitality.

Lodging and camping

The towns of Tan-Tan, El Ouatia, Laayoune, Boujdour and Dakhla have hotels for all budgets; elsewhere you get what you're given and that won't always add up to much. Motel Barbas (KM1056) is about 86km before the border.

At the time of writing camping sites were few and included a spot 90km south of Tan-Tan just after the Oued el Oua'ar bridge by the ocean

(N28° 10.47′ W11° 52.92′); *Camping Le Roi Bedoin* (N27° 27.70′ W13° 03.09′) west of the N1 and about 35km before Laayoune (see KM272); *Camping Lamsiyed* (N27° 02.49′ W13° 05.70′) about 15km south-east of Laayoune on the road to Smara (with an excellent view over the Saquia al Hamra valley); *Camping Nil* west of Laayoune (see KM320) and *Camping Moussafir* in Dakhla after KM807.

Bush camping is also an option, but do it well away from the road as traffic runs all night long. If you decide to bush camp after dark it's better to turn inland, away from the windy cliff edge. Bush camping is not advisable south of Dakhla due to the small risk of landmines. If you plan to do so, stick to well-defined tracks but recognise that the absence of warning signs doesn't mean mines are not present.

Driving and traffic

From Tan-Tan to Laayoune traffic is regular with the usual menace of West Africa-bound car dealers pulling kamikaze overtaking moves on ancient Land Rover Santanas. New or old, vehicle lights can often add up to merely the reflected glow of a cigarette so, along with the danger of wandering dromedaries it's best **not to drive at night**. Beware of sunset glare when southbound.

South of Laayoune traffic decreases, although there's enough to help in a breakdown. Beyond Dakhla junction traffic drops right off and the formerly wide road from Tan-Tan becomes narrow.

Police checkpoints

There are several police checkpoints along the road as well as either side of larger towns like Laayoune, Boujdour and Dakhla. Passing these checkpoints can be expedited by handing out pre-printed copies of your details or *fiches* which will be laboriously entered into a ledger once you're on your way. See 'Documents' on the website for a Word template to fill out and print off; at least a dozen will be useful on the Atlantic Route. As with much of the N1 right up to Tangiers, watch out for **speed traps** too; a typical spot is on the southern exit of Laayoune. The route **maps** are on pp230-1.

TAN-TAN TO THE MAURITANIAN BORDER   1147KM
January 2008 ~ BMW R1200GS Adventure (Tim Cullis)

0km   N28° 26.03′ W11° 04.75′
Fuel station at the eastern end of **Tan-Tan**. South of here you're unlikely to find unleaded petrol however, from KM113 fuel prices are subsidised by about 40%.

Head west towards El Ouatia, aka: Tan-Tan Plage.

26 (1121)   N28° 29.12′ W11° 19.37′
At the **El Ouatia** turn-off keep left at the junction for the N1. El Ouatia is a pleasant little beach resort. Over the next 80km the road runs along low cliffs broken by three river estuaries.

113 (1034)   N28° 06.42′ W12° 02.28′
Sidi Akhfenir is the first point south of

Tan-Tan with **cheap fuel**. Immediately after a naval building on the right and before the town, you can pull over to see the Gouffre d'Akhfenir, a large sea cave with a collapsed roof.

137 (1010)   N28° 00.25′ W12° 14.57′
A sandy track heading north leads to the **Naila** flamingo sanctuary at N28° 02.06′ W12° 14.15′ situated at a lagoon on the estuary of the Sebkha Tarzgha.

146 (1001)   N27° 56.48′ W12° 17.46′
You're now at the same level as the Sebkha Tarzgha, a smooth, flat plain only 5m above sea level and which can get flooded after rain. In 6km you rise from

MO - OCEAN

Route MO2
NORTH

MO — OCEAN

To Sidi Ifni

MO1 *MW3* To Assa

El Ouatia **TAN-TAN**

MO2

MW1
MW2

Mseid

N 28°00'

Abetteh

Gouffre d'Akhfenir

Flamingo turn-off

Cape Juby

Salines Tarzgha

Tarfaya

Khawi Nam cascades

To Assa

MW6

E

Tah

Sebkha Tah, -55m

N 27°00'

Camping Le Roi Bedouin

Smara

Tbeila Rock

LAAYOUNE

Laayoune Plage

El Marsa

N 1

Bou Craa (mine)

N 26°00'

trailblazer

Lemsid

W E S T E R N   S A H A R A

Boujdour

N 25°00'

MO2

N 1

0   25   50   75   100km

TO SOUTH MAP

Echtoucan

S

Atlantic Ocean

N (compass)

W (compass)

W 12°00'

W 13°00'

W 14°00'

W 15°00'

Route MO2
SOUTH

the depression and can overlook the Tarzgha saltworks. The last 30km before Tarfaya has sandy beaches.

211 (936)   N27° 56.91' W12° 52.93'
Tarfaya junction. Keep left for the N1. Straight on leads to the fishing town of **Tarfaya (fuel)**, site of a former trading post called Port Victoria built by Scottish adventurer Donald Mackenzie in 1879. His original fort lies just offshore at Cape Juby, overlooked at N27° 56.70' W12° 55.53' and alongside a memorial to Antoine de Saint-Exupéry (there's also a Saint-Exupéry museum in town).
    South of Tarfaya the road moves away from the coast running alongside the **Sebkha Tah**, at 55m below sea level, the lowest point in Morocco.

244 (903)   N27° 40.28' W12° 57.36'
Tah or **Hassi Laoroud (fuel)**, once the frontier between Spanish Morocco to the north and Spanish Sahara to the south.

252 (895)   N27° 35.63' W12° 57.09'
To the west of the road is the northern rim of **Sebkha Um Ed Deboaa**, another massive salt depression some 30m below sea level. The piste that leaves the road here heading west then south along the southern rim of the depression eventually leads to the campsite mentioned off KM272.

272 (875)   N27° 26.43' W13° 01.38'
Heading west from this point along the track for 4km brings you to *Camping Le Roi Bedouin* (N27° 27.70' W13° 03.09'), a popular stop for overlanders, situated next to a calcified waterfall on the southern edge of Sebkha Um Ed Deboaa.

305 (842)   N27° 11.77' W13° 10.39'
Laayoune junction. Take the right fork to continue on the N1 into **Laayoune (fuel)**. As you approach the town you come to the Saguia el Hamra which has been dammed to create a shallow lagoon. The N1 turns west here; turning inland leads 240km to Smara and MW6.
    You leave Laayoune on a four-lane highway between the dunes of Erg Lakhbayta which sometimes overwhelm the road.

320 (827)   N27° 09.57' W13° 20.19'
About 15km west of town, following a left

bend to the SW and just after a **fuel** station, turn right and then first left and follow the road for 5km to *Camping Nil* (N27°10.60' W13° 23.55'), a shadeless **campsite** by Laayoune Plage more suited to motorhomes. There are said to be more hotels down here too.

336 (811)   N27° 06.13' W13° 24.56'
The road approaches the ocean at El Marsa where a beltway crosses the road from the huge jetty to the Bou Kra phosphate mine 100km inland.

405 (742)   N26° 36.00' W13° 43.62'
The only place on the 164km between El Marsa and Boujdour is **Lemsid (fuel)**.

500 (647)   N26° 07.60' W14° 29.05'
The entrance to **Boujdour (fuel** and other services) is marked by an archway and massive sculptures of leaping swordfish and ostriches (above).

644 (503)   N24° 54.65' W14° 49.19'
A few shacks mark **Echtoucan** (or Nwifed), little more than a pair of fuel stations and a café. There's more **fuel** in the Gor Touf area (N24° 40.00' W14° 52.32').

784 (363)   N24° 03.64' W15° 34.21'
Entayreft fuel station.

807 (340)   N23° 53.56' W15° 40.38'
Dakhla Junction, checkpoint and **fuel**. Turn right for Dakhla (45km); continue straight on for Mauritania. Formerly 'Villa Cisneros' Dakhla was the capital of Spain's Rio de Oro province.
    You can wild camp at N23° 54.03' W15° 47.24' and N23° 49.86' W15° 51.92' or *Camping Moussafir* is 5km from town.

846 (301)   N23° 36.29' W15° 52.19'
Back on the N1, **El Argoub (fuel**, and again 5km later) is now a quiet little town a couple of kilometres off the main road and directly across the bay from Dakhla.

868 (279)   N23° 26.00' W15° 58.20'
You've just crossed the Tropic of Cancer. From here on you'll see many signs warning of **minefields** either side of the road.
    Over the next 180km the road runs mainly along cliffs overlooking the ocean.

898 (249)   N23° 12.48' W16° 05.75'
Cliyeb fuel station. The next attraction is the huge Gulf of Cintra with more than 40km of coastline opening to the ocean in an almost perfect semi-circle.

1056 (91)   N22° 03.27' W16° 44.84'
Motel Barbas is a haven in the middle of nowhere with two **fuel** stations and a hotel, café and shop as well as unofficial money-changing services. Many choose to overnight here and get stuck into the border as soon as it opens next morning.

1142 (5)   N21° 21.80' W16° 57.64'
Moroccan **border post**. Exit procedures can take between one and two hours: first register with the gendarmerie, then let the police stamp your passport, then the *Douane* (Customs) will formalise the exit of your vehicle. Once that's done move 50m down the road to register with the military. Finally your passport is checked again and you're let loose to navigate the 5km of piste to the Mauritanian counterpart.

Either side of the clearly defined but braiding tracks are minefields so don't stray. Tourists have got themselves killed while doing so (entirely unnecessarily it must be said). Despite this, it's all much less perilous than it sounds and regular 2WD cars and road bikes easily manage the track.

On the way through No Man's Land you may be waved down by **money changers**. If you're after buying ouguiyas they prefer euros over dirhams.

1147   N21° 20.02' W16° 56.83'
Mauritania border post: police, Customs as well as official money changing and motor insurance.

Hopefully you'll have arrived here with a visa which you got on the same day from the consulate in Rabat, if not in your home country (see 🖥 www.sahara-overland.com/country for the latest details).

After the border the next **fuel** is Nouadhibou, 70km to the SW, or at Bou Lanouar, 45km along the road south to Nouakchott (450km).

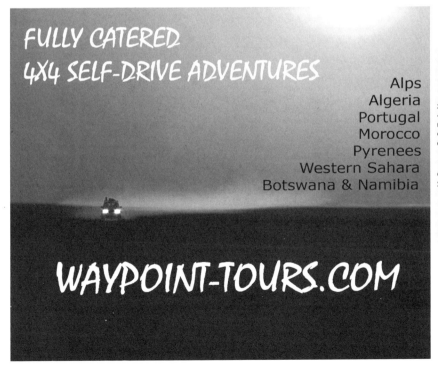

MO – OCEAN

Overlander - 60

Innovative panniers designed for the toughest of adventures. Platform design accepts Kriega Overlander packs or Rotopax fuel/water containers. Ultra-secure cam levers mount to 18mm pannier frames with quick-release for when the going gets really tough.

IT'S TOUGH OUT THERE

PHOTO: Alessio Corrandini

Overlander - 60

60-litre capacity (4 x 15L packs)

100% water, dust & sand proof

Double stiched 1000D Cordura

LDPE - Adventure platforms

ROTOPAX compatible

6061-T6 alloy hardware

10-year guarantee

kriega.com

Adventure luggage Hydration packs Waistpacks Backpacks Tool rolls Haul loops Fork seals

INDEX

TRAILBLAZER

OTHER GUIDES FROM TRAILBLAZER – see p244 for full list

Moroccan Atlas – the trekking guide
Alan Palmer, 268pp, 54 maps, 40 colour photos
ISBN 978 1 873756 77 5, *1st edition*, £12.99
The High Atlas in central Morocco is the most dramatic and beautiful section of the entire Atlas range. Towering peaks, deep gorges and huddled Berber villages enchant all who visit. With 44 detailed trekking maps, 10 town and village guides including Marrakech.

Sahara Overland – a route & planning guide
Chris Scott, 640pp, 24 colour & 170 B&W photos
ISBN 978 1 873756 76 8, Hardback, *2nd edition*, £19.99
Covers all aspects Saharan, from acquiring documentation to vehicle choice and preparation; from descriptions of the prehistoric art sites of the Libyan Fezzan to the ancient caravan cities of southern Mauritania. How to 'read' sand surfaces, using GPS – it's all here along with detailed off-road itineraries covering 26,000kms in nine countries. '*THE essential desert companion for anyone planning a Saharan trip on either two wheels or four.*' **Trailbike Magazine**

Overlanders' Handbook – a worldwide route & planning guide
Chris Scott, 752pp, 30 colour & 400 B&W photos
ISBN 978 1 905864 07 2, Hardback, *1st edition*, £24.99
Chris Scott and his band of globetrotting contributors have put together the definitive manual for planning and undertaking a vehicle-dependent overlanding adventure across the wilds of Africa, Asia and Latin America. The *Overlanders' Handbook* is written in the same entertaining yet clear jargon-free language for which Chris's other books are known.
'*I cannot recommend this book highly enough. It is the first word, the last word, and if there is such a thing, the middle word, on overlanding.*' **4x4 Magazine**

Adventure Motorcycling Handbook – a route & planning guide
Chris Scott, 400pp, 30 colour & 100 B&W photos,
ISBN 978 1 905864 46 1, *6th edition*, £15.99
Every red-blooded motorcyclist dreams of making the Big Trip – the updated sixth edition of this classic shows you how. Choosing a bike, deciding on a destination, bike preparation, documentation and shipping, trans-continental route outlines across Africa, Asia and Latin America. Plus – first hand accounts of biking adventures worldwide. '*The first thing we did was to buy the Adventure Motorcycling Handbook*'. Ewan McGregor, **The Long Way Round**

Adventure Cycle-Touring Handbook – a route & planning guide
Stephen Lord, 312pp, 28 colour & 180 B&W photos
ISBN 978 1 905864 25 6, *2nd edition*, £14.99
Escape the backpacker circuit and expand your horizons with the *Adventure Cycle-Touring Handbook*. Turn your bicycle into a travelling machine capable of taking you on the trip of a lifetime – across a country, across a continent or even right around the world. '*The definitive guide to how, where, why and what to do on a cycle expedition*' **Adventure Travel**

Himalaya by Bike – a route & planning guide
Laura Stone 368pp, 28 colour & 50 B&W photos, 73 maps
ISBN 978 1 905864 04 1, *1st edition*, £16.99
An all-in-one guide for Himalayan cycle-touring. Covers the Himalayan regions of Pakistan, Tibet, India, Nepal and Sikkim with detailed km-by-km guides to main routes including the Karakoram Highway and the Friendship Highway. '*Inspirational guide*' **Cycle Magazine** '*Rammed full of in-depth information*' **Adventure Travel Magazine** '*Indispensable*' **LCC Magazine**

Sinai – the trekking guide
Ben Hoffler, 288pp, 30 colour photos, 74 maps
ISBN 978 1 905864 41 6, *1st edition*, £14.99
Trek with the Bedouin and their camels and discover one of the most exciting new trekking destinations. The best routes in the High Mountain Region (St. Katherine), Wadi Feiran and the Muzeina deserts. Includes guides to the nearby coastal resorts of Sharm el Sheikh, Dahab and Nuweiba. **Due Aug 2013.**

TRAILBLAZER

Adventure Cycle-Touring Handbook
Adventure Motorcycling Handbook
Australia by Rail
Australia's Great Ocean Road
Azerbaijan
Coast to Coast (British Walking Guide)
Cornwall Coast Path (British Walking Guide)
Corsica Trekking – GR20
Cotswold Way (British Walking Guide)
Dolomites Trekking – AV1 & AV2
Dorset & Sth Devon Coast Path (British Walking Gde)
Exmoor & Nth Devon Coast Path (British Walking Gde)
Hadrian's Wall Path (British Walking Guide)
Himalaya by Bike – a route and planning guide
Inca Trail, Cusco & Machu Picchu
Indian Rail Handbook
Japan by Rail
Kilimanjaro – the trekking guide (includes Mt Meru)
Mediterranean Handbook
Morocco Overland (4WD/motorcycle/mountainbike)
Moroccan Atlas – The Trekking Guide
Nepal Trekking & The Great Himalaya Trail
New Zealand – The Great Walks
North Downs Way (British Walking Guide)
Norway's Arctic Highway
Offa's Dyke Path (British Walking Guide)
Overlanders' Handbook – worldwide driving guide
Peddars Way & Norfolk Coast Path (British Walking Gde)
Pembrokeshire Coast Path (British Walking Guide)
Pennine Way (British Walking Guide)
The Ridgeway (British Walking Guide)
Siberian BAM Guide – rail, rivers & road
The Silk Roads – a route and planning guide
Sahara Overland – a route and planning guide
Scottish Highlands – The Hillwalking Guide
Sinai – the trekking guide
South Downs Way (British Walking Guide)
Tour du Mont Blanc
Trans-Canada Rail Guide
Trans-Siberian Handbook
Trekking in the Annapurna Region
Trekking in the Everest Region
Trekking in Ladakh
Trekking in the Pyrenees
The Walker's Haute Route – Mont Blanc to Matterhorn
West Highland Way (British Walking Guide)

www.trailblazer-guides.com

ROUTE GUIDES FOR THE ADVENTUROUS TRAVELLER